2011

THE
VIOLENCE
of PEACE

THE
VIOLENCE
of PEACE

America's Wars in
the Age of Obama

STEPHEN L. CARTER

William Nelson Cromwell Professor of Law
Yale University

New York

Published by Beast Books
Beast Books is a co-publishing venture with the Perseus Books Group

Books published by Beast Books are available at special discounts for bulk purchases in the United States by corporations, institutions, and other organizations. For more information, please contact the Special Markets Department at the Perseus Books Group, 2300 Chestnut Street, Suite 200, Philadelphia, PA 19103, or call (800) 810-4145, ext. 5000, or e-mail special.markets@perseusbooks.com.

Editorial production by *Marra*thon Production Services. www.marrathon.net

DESIGN BY JANE RAESE
Text set in 12-point New Baskerville

A CIP catalog record for this book is available from the Library of Congress.

ISBN 978-0-9842951-7-3

10 9 8 7 6 5 4 3 2 1

To the unknown soldier, and his colleagues,
with gratitude

CONTENTS

PREFACE:

OBAMA'S INVITATION

THIS BOOK IS a meditation on the morality of war—in particular, the views of Barack Obama about the morality of war. As President of the United States, he controls the mightiest military machine on the face of the planet. More than forty cents of every dollar spent on defense around the world is spent by the government he leads. At this writing, the United States is fighting simultaneously a war in Afghanistan and a global war against terrorism. Even in Iraq, where the war is being wound down, some 50,000 American troops remain on the ground. If history is any guide, more conflicts are in the offing, some in places we cannot now predict. President Obama may have inherited this world, but the American military is now in his charge. When he makes decisions on when and how to fight, he will be deciding who lives and who dies. Consequently, it matters a great deal what he believes is worth fighting for, and what he is willing to do to win. That is my subject.

At the midpoint of Obama's first term, we have copious material upon which to base a judgment. He did not start the wars he now runs—indeed, he was adamant in his opposition to the invasion of Iraq—but his conduct of those wars has required him to answer any number of thorny questions about when and how wars should be fought. Despite press reports of disarray among the President's advisers, and of conflicts between the White House and the Pentagon, Obama, as commander in chief, has been firmly in charge. Any doubts should have been dispelled by his decision to dismiss Stanley McChrystal, a four-star general, as head of American forces in Afghanistan. Thus, what the military has done under President Obama's leadership can be treated, by extension, as his own acts.

His actions are of course the most important indicator of what he really believes. But the President's words matter too—they are the justifications for his actions—and Obama has spoken several times on the subject of war. Most notable among his public comments is the address he delivered on the occasion of receiving the Nobel Peace Prize in December of 2009. In that speech, he suggested that the proper way of evaluating the morality of war is the just war tradition, a part of Catholic natural law thinking that over the centuries has made its way into scholarly as well as mainstream public dialogue. The just war tradition is among the most powerful tools ever developed for the moral study of war. So it seems appropriate to accept the President's invitation and use the tools of that tradition to scrutinize his own arguments on behalf of the morality of war.

Some of my conclusions may be predictable. Others might be more troubling. President Obama's efforts to undergird America's military adventures abroad with a larger moral justification than self-interest is itself attractive. So is his emphasis on expanded research on future weapons systems. At the same time, his assertions of executive authority to prosecute warfare seem to me significantly broader than those of his predecessor, George W. Bush. President Bush, to take a single example, never claimed the power to target American citizens for assassination. President Obama has. He has also expanded the battlefield, both geographically and technologically, and is prosecuting America's wars with a stunning ferocity. Obama, like Bush, describes the work that our military is doing abroad as defense of the American people. This claim, as we shall see, already presses the boundaries of the traditional understanding of the just war. Obama has adopted many of the controversial tactics of his predecessor—assassinations, rendition of suspects to other countries, and, possibly, secret prisons—and here, too, important moral questions arise. Obama, moreover, may even have adopted a rarely articulated theory of the previous Administration that holds, in the bald and tragic terms of just war theory, that it is not possible to wage just war against the United States.

Yet none of this is necessarily a criticism of President Obama. It may instead be a signal that the vehement attacks on his predecessor were overblown. As I discussed, in various venues, the ideas presented in this book, I was surprised and a bit depressed to discover how many quite thoughtful people are so steeped in a hatred of President Bush that the merest suggestion that President Obama has followed any of his policies, on any matter, is considered an insult to Obama. But in so dangerous an age, we dare not treat arguments over warfare as opportunities to indulge our partisan side. There is not a Bush way to fight, adopted by Obama; there is an American way to fight, common to many of the nation's wars, adopted by them both. Put most simply, we fight to win. I have chosen the title *The Violence of Peace* because I believe that President Obama has learned what so many of his predecessors were also brought unwillingly to accept: that America faces real enemies in the world, and keeping the nation at peace, ironically, sometimes requires battle.

I have been teaching and writing about the ethics of war for many years, but the events of the past decade raise particularly urgent questions under just war theory. This book actually began as a study of the views of President George W. Bush, who will feature frequently in its pages. But I certainly do not mean to suggest that there are no differences between President Obama and his predecessor. We will be better able to assess their similarities once Obama is faced with a decision on not how but whether to fight. We may see this moment arrive sooner than any of us would like as the President and his advisers continue debate over how to deal with the nuclear ambitions of Iran. At the same time, Obama has suggested, more than once, the possibility of going to war not to defend the United States from attack but to defend strangers from oppression by their own governments. If the President means what he says, this would represent a significant, and positive, change in the American conception of just war, moving it closer to the view of early just war thinkers, who argued that the purpose of war is not defending the self but establishing justice. Alas, given the state of the world today, President Obama already faces many opportunities, should he choose to take them, to persuade us to fight for strangers, and we will learn much about ourselves by how we respond.

Let me be clear. This is not a book about international law, although I will certainly make occasional references to it.* Nor is the book about foreign policy as such. It is about President Obama's views on the ethics of war, and how his views square with the Western tradition of just and unjust wars that he invoked in his Nobel Address. Along the way, we will visit such controversial practices as drone missile attacks and torture, and see why fighting a war on terror tempts us to apply both. We will deal with the Obama Administration's approach to everything from interrogation to assassination, from nuclear arms to cyberwar. We will see why the wars in Afghanistan and Iraq are more similar than one might think. We will ask whether the world might sometimes have an obligation to use war to stop a

---

*I do not mean to suggest that international law is devoid of moral content. This book, however, is an effort to use the moral tools deployed by the President himself in his Nobel Address: the tools of just war theory.

great horror from taking place, and why powerful nations are reluctant to do so. We will try to understand, in short, when war—the vast and organized destruction that is among the most horrendous and most ubiquitous of human institutions—can be justified in moral terms.

The book is divided into four parts. In Part I, I examine the President's words and actions to understand what he considers a just cause for war. In Part II, I discuss the means by which he evidently believes war can justly be fought. Part III asks what might be different if Obama means seriously his words about defending strangers. Part IV notes the weaknesses in our national dialogue about war. In presenting my argument, I am less concerned with law than with morality, less worried about what the President thinks legally permissible than what he thinks morally right. If we know what Obama thinks about the present crises, we can better predict what decisions he will make when the next one strikes.

Public moral argument is crucial to democracy. Too often, we debate difficult questions using slogans and placards, a questionable way to make up our minds about anything and, certainly, war. Given America's worldwide responsibilities, and its status as the only superpower, Americans need to cultivate a shared understanding of what we do and don't want our military to do; when we do and don't want to risk the lives of our children; when we do and don't want to kill strangers. We should debate these questions with the solemnity the subject deserves. The answers matter. A war without a philosophy is not mere tragedy; it is, in a sense, organized murder. The flight from serious ethical argument in our public culture is frightening enough, without presuming to exempt from moral criticism the most deadly activity we undertake. In an era of war—as every era is!—the responsible citizen dares not stand on the sideline.

While working on this book, I gave a talk at the Yale Club in New York City on the subject of just and unjust wars. In the audience was a veteran of Iraq, who had seen friends killed in battle. He stood up during the question period to tell us that he was uneasy about going off to war for a theory. Here history has admittedly been an unkind teacher. Millions of lives have been lost over the years for ideas, many of them very bad ones. But there are good ideas, too, ideas worth fighting for: ideas about justice, and humanity, and the protection of those we love. In the end, sad to say, every war is about a theory, because someone somewhere has concluded that the matter in question is worth dying for, and worth killing for. This book is dedicated to that soldier, whose name I do not know, and his colleagues.

President Obama, in his Nobel Address, as well as in other words and actions, has tried to provide a theory about what is worth killing and dying for. This is a part of the responsibility of any wartime President. My purpose in this book is to reflect on how well that work has been done.

ELIMINATING ENEMIES

President Obama on *Jus ad bellum*

THE PEACE CANDIDATE

Near the end of 2009, in Khost Province in southeastern Afghanistan, a suicide bomber made his way inside a protected military installation and killed seven employees of the Central Intelligence Agency. Relative to the size of the Agency, the loss "was the equivalent of the Army losing a battalion."[1] President Obama, speaking in February of 2010 at the memorial service for the slain officers, summarized their work this way:

> They served in secrecy, but today every American can see their legacy. For the record of their service—and of this generation of intelligence professionals—is written all around us. It's written in the extremists who no longer threaten our country— because you eliminated them. It's written in the attacks that never occurred—because you thwarted them. And it's written in the Americans, across this country and around the world, who are alive today—because you saved them.

Notice what the President lauds the Agency for doing in secrecy: saving Americans, thwarting attacks, and eliminating extremists. That is what one does in war, and the nation is at war. Killing is an ugly business. Killing in battle is uglier still. Four centuries of international law and two millennia of just war thinking have not changed that simple fact.

War is not pleasant. War is not tidy. War is not nice. We spend a remarkable amount of time in America arguing over the conduct of war, as if war were just like every other human activity. But it isn't. The ethicist may safely say, of just about everything we do, "Winning is not a virtue." In war, however, winning is a virtue, assuming that the war is just. This does not mean that it makes no difference what we do in order to win; it does mean, however, that winning matters. And war is not the same as law. The two are antitheses.[2] Law is what the nation does at its leisure, battling titanically from the safety of its living rooms and laptops and congressional offices over whether to raise or lower the capital gains tax half a point or so. War is how the leisure to engage in robust democratic argument is protected. In ordinary political argument, when we say someone is an enemy, we are being silly: all we really mean is that he has a different point of view and we wish he would shut up. In war, when we say someone is the enemy, we are being serious: we mean that we are willing to kill him.

This is why we should take the time to understand what President Obama thinks just and unjust about war. For make no mistake. With his Nobel Prize acceptance address in December of 2009—and with his words and conduct before and since—the man who many considered the peace candidate in the last election was transformed into a war President. He opposed the Iraq War and supported the Afghan War, but he now owns them both. Indeed, with respect to both wars, he has largely adopted the policies of his predecessor; but the word "largely" hides some intriguing differences.[3]

In Iraq, as of this writing, President Obama has implemented the Status of Forces Agreement reached between the Bush Administration and the government of Iraq, but executed a somewhat swifter withdrawal. (Although not nearly as fast as he envisioned when, as a freshman Senator, he declared the war unwinnable and demanded that all American forces exit by mid-2008.) Obama has reduced American forces in Iraq to about 50,000, and ordered that American troops depart by the summer of 2011. At the same time, military commanders have made clear that they are leaving open the option of keeping American troops on the ground after the deadline for withdrawal, depending on how events unfold, and the White House has not contradicted them. Indeed, according to news reports, this Administration, like its predecessor, envisions the possibility that a substantial residual force, perhaps in the tens of thousands, might remain in Iraq indefinitely.

In Afghanistan, President Obama ordered a "surge," a temporary increase in troop levels to improve efforts to drive insurgents out of key areas of the country, evidently emulating his predecessor's surge that turned the tide in Iraq. The President has also greatly expanded the use of missiles fired from Predator and Reaper drones against suspected leaders of the Taliban and al-Qaeda, and has consistently allowed strikes across the border into Pakistan, a widening of the war that his predecessor was reluctant to permit. The first year of the Obama Administration saw nearly 250 attacks in Afghanistan by missiles and bombs fired from drones, and perhaps a third that number in Pakistan, both substantial increases over the final year (or any year) of the Bush Administration.[4] The President promised on the campaign trail to work hard to win the Afghan War, and he seems to be doing precisely that.[5]

To gain a clue to Obama's understanding of his role as commander in chief, it is useful to consider not just his actions, but also his public explanations and justifications. A doctrine, after all, is both actions and the arguments that justify them. The best way to get a sense of the nascent Obama Doctrine is to examine the President's own words. But words are not everything. President Obama, for example, does not like to acknowledge the existence of what his predecessor called the Global War on Terror.* Yet, Obama is fighting that war all the same, not only in Afghanistan and Pakistan, but in Yemen, in Somalia, and here at home; and perhaps elsewhere, for the Terror War has always had its secret side.[6]

As we shall see, on most matters relating to war the contrast between President Obama and his predecessor is quite a bit smaller than most observers expected. When I presented this conundrum to my students late in the first year of the Obama Administration, they had trouble coming up with significant differences. Their instinct, to be sure, was that the two men have propounded very different policies, and on foreign policy generally this instinct was undoubtedly sound. On how to fight a war, however, my students, like many Americans, seemed to have mistaken style for substance. They thought that the 2008 election had brought to the White House the peace candidate.

Indeed, the election that brought Barack Obama to the White House overturned an odd bit of conventional wisdom, that Americans had never, in the midst of war, elected an anti-war candidate. In truth, few presidential elections have been

---

*Many scholars dislike the term "terrorism" because it is politically freighted and inexact. Terror, after all, might more fairly be described as a device or a tactic. If we consider terrorism to be the intentional targeting of civilians, for example, then states, too, can be terrorist. However, in political usage (and in the usual usage of diplomacy as well), terrorism is committed only by nonstate actors. A state that targets civilians intentionally may be guilty of a war crime, because the state otherwise has the right under international law to fight. According to this line of reasoning, the terrorist has no right to fight in the first place. Thus the term "terrorism" in a sense signals not only the tactic (targeting civilians) but the identity of the actor. For a brief period early in his presidency, Obama seemed to be trying to avoid the word. But he has now yielded. And so shall I. Yes, the word "terrorism" is inexact, but other coinages would add accuracy at the cost of clarity.

held in the midst of wars. The sample is too small to allow serious conclusions to be drawn. In 1864, when Abraham Lincoln was reelected (after everyone, all summer long, thought he was doomed), the European papers could scarcely conceal their astonishment. They could scarcely believe that the man they considered the pro-war candidate had won. A British paper mockingly labeled him "Abraham Lincoln II," and predicted that he would be overthrown before the end of his second term.[7] Wars, the Europeans contended, must never be put to the people for a vote, because the people will always vote no. One French paper, an avowed supporter of the war, went so far as to insist that never before in history had a democracy laid its war policy before the people.[8]

Wars, as a rule, are clever enough to bracket election years. Another presidential election held in the midst of a large war was in 1944, when Franklin Roosevelt won, certainly, and with ease; but two examples do not a trend make. And, even there, had the Allies not invaded Europe before the election, he might have had more trouble, for the perception at home was that the war was stalemated. Roosevelt, in any event, had run in 1940 on the promise not to get the United States involved in what was then termed the European War. Woodrow Wilson ran and won on a similar platform in 1916. Both men are remembered as war Presidents. Richard Nixon, although he is not remembered this way, ran and won as the peace candidate in 1968, at the height of the Vietnam War.

But perhaps the best example is Lincoln again. Lincoln was elected President in November of 1860, a few months before the Civil War formally began. The nation was terrified of war. The two Republican candidates viewed as pro-war, William Seward and Salmon Chase, both lost out at the convention, where Lincoln's managers put him forth as the peace candidate. And so he presented himself to the nation, as the man whose election would avoid war. Many voters likely believed it. But not the Southerners: as soon as Lincoln won, they began to secede. Whether Lincoln, as some historians believe, was secretly preparing for war all along is beside the point. The minority of voters who elected him could hardly have expected him to lead the nation into a conflict that would take more than half a million lives. They thought they were voting for peace.

So it is simply not true that the nation never elects the peace candidate. The better interpretation of the history—an interpretation that makes perfect sense of President Obama's Nobel Address—is that there are no true peace candidates. Not among those with the serious possibility of winning. When war looms, the ideal candidate may be the one viewed as most likely to build the bridge, to remain sensitive to the ideals of those who want peace at any price—always a significant group in American history—while at the same time doing what is necessary to prevail.

And what does President Obama think is worth fighting for? In his best-selling book *The Audacity of Hope,* a younger Barack Obama warned of the dangers of fighting "war without sacrifice."[9] And yet, he pointed out, "War might be hell and still be the right thing to do."[10] Fair enough. But how do we know when war is "the right thing"? The philosopher Thomas Nagel, in his classic article "War and Massacre," set forth a challenge for future warriors, proposing that a war must not be undertaken unless its supporters believe they could, in theory, sit down with the soldiers on the other side and explain why their deaths were necessary to some larger cause.[11] In a sense, this book is an effort to take up his challenge, only I am trying to explain not my own views, but President Obama's. Again, he is fighting three wars—the Iraq War, the Afghan War, and the War on Terror—and, even if he inherited them from his predecessor, the wars nevertheless now belong to him, and to his legacy. That is a burden of the office. And Obama himself, although doing his best to distance himself from Iraq, has embraced the other wars. He is a wartime President. And so, in Nagel's terms, Obama owes those he is willing to kill an explanation of why they must die.

WAR AND EVIL

Six months after the 9/11 attacks, President George W. Bush told the nation: "My most important job as your President is to defend the homeland; to protect American people from further attacks."[12] Seven and a half years later, in his Nobel Prize Address, President Barack Obama said: "I face the world as it is, and cannot stand idle in the face of threats to the American people."* Two Presidents, one mission: keeping their fellow citizens safe from harm.

I begin here because it is easy to forget, in the midst of our many heated political debates, that the first and most vital task of government is the security of the nation. This principle comes down to us from the Enlightenment, although it has been accepted widely throughout recorded history. In the United States, the responsibility for national security devolves almost entirely upon the executive branch. Whatever scholars might say about the balance of powers established by the Constitution, we have come to accept as a given that the President has charge of protecting us from external threats.[13]

President Obama, in his Nobel Address, recognized this proposition:

---

*President Obama's Nobel Address appears as an appendix. In general, I do not include citations for presidential speeches that are widely available.

I know there's nothing weak—nothing passive—nothing naive—in the creed and lives of Gandhi and King.

But as a head of state sworn to protect and defend my nation, I cannot be guided by their examples alone. I face the world as it is, and cannot stand idle in the face of threats to the American people. For make no mistake: Evil does exist in the world. A non-violent movement could not have halted Hitler's armies. Negotiations cannot convince al-Qaeda's leaders to lay down their arms. To say that force may sometimes be necessary is not a call to cynicism—it is a recognition of history; the imperfections of man and the limits of reason.

Thus did the President state his duty, and the statement is one with which few would disagree. Indeed, President Bush, in setting forth the doctrine that came to bear his name, said something quite similar:

Some worry that it is somehow undiplomatic or impolite to speak the language of right and wrong. I disagree. Different circumstances require different methods but not different moralities. Moral truth is the same in every culture, in every time and in every place. Targeting innocent civilians for murder is always and everywhere wrong. Brutality against women is always and everywhere wrong.

Added Bush:

There can be no neutrality between justice and cruelty, between the innocent and the guilty. We are in a conflict between good and evil. And America will call evil by its name.

President Obama's insistence that it is not possible to negotiate with the leaders of al-Qaeda might have seemed counterintuitive to Western liberals raised to believe in the primacy of reason in human affairs. But it isn't. On the contrary, he stands in a long American tradition of dualism, of dividing the evils with which one must live from those that must be fought because reason has reached its end. Consider the Declaration of Independence, where Jefferson's argument pivots not on a statement about self-evident truths, but on this neat bit of prose:

> Prudence, indeed, will dictate that Governments long established should not be changed for light and transient causes; and accordingly all experience hath shewn that mankind are more disposed to suffer, while evils are sufferable than to right themselves by abolishing the forms to which they are accustomed. But when a long train of abuses and usurpations, pursuing invariably the same Object evinces a design to reduce them under absolute Despotism, it is their right, it is their duty, to throw off such Government, and to provide new Guards for their future security.

We have had enough, the Declaration announces. We have tried everything, even negotiation:

> In every stage of these Oppressions We have Petitioned for Redress in the most humble terms: Our repeated Petitions have been answered only by repeated injury.

War, then, is the last resort, says Jefferson; the only way to combat evil when dialogue fails.

Or consider the struggle over slavery, when the leading abolitionist William Lloyd Garrison could declare: "My crime is, that I will not go with the multitude to do evil. My singularity is, that when I say that Freedom is of God, and Slavery is of the devil, I mean just what I say."[14] The arguments in favor of slavery, he contended, were not arguments at all: "They are the logic of Bedlam, the morality of the pirate ship, the diabolism of the pit."[15] The time has passed, said Garrison, for dialogue, because compromise is the device through which slavery "has grown to its present enormous dimension." The only way slavery could be "exterminated" was "by an uncompromising spirit."[16] One should not even entertain the possibility that there was anything to be said on the pro-slavery side: "[I]f a man should propose to me a discussion on the propriety of picking pockets, I would turn him out of my study."[17] Nor would he countenance any form of negotiation with the South that would allow slavery to survive, anywhere, even for a brief while:

> I will not try to make as good a bargain for the Lord as the Devil will let me, and plead the necessity of a compromise, and regret that I cannot do any better, and be thankful that I can do so much.[18]

Between the two sides, pro-slavery and abolitionist, stands "an impassable gulf" that negotiation will not bridge.[19]

Consider next this passage from President Franklin Roosevelt's radio address of December 29, 1940, on the "Arsenal of Democracy," bearing in mind that at this time America had not entered the Second World War, and isolationist sentiment at home ran strong:

> The Nazi masters of Germany have made it clear that they intend not only to dominate all life and thought in their own country, but also to enslave the whole of Europe, and then to use the resources of Europe to dominate the rest of the world.

For Roosevelt, the consequence of this understanding was simple:

In view of the nature of this undeniable threat, it can be asserted, properly and categorically, that the United States has no right or reason to encourage talk of peace, until the day shall come when there is a clear intention on the part of the aggressor nations to abandon all thought of dominating or conquering the world.

Thus, said Roosevelt, negotiations with the Nazis would be pointless. You do not, he argued, talk to those determined to conquer: you defeat them. Indeed, Roosevelt had strong words for those who argued that one should sit down with the Nazis:

> There are also American citizens, many of then in high places, who, unwittingly in most cases, are aiding and abetting the work of these agents. I do not charge these American citizens with being foreign agents. But I do charge them with doing exactly the kind of work that the dictators want done in the United States.
>
> These people not only believe that we can save our own skins by shutting our eyes to the fate of other nations. Some of them go much further than that. They say that we can and should become the friends and even the partners of the Axis powers. . . . But Americans never can and never will do that.

Sixty years later, rhetoric of this kind might seem to many unnecessarily warlike and confrontational. But President Obama, now that he is no longer candidate Obama, seems to have discovered the same truth that President George W. Bush discovered once he was no longer candidate Bush: there are forces in the world that must not be allowed to triumph. Sometimes matters really are as simple as that. Indeed, in presenting the choice between battling evil with force of arms and allowing it to flourish, the President was returning to the roots of the Western theory of just war. That theory has its origins in the effort by early Christians to work out what sorts of evils were sufficiently great that followers of an essentially nonviolent religion might be justified in taking up arms against them. But before we consider that theory in detail, let us take a moment to examine President Obama's views on the wars in which America is currently involved and how those views square with the just war theory he had invited us to invoke. After that, we will consider how President Obama's vision of what is worth fighting for squares with the tradition he cites.

The Justness of Self-Defense

America has long accepted that there are issues on which there is only one side, with the other only evil; that has been, through the nation's history, the very definition of the cause worth fighting for. President Obama's argument stands firmly in this tradition. But what kind of evil matters? What kind of evil gives rise to the moral right to go to war? In his Nobel Address, the President answered with a summary of the theory of just and unjust war—which, perhaps understandably, he somewhat oversimplified for his audience—and he was careful to include a right of self-defense:

> And over time, as codes of law sought to control violence within groups, so did philosophers and clerics and statesmen seek to regulate the destructive power of war. The concept of a "just war" emerged, suggesting that war is justified only when certain conditions were met: if it is waged as a last resort or in self-defense; if the force used is proportional; and if, whenever possible, civilians are spared from violence.

The President's brief summary does not really get to the heart of the just war tradition, but at least he makes clear which tradition he has in mind. The Western tradition of sorting just wars from unjust has its origins in Catholic theology, particularly the work of Augustine in the fourth and early fifth centuries and Aquinas in the thirteenth.[20] Aquinas and Augustine, like other thinkers of their eras, puzzled over when and how the Christian ruler could resort to the sword. After being secularized, so to speak, in the late sixteenth and early seventeenth centuries, the essentially religious understanding of just war developed by the church became the foundation of modern international law. In its early development, as we shall see, the idea of the just war had less to do with self-defense than with using the power of the sword to achieve justice and order in the world. Over the centuries, however—especially since the secular philosophers got their hands on the theory—the right of self defense has come to the fore.

The right to self-defense feels natural. It is all but axiomatic. If you are walking down the street and a mugger attacks you, you might try to flee. If you can't get away, you will likely try to defend yourself. If you injure your attacker in the process, no jury is going to convict you. No prosecutor is going to try. The law follows what has come to be our shared ethical understanding: you have the right to defend yourself.

So does your nation. If Country A invades Country B, Country B is like the one being mugged, and has the same right to fight back against the invader. In our modern understanding, it is war itself, not injustice, that is the evil we must avoid. The traditional conception of war as a tool of justice is one that we, at least in our rhetoric, tend to reject.[21] But war as a tool of self-defense is something we instinctively understand, and accept. That is the import of what the President, in his Nobel Address, said of the two major wars the United States is fighting:

> I am the Commander-in-Chief of the military of a nation in the
> midst of two wars. One of these wars is winding down. The
> other is a conflict that America did not seek; one in which we
> are joined by 42 other countries . . . in an effort to defend our-
> selves and all nations from further attacks.

Let us parse this a bit. Here, the President plainly means to distinguish between the Iraq and Afghan Wars. He took the same
position even before his Nobel Address, insisting that the
Afghan War (in his view, unlike the Iraq War) is a war of necessity.[22] His method has been to squeeze Afghanistan into the
moral space set aside for the use of force in self-defense. Every
version of the ethics of war, after all, accepts the justice of a war
to defend your country. (Much less important, the United Nations Charter accepts it, too.) True, the right of self-defense has
serious intellectual challengers—the philosopher Richard Norman[23] and the theologian Stanley Hauerwas[24] come to mind—
but they are plainly the outliers. And self-defense entails knotty
problems, not yet fully thought through, such as the relevance
of your attacker's motivation, and whether you have the same
right to shoot a man who is about to kill you by accident as you
do to shoot a man who is about to kill you on purpose.[25] Nevertheless, there exists a broad consensus, in law and philosophy,
that we as individuals have the right to defend ourselves, at least
when our own lives are at stake, and a similar consensus, in international law and the ethics of war, that countries, too, have
the right to defend themselves from attack. Indeed, at least
since the effective date of the United Nations Charter, a significant minority of scholars has argued that self-defense is the
only legitimate ground for war.

    This, then, is the moral and legal context for President
Obama's insistence (and the insistence of President Bush before him) that the Afghan War is a war for the defense of the

country. By labeling the war defensive, Obama is drawing it within the ambit of the just war tradition. By omission, Iraq becomes a war of some other kind—an unjust war, presumably. Ever since Barack Obama launched his presidential campaign, this argument has been a linchpin of his analysis. Many other commentators draw the same distinction between Afghanistan and Iraq. But the distinction is a good deal less sharp than it may appear.

Put aside for the moment whether we should accept the notion of the war of self-defense as the most obvious case of a just war. Consider instead what purportedly makes Afghanistan a war of self-defense in the first place. The argument would run something like this: The Taliban government harbored the al-Qaeda organization. Al-Qaeda trained and launched the fanatics who destroyed the World Trade Center and attacked the Pentagon on 9/11. Al-Qaeda had also sponsored or organized other attacks on Americans in the past. The United States warned the Taliban regime to throw open the al-Qaeda camps to American inspection or be overthrown. When the Taliban refused, the United States and its Coalition allies invaded.

Not bad, except for one small detail: At the moment of the American invasion, no actual attacks were being launched; and if any major attacks were, at that moment, near fruition, we have yet to learn of them. True, everyone, or nearly everyone, agreed that al-Qaeda would not stop unless forced to: a reasonable argument can be made that the war to overthrow the Taliban was just. Nevertheless, the war was, at best, of the preemptive variety, and possibly of the preventive variety.

In just war thinking, as in international law, a preemptive attack occurs when you strike an enemy who is on the verge of attacking you: when, say, the tanks are massed on your border, about to invade. Historically, preemption has been one of the most commonly asserted grounds for war: every aggressor claims that it had no choice because its neighbors were about to attack. Perhaps the most infamous example is Hitler's invasion of the Soviet Union in 1941, planned for months, which the Nazi regime justified to the world as necessary to keep Stalin from attacking first.[26] Arguably, the American Revolution was preemptive, too: Britain launched the war because of a fear that the colonies were about to stage a rebellion.[27] Indeed, from the point of view of the South, which started it, the Civil War was a preemptive war, for the secessionists whipped up fears that the North was about to confiscate their property—that is, the slaves—if necessary by force.[28]

A preventive attack occurs when your purpose is to keep your enemy from achieving the means to attack you at some future and unspecified date: if, for example, you attack his factories because you believe he is going to build a weapon of mass destruction and use it against you. The Israeli bombing of Iraq's Osirak nuclear reactor in 1981 is the classic modern example of a preventive attack: the idea is to set back your enemy's progress. Preventive war as commonly understood is very much a creature of modern technology. Nevertheless, one of the principal justifications for conquest of surrounding territory was security, and so empire building might be viewed as a sort of preventive war: if you take over the country next door, its rulers, presumably slain, will never be able to organize an invasion of your homeland. Indeed, this was the explicit reasoning of the Roman Republic in launching its various wars of expansion, in Greece, in eastern and northern Europe, and of course in Africa, where the Third Punic War resulted in the destruction of Carthage—at the time, Rome's principal rival. Consider Cicero's generous endorsement of the military conquests of the Republic:

Let me add, however, that as long as the empire of the Roman People maintained itself by acts of service, not of oppression, wars were waged in the interest of our allies or to safeguard our supremacy; the end of our wars was marked by acts of clemency or by only a necessary degree of severity; the senate was a haven of refuge for kings, tribes, and nations; and the highest ambition of our magistrates and generals was to defend our provinces and allies with justice and honour. And so our government could be called more accurately a protectorate of the world than a dominion.[29]

Safeguarding supremacy: this sounds very much like the language of preemption. The idea was to reduce potential rivals to the point where an attack on Rome would be unthinkable; and this policy, for a long time, kept safe first the Republic, then the Empire.

Yet one need not delve very far into just war theory to find a broad scholarly consensus that preemptive attacks are morally shaky but often necessary, whereas preventive attacks are almost always morally objectionable.[30] The principal concern with preventive attacks is the slippery slope problem: once you begin the work of prevention, it is not clear where to stop. (James Russell Lowell referred to the bombardment of Fort Sumter, the preventive attack that started the Civil War, as stemming from "the impatient vanity of South Carolina."[31])

Consider, for example, the passionate debate over whether the United States should accept the seeming inevitability that Iran will develop nuclear weapons, or take military action to prevent it. One form of the prevention argument holds that an attack on nuclear facilities would be justified because of the importance of keeping those weapons out of the hands of a regime thought likely to use them. Another holds that a nuclear-armed Iran would set off an arms race throughout the Middle East. The more nations that possess nuclear arms, the argument runs, the greater the chance that they will be used. No doubt this is so. Perhaps the argument is even correct. But one can see how attenuated the case can become, as the potential for harm recedes further into the future.

The reason it is worth pursuing this point is that the President is mistaken: the Afghan War was not actually forced upon the United States. It is a war that the nation chose to fight, a decision America's leaders made about how best to prevent al-Qaeda from launching future attacks. The decision might have been correct—the Afghan War might therefore be just—but to call the war "forced" reduces questions of judgment and prudence to analytical sideshows in a world in which we are controlled by events. America and its leaders possess both the capacity and the responsibility to act reflectively, not reflexively, when taking up arms.

Let us take a moment to unpack this proposition further.

After the attacks on the Pentagon and the World Trade Center, the nation's leaders concluded, as the 9/11 Commission noted, that al-Qaeda was a continuing threat, and that neither diplomacy nor limited attacks by standoff missiles had proved capable of stopping the group. Thus, wrote the commission, it was crucial to the nation's security that the military continue to "attack terrorists and their organizations," all over the world.[32] This understanding formed a cornerstone of the Bush Doctrine and has been adopted wholesale by the strategists of the Obama Administration as well. Again, recall President Obama's February 2010 eulogy, where he praised the Central Intelligence Agency for "the extremists who no longer threaten our country—because you eliminated them." Compare this with President Bush's language in his June 2002 speech to the graduating class at West Point, setting forth the Bush Doctrine: "[T]he war on terror will not be won on the defensive. We must take the battle to the enemy, disrupt his plans and confront the worst threats before they emerge." Bush added: "In the world we have entered the only path to safety is the path of action. And this nation will act."

The similarity is patent. Both Presidents reached the same conclusion. But why? Why must we attack terrorists all over the world? Because of the threat they pose to our security, obviously. And what is the threat? That, unstopped, they will launch future attacks. We do not know where and when, so the war against the terrorists is not preemptive. It is preventive. And this is true whether the terrorist leaders are being pursued by Special Forces in Afghanistan or Yemen, or blown to bits by missiles fired from Predator and Reaper drones in Somalia or Pakistan. Far from being forced upon us, then, the Afghan War is part of a larger policy of getting them before they can get us.

In this sense, contrary to President Obama's implication, the Afghan War and the Iraq War are justified by precisely the same theory: the need to prevent future attacks. Supporters of the Anglo-American invasion of Iraq believed that Saddam Hussein was developing weapons of mass destruction outside the prying eyes of the United Nations inspectors whose mission he did his best to frustrate. True, other justifications were offered for the invasion, such as the role played by Saddam Hussein in fomenting discord in the region, and his brutal attacks on his own people—but, for the moment, let us stay with the concern about future attacks on the United States. If this was indeed the motivation, then the war becomes preventive—much like the war in Afghanistan.

Why, then, the broad sense that the two wars are so very different? Because, in the case of Iraq, the evidence of intent was weaker. Most people—most countries—believed that al-Qaeda meant to strike America again. Many fewer people believed that

Saddam Hussein had any such intention; and fewer probably believe it today than believed it when the Iraq War began in 2003. Note that this conclusion is entirely independent of the question whether Saddam possessed a working supply of weapons of mass destruction. He could, after all, have possessed them and yet had no intention of using them against the United States, in which case a belief in the existence of the weapons would not have been a sufficient argument in favor of a preventive war of self-defense.

Let me be quite clear. It is an article of faith among many on the left that there exist on the right some who were chomping at the bit to strike Iraq, and that any evidence, however specious, would do. It is an article of faith among many on the right that there exist on the left some who will never find any war to their liking, and will seize upon any evidence, however specious, to justify their disapproval. Perhaps there is something to these ad hominem fears, but they are uninteresting to the scholar and, in a wiser world, would be equally uninteresting to politicians and pundits. Evidence and argument, not preexisting prejudices, should guide us in our moral lives, particularly when we ponder so momentous a moral decision as whether to move a nation to war. My point is that, from the point of view of reason, the essential argument for the Iraq War and the Afghanistan War was the same: we must do this, or they will sooner or later come after us. The difference between the two is empirical, not theoretical. Both wars were conceptualized as preventive. It is simply that, in the case of Iraq, there was probably a good deal less to prevent.[33]

That is not to say the invasion of Iraq cannot be justified. There are arguments on either side. Those among my students who support the Iraq War tend to refer to Saddam Hussein as a murderous tyrant, as no doubt he was, who fomented unrest in countries around him, as no doubt he did. Are these sufficient grounds? Jean Bethke Elshtain, a strong proponent of the

War on Terror, refers to the Iraq invasion as "a judgment call,"[34] and it is in the nature of judgment calls that reasonable people of good will can come out on different sides. Thus, President Obama believes that his predecessor exercised poor judgment. The war's supporters believe there was little choice. Some theorists would deny the moral right of one nation to make war on another when the question is close. Wars must be necessary, the argument runs, or they are forbidden. If one agrees with this theory, then if the war in Iraq was not necessary, but merely a war of choice, it could not properly be fought at all. I am skeptical of the argument, but it seems to have a growing number of adherents. The trouble is, if one truly believes that all wars of choice are organized mass murder, the claim cannot be limited to Iraq; it applies equally to Afghanistan; and this President of the United States is committing a crime. The antiwar activist Cindy Sheehan, among others, has lately described Obama in precisely these terms, labeling him a war criminal.[35] Sheehan is of course entitled to her opinion, but here her opinion is simply wrong. Indeed, such an accusation is contemptible nonsense, just as it was when the President was George W. Bush.

THE JUST WAR TRADITION

To understand why fighting a war does not make one a criminal, one must have a view about what makes a war just. I have already laid out the President's view—that the justice in a war arises because the war is fought in self-defense—and now I would like to contrast his theory with the actual tradition of just and unjust wars.

The just war tradition is not only the basis of international law but has become, in recent years, a part of everyday ethical conversation, as it should be. Commentators argue over whether a particular war has been launched as a last resort, or whether too many civilians are dying, or whether the amount of force being used is proportional to the end in view. So common are discussions of the criteria that the philosopher Michael Walzer has referred to the "triumph" of just war theory.[36] It is difficult to imagine a time when such conversations did not preoccupy public discourse about war. But systematic Western thought about when and how a war can ever be just did not begin with the secularists. The traditions, as I've indicated, developed among Christian thinkers who hesitated to suggest the permissibility of violence, and yet believed that there were times when the prince had an obligation to fight—as long as his goal was God's peace. The point was nicely captured by Martin Luther in the sixteenth century: "What men write about war, saying that it is a great plague, is all true. But they should also consider how great the plague is that war prevents."[37] As we shall see, the tradition was more sensible—and more morally attractive—before the secularists got their hands on it.

Consider again how President Obama summarized the just war tradition in his Nobel Address:

> And over time, as codes of law sought to control violence within groups, so did philosophers and clerics and statesmen seek to regulate the destructive power of war. The concept of a "just war" emerged, suggesting that war is justified only when certain conditions were met: if it is waged as a last resort or in self-defense; if the force used is proportional; and if, whenever possible, civilians are spared from violence.

The President thus named three characteristics of just war: self-defense; last resort; and proportionality. The structure of the sentence implies that self-defense is one thing and last resort another, suggesting, perhaps, that one need not wait until the last resort to launch a war of self-defense. Unless Obama was simply careless, which is unlikely in so carefully worded a speech, one can see how this vision would permit the Afghan War, even if, as I have suggested, that war is itself preventive in nature. The invasion of Afghanistan might not have been a last resort, but, according to Obama, it may have been justified nevertheless as an act of self-defense.

Fair enough. Still, there is much more to the just war thinking than the President mentioned. The tradition distinguishes between a set of questions to ask in determining whether or not a war is just, and a different set of questions to ask in determining whether or not a war is being waged in a just manner. President Obama, interestingly, drew a bit from each column— and what he left out is as important to the tradition as what he left in.

The rules for analyzing the justice of the war itself are known as the rules of *jus ad bellum:* literally, justice for war. In secular moral thinking, these include the following: the underlying cause must be just; the war must be a last resort; the war must be proclaimed by a legitimate authority; and there must be a reasonable hope of success. (Catholic theology also includes the notion that one must go to war with the "right intention." As we shall see, the decision of most secular thinkers to reject this criterion has led to difficulties.) From this list, the President mentioned only last resort, perhaps omitting the others as an indirect slap at the invasion of Iraq. He also mentioned self-defense, but that is, in just war theory, simply an example of a just cause. True, there are many thinkers who believe that self-defense is the only just cause for war, but, as we shall see, President Obama is not necessarily among them.

The just war criteria, especially since being taken over by secular policymakers and their apologists and critics, are often poorly understood. Put aside for the moment the criterion of just cause. Consider two of the most misused: the requirements that the war be a last resort and that it be waged by legitimate authority.

War as last resort is sometimes mistaken to mean that one should never wage war if there is any possibility of resolving differences peacefully. By this token, no war could be fought. The tanks might cross your border, the slaughter of your people might already have begun, but the invader might change its mind—thus there still remains a possibility that you need not resort to war. This view is very close to pacifism, and pacifism, as we shall see later on, has a respectable intellectual provenance. But pacifism is not a part of the just war tradition, which holds that there are times when it is indeed morally appropriate to take up arms. Thus the "last resort" of which just war theory speaks implies only the reasonable exhaustion of alternatives. You might try to avoid war, but if a time comes when you believe to a moral certainty that there is no peaceful way to obtain your just objective, then war becomes a permissible option.

And what about the requirement (omitted by the President) that war be waged only by the command of legitimate authority? This traditional rule of just war is badly misunderstood in contemporary America, as people confuse moral theory with domestic law, and therefore conclude that war cannot be just unless Congress authorizes it; or, for some critics, unless the United Nations does so. This misapprehends the purpose of the legitimate authority criterion. Let us go back to the first serious systematizer of the theory, Thomas Aquinas, who wrote, in his *Summa Theologica,* that war could only be fought by "the authority of the sovereign" because "it is not the business of the private individual to declare war."[38] The point was to ensure that war was a public not a private enterprise, because the power to redress grievances through the sword was given, said Aquinas, only to the sovereign.

In the Middle Ages, this problem was no small concern. It was not at all uncommon for various lords or even brigands to raise armies and purport to declare wars.[39] Aquinas's point was that these wars were not legitimate. The sovereign to whom the various lords owed fealty might declare war, and require them to fight for him, but the individual lords should not be doing battle against each other except on the sovereign's behalf. Aquinas's notion was that the power of the sword was placed by God in the hand of the legitimate ruler, and nobody else. The brigand could do only private violence, for private gain, an act that was never justified. In modern terms, the legitimate authority criterion means that only nations, not individuals or groups within them, are permitted to do battle. Today's inheritor of this mantle of lawless war making is the pirate. As we shall see later on, some contend that the terrorist, too, belongs in this category.

Consider next the requirement (also not mentioned by Obama) that war must not be undertaken unless you have a reasonable hope of success. The idea is to avoid unnecessary violence. If you cannot win, the argument runs, you should not fight. When I teach just war, my students always have a problem here. There is after all something most of us find admirable in, for example, the Warsaw Ghetto uprising. But desperate resistance in the face of overwhelming odds is not the moral problem that just war theory should restrict. Were nations unable to defend themselves whenever their attackers were mightier, there might be a new war every week. The likelihood of success is a more important consideration for the leader pondering a war that is not a war of necessity.[40]

And what about the requirement that the cause itself be a just one? Aquinas, the principal systematizer of the ethics of war, argued that only one goal is ever truly just: "Those who wage war justly aim at peace." Thus, for Aquinas, the enemy "should be attacked because they deserve it on account of some fault (*causa*)."[41] Nowadays, the most widely accepted example of a just cause is self-defense, and it is upon self-defense that President Obama has consistently relied in explaining the necessity of the Afghan War. In his Nobel Address, the President also left open the possibility of going to war for humanitarian purposes—that is, fighting for the defense of someone other than one's own people—a point to which we shall return in Part III. Suffice to say here that there were those among the church fathers who considered defense of others a more worthy cause than self-defense. Augustine, for example, warned that we should never kill out of love of self, but only out of love for others.

The President also made reference to trying to spare civilians from violence. Here Obama was reworking one of the two criteria of what the tradition calls *jus in bellum* —"justice in war," a reference to the way in which the war is conducted. The just war tradition holds the just and the unjust sides to the same standards of conduct, and these are two, not one as the President suggested. First, one must target only the enemy's soldiers and military facilities, never civilians, a rule known as discrimination. Second, one must not do more damage than is reasonably necessary to gain the just end, a rule known as proportionality (the one the President did mention). Thus, a more accurate summary of just war theory would include the following requirements: just cause, last resort, legitimate authority, reasonable hope of success, proportionality, and discrimination.

There is a tendency, in our law-happy world, to view the theory of just and unjust wars as a legal structure, a set of rules with which a sovereign power must comport.[42] The traditional understanding of the idea, however, was that the principles of justice with which a war should comport were simply part of a larger conversation about how to live justly. This was how the problem was understood by Augustine, the intellectual progenitor of just war thinking, who saw the question of war as a subset of the larger question of politics. The state does exist, Augustine reasoned, and the state does act. We cannot wish it away. Therefore, in Augustinian thought, a question of first moral importance is always how the state should act: bearing in mind, always, that whenever the state acts, whether in war or in law, the state is acting coercively, bearing the sword against those who disagree.[43] Seen this way, war is not a radical departure from other aspects of human practice, but is instead an activity that, like all human activities, must be dedicated to the search for justice and peace. Peace to Augustine meant not the entire absence of violence (although one could hope for that), but rather life in accord with good order. War, like law itself, was placed by God in the hands of the sovereign so that the sovereign might move us closer to that good order.

How does all of this relate to President Obama's assertion that there are those in the world who are not amenable to reason? The fit is perfect. At the heart of the just war tradition is the belief that evil exists in the world, and must be combated. Not merely other ways of seeing reality, or other points of view, but actual evil. This simple fact is widely misunderstood. Some theorists see the just war tradition as mainly about the preservation of peace. Others insist that it stems from the need to achieve justice. But to understand its origin, back in the early centuries of Christianity, one must also understand the way that the world view of the early Christians was characterized by a sharp dualism, a belief in the inevitable conflict of the forces of evil and the forces of good. As the biblical historian Wayne Meeks has put it: "The realm of Satan and his host of daimonia or 'unclean spirits' stands over against the realm of God and of the good, until at last the one will destroy the other."[44] Augustine warned of the constant danger of attack by "deserters from the heavenly army."[45]

Of course this language is partly metaphorical; more to the point, spiritual. The war is internal, the constant battle of conscience and desire. But there is an external manifestation to our unsettled spiritual selves, and that is the constant cruelty and injustice to which we mortals subject our fellow man. The war might be forestalled but cannot finally be avoided. The battle is a constant: thus the need, in the words of Paul's letter to the Ephesians, to put on the armor of God. The early Christians saw themselves as under constant "threat from human and superhuman opponents," standing with God in the midst of "vast forces of evil arrayed against them."[46] And even if the threats were, for the most part, spiritual rather than temporal, the need to be ready for the battle was a constant.

The church fathers, the originators of just war thinking in the West, understood our daily choice as between not war or peace, but justice or injustice. This is another reason that just war theory was richer before the secularists got their hands on it.[47] Here we should pause for a historical note. Hugo de Groot, known as Grotius, revered as the father of international law, decided in the seventeenth century to strip away what had been, for Aquinas, a central tenet of the ethics of warfare: that the sovereign who makes war, in addition to meeting all the other tenets of *jus ad bellum* and *jus in bello*—"justice for war" (the cause, and the process) and "justice in war" (the manner of fighting)—had also to act with right intention. To the church fathers who labored so many centuries over the agonizing move from a Christianity of pacifism to a Christianity in which the believer could take life, it was crucial that the sovereign go to war, as Aquinas wrote, with "a rightful intention," by which he meant that the sovereign must intend "the advancement of good, or the avoidance of evil."[48] That intention was bound up with the concept of Christian peace, born of love of neighbor, which is why, paradoxical though it may seem to the modern mind, the church fathers tended to discuss war and love together in their treatises.[49] Thus a war, say, to expand one's territory, or to gain resources, or simply for glory, would never be just. But as long as the aim of the war was peace, there was no requirement that the fault, the *causa,* be committed against the sovereign that decided to wage war. Augustine's view was similar. "For it is the wrongdoing of the opposing party," he wrote in *The City of God,* "which compels the wise man to wage just wars."[50] The prince could perfectly well go justly to war to protect the innocent.

In time, secular just war theory would largely dispense with the requirement of a right intention, on the theory that no state, even a monarchy, ever acts with a single motive only.[51] This is of course a familiar truth of modern political theory, but has been known for centuries. As Benjamin Franklin put it, "[W]hile a Party is carrying on a general Design, each man has his particular private Interest in View."[52] And yet, in evaluating the justice of a war, it may after all be advisable to take intention into account, at least in the sense in which Aquinas meant it: to be just, your war must be intended to advance good, or avoid evil.

All of which is to say that President Obama's insistence that there are evils in the world that must be combated with force rather than reason is not in any sense a violation of the just war tradition. On the contrary. The President is making precisely the sort of claim that the originators of the tradition thought the sovereign was obliged to make. He is differentiating between the evils with which you can negotiate and the evils with which you cannot. He may be right or wrong in his conclusion that there is no point to negotiating with al-Qaeda and other terror groups—as Roosevelt might have been right or wrong in concluding the same about the Nazis. Indeed, it may be that there are no forces anywhere in the world so wicked that they must be combated with force of arms. Given the path of human history, however, the burden of proof surely rests upon the critics.

THE NEED FOR INTELLIGENCE

Very well: let us concede President Obama's view of the world. The terror threat is real. The intention to do us harm is real. The notion, occasionally broached, that we have brought the threat upon ourselves by our foreign policy is a non sequitur. If our policies are wrong, the reason to change them is that they are wrong, not that they make some people in the world angry. If our policies are right, then we are fighting in defense of them. Either way, if the threat is real, the most relevant question is what to do about it. One answer is to try, in effect, to figure out what terrorists want, and give it to them. The problem, of course, is that giving someone what he wants creates an incentive for him to keep doing what he is doing.[53]

As we have seen, the President's response is to insist that we have the right, in defense of the nation, to launch a war that is at best preemptive and possibly preventive. The puzzle that just war theory has not yet resolved is how real the threat must be before a preventive or preemptive war can be declared a war of self-defense. Intelligence flows in all the time, from all around the world. Some of it seems reliable, some of it less so. Constructing from these myriad clues a coherent threat assessment is, according to many in the field, the toughest aspect of intelligence work. If Obama is right—if the United States has the right to strike the enemy before the enemy strikes us first—how certain do we have to be of the enemy's intention before we act?

One answer that appears often in the literature is, as the scholars would say, to discount the harm by the likelihood of its occurrence. Thus, the greater the harm a particular threat would cause, the less evidence you need to act upon it. This approach, common to other areas of state action, would here produce interestingly counterintuitive results. This would mean that if we suspected another nation of developing catastrophically powerful weapons of mass destruction, we could act on a smaller quantum of evidence than if we were worried about some lesser harm. Thus, for example, Richard Cheney, former vice president of the United States, has argued that we should apply to the nation's defense what amounts to a version of what is known in environmental law as the "precautionary principle": that we should, in effect, be prepared for the possible use of force against a potential adversary even if the likelihood of its launching a catastrophic attack is only 1 percent.

The discounting idea does not apply merely to potential future adversaries, such as the Islamic Republic of Iran. One of Cheney's specific concerns, according to journalist Ron Suskind's best-selling book, *The One Percent Doctrine,* was the possibility that al-Qaeda was developing a nuclear weapon, a threat to which he argued we should respond even if the probability was only 1 percent. He made the same argument, evidently, about the possibility that Saddam Hussein possessed weapons of mass destruction.[54] It was precisely this discounting process, however, that got us into trouble in Iraq, where much of the intelligence turned out to be less compelling than President Bush and his advisers believed. Cheney developed the notion in part as an answer to critics of the intelligence on which much of the case for war was based, and here, again, he is half right. A decision must be made on the evidence as presented, not the additional evidence you discover later, long after the deadline has passed. In retrospect, the decision to concentrate the American fleet at Pearl Harbor to avoid Japanese attack today looks absurd, but on the information available to military commanders in the fall of 1941, the choice seemed a sensible one.[55] Similarly, the argument against the invasion in Iraq cannot be that no weapons of mass destruction were *found.*[56] The decision makers had no opportunity to look at the answers, as it were, in the back of the book. If the presence of weapons of mass destruction matters, then the argument against the invasion must be that the information at the time did not justify the precaution—that is what it was, a precaution—of launching an attack. This, it seems to me, is Cheney's point.*

The 1-percent theory has been the subject of a good deal of foolish ridicule, and some very effective academic criticism, including by Cass Sunstein, now an adviser to President Obama.[57] Yet there is a certain elegance to the idea, the flip side, if you will, of the remark attributed by various authors to various terror suspects from different parts of the globe, explaining the difference between committing acts of terror, and defending against them: "We win if we get through 1 percent of the time. You lose if you stop us 99 percent of the time." (Or words to that effect.[58]) One sees the point. When we contemplate disaster, our heuristics misfire. Catastrophic harms tend to be treated, in our minds and in our regulations, as far more likely than they are. And, certainly, successful terror attacks are considered catastrophic. The public position is, in effect, zero tolerance. If no attacks are permitted, then no risks can be taken. Thus a risk of 1 percent becomes too high.

The point is not merely heuristic. It is also arithmetical. Suppose we have a 50 percent chance of suffering an attack that would kill 100 people. Everyone would agree that the government should take steps to stop it. The expected harm (.5 chance × 100 deaths = 50 deaths) is, however, precisely the same in the case of an attack with a 25 percent chance of oc-

---

*I should make clear that I never considered the supposed weapons of mass destruction, even had they existed, to be adequate *casus belli,* and, therefore, their nonexistence is, in a sense, beside the point. The mere existence of the weapons would not by itself have been evidence that the United States or its allies were in danger. The problem the Bush Administration faced in justifying the Iraq War was not so much the intelligence as tying what the intelligence taught to the national interests of the United States and its allies.

currence that would kill 200 people (.25 × 200 = 50), or the
case of an attack with a 1 percent chance that would kill 5,000
people (.01 × 5,000 = 50). The expected harm from all three
attacks is the same. The 1-percent principle, in short, was never
ridiculous. Indeed, it provides a useful example of a place
where we could do with more serious reflection and less hate-
mongering. An idea can be worrisome, or even wrong, without
being evil or absurd.

And the 1-percent notion *is* worrisome. Cass Sunstein has
pointed out that it produces the same paradoxes as the precautionary environmental principle it imitates, a tendency, if taken
seriously, to freeze us into utter inaction, since we never know
for sure what any regulation will do, meaning that some small
risk of harm is present no matter what we decide.[59] Putting the
practicalities aside, the 1-percent idea is politically untenable,
and morally indefensible. We are speaking not of regulation but
of war; not of using law to control people's actions but of using
violence to take their lives. Consider all the different terror
groups and hostile governments around the world that might
obtain weapons of mass destruction. Imagine that each has at
least a 1 percent chance of success. One sees at once that the
need for military action would never abate. A theory that, taken
seriously, would require near-constant offensive warfare forces
us to search for the second- or third-best idea. One hopes that
Cheney meant the proposal as a thought experiment. No government could undertake to turn it into policy.

And yet one does not want to carry this form of argument
too far. A common assertion made against both the Afghan and
Iraq wars was that each would lead to unpredictable consequences. There is the whiff of tautology in this criticism. As
Thomas Schelling pointed out at the height of the Cold War,
every war possesses that characteristic, and modern warfare,
with its remarkable array of weaponry, ironically has a greater

not a smaller tendency to veer in unexpected directions.[60] The wary cautioned that Vietnam would lead to foreign policy ca-tastrophe, and they were right. The wary cautioned that the invasions of Panama and Grenada would lead to continent-shaking consequences, and they were wrong.[61] As it turned out, the "war" part of the Iraq invasion went smoothly. The Iraqi army collapsed with remarkable swiftness, including the Revo-lutionary Guards, supposed on the eve of the conflict to be a formidable fighting force.[62] The peace, on the other hand, was considerably tougher than the Administration expected, a re-minder of the wisdom of the principle of international law re-quiring a conqueror to keep order once the regime has been toppled.

When one adds in the War on Terror, however, the argument for unpredictable consequences becomes more powerful, in part because of the difficulty of specifying precisely whom the war is against. "Those who mean us ill," and similar phrases, are too broad, and too vague. It would be easy for one who listens only to the sound bites to come around to the view that some supporters of the Terror War view Islam itself as at least suspect and, in some of its forms, as the enemy. And it is true that if one reads the fiery sermons of some of the most fanatical imams, (something I have spent a great deal of time doing), one cannot help but be struck by how little time they spend attacking our policies, and how much time they spend attacking the con-sumerism, sexual freedom, and gender equality that are hall-marks of the West. But so what? One cannot fight a war against words, and one must not fight a war against a faith. In Afghan-istan and in Iraq, at least it is clear who the enemy is. In pursu-ing the broader War on Terror, which so far has taken aim principally at violent Islamist groups, we must take pains to dis-tinguish those who hate us from those willing to act on their hatred; and we must never fall into the odious trap of treating

Muslims as objects of suspicion, rather than fellow human be-ings—and, increasingly, fellow citizens. President Obama and President Bush have both stressed that Islam is not the enemy, and they are right to do so.

And what of those missing weapons of mass destruction? There is a tendency nowadays to respond to *realpolitik* with epic poetry, to search for the seeds of every wrong decision in some-one's grand design. Because no large stores of weapons of mass destruction were found in Iraq, the argument runs, there had to be a conspiracy afoot, an effort by the Bush Administration to lie and cheat in order to launch the war. The trouble with the theory is that the war has no obvious American beneficiar-ies. (The dreaded oil companies, for example, supposedly able to manipulate American foreign policy at whim, would have preferred that the sanctions keeping Iraqi oil off the market simply be dropped. More on this later.) It is easy to invent con-spiracies, but it is logical to apply Occam's Razor. More likely, the intelligence failure that helped lead to the Iraq War was pre-cisely what it seems: an intelligence failure.[63]

This is a proposition that matters. If, as President Obama ev-idently believes, America's leaders have an obligation to attack the terrorists wherever they may be found, correct intelligence is crucial. Unfortunately, correct intelligence is also very diffi-cult to obtain. That is why we read stories of Hellfire missiles fired from Predator and Reaper drones all too often blowing up not a secret al-Qaeda strategy session but a wedding party. John Keegan, the world's preeminent military historian, argues in his fine book *Intelligence in War* that the military intelligence that is most-prized—the "gold standard"—is real-time informa-tion on enemy actions: Where is this ship headed? What time are the planes launching? But, says Keegan, until fairly recent history, real-time intelligence was almost impossible to come by. Indeed, in the medieval age, it was all but unheard of.[64] One had to deduce the enemy's intentions, and wrong guesses led to great military disasters.

But times changed. Any history book will recount, for example, Admiral Nelson's famous three-month pursuit of the French fleet. Nelson found the fleet and destroyed it, effectively putting an end to the war with Napoleon. Was the victory merely a tribute to Nelson's superior seamanship? Keegan thinks not, attributing the outcome largely to the British advantage in patiently cultivating sources of intelligence that helped indicate where the French were headed. At that time, the real-time use of information was almost unheard of in war, because the distances between source and analyst, then analyst and general, were so vast. But Nelson had set up an extensive system of relays to bring information to his own ships as swiftly as possible. He was able to use the information to corner and destroy Napoleon's ships. This was the origin of military intelligence in the modern sense.

Plainly, if the War on Terror is going to proceed largely by drone missile attack, accurate real-time intelligence is crucial. The targeters must know where to find their targets. And therein lies the problem. In recent history, signals intelligence—intercepted messages and calls and the like—has been more easily gathered than human intelligence. Yet, as Keegan points out, human intelligence often yields more extensive and accurate information. The trouble is, the organizations targeted in the War on Terror are so difficult to penetrate that signals intelligence is often all there is. Terror groups have learned from bitter experience to keep their electronic communication brief, or to avoid it altogether.

But creating live sources within terror groups has proved nearly impossible; and, even once recruited, they often prove unreliable, or worse. Consider again President Obama's eulogy for the seven of the Central Intelligence Agency killed by a suicide bombing inside a protected military installation in Khost Province in southeastern Afghanistan. How did the bomber breach security? According to press reports, the CIA officers at the base "were responsible for collecting intelligence on militant networks in Afghanistan and Pakistan and plotting missions to kill their top leaders."[65] The bomber who killed them had been identified by the Jordanian secret service as a potential source on the whereabouts of the al-Qaeda leadership. He turned out to be, in the argot, doubling.[66] As of this writing, the Agency has yet to issue a public report on its investigation, and perhaps it never will. But a sound supposition is that the bomber's access, with all the risk involved, resulted in part from the pressure to find live sources.

The journalist Tim Weiner, in his history of the Agency, tells the story of Ali Hassan Salameh, the intelligence chief of the Palestine Liberation Organization during the 1970s, who (with the consent of Yasir Arafat) provided information to the United States for years. "During that time," reports Weiner, "the CIA's reporting on terrorism in the Middle East was better than it ever had been, or ever would be again."[67] Alas, Salameh may have been a good source, but he was not a good man. He had been an architect of the massacre of Israeli athletes at the Munich Olympics in 1972, an act that led to his end, and the end of the stream of intelligence he provided: the Israelis assassinated him in 1978.

And therein lies the conundrum of seeking human sources during the Terror War. If they are placed highly enough to know anything important, the likelihood is that they have innocent blood on their hands. Indeed, it is possible, perhaps probable, that even while providing information, they will continue to ply their trade. The United States has been understandably reluctant to recruit sources who kill. One lesson of the past decade is that nobody else has the intelligence we need.

Throughout the Middle East and the Persian Gulf, more-over, America's own intelligence officers are also at high risk: by most estimates, at higher risk than during the Cold War. In 1983, an explosion tore through the American embassy in Beirut, a blast so gigantic that it rocked an American warship five miles off the coast.[68] Six employees of the Central Intelligence Agency were killed (including the chief of station and his wife) and the CIA station was for practical purposes wiped out. After the attack, the Agency's capacity to gather hard intelligence in the region was crippled, for several years practically destroyed.[69] Two years later, William Buckley, the new Beirut station chief, was kidnapped and, over a captivity lasting a year and a half, tortured to death. (In a bizarre coincidence, five years later, another senior CIA officer assigned to Beirut station died in the bombing of Pan-Am flight 103 over Lockerbie, Scotland.)

More recently, in 2001, Mike Spann, a member of the Agency's Special Activities Division, was killed by prisoners he had been questioning at the Qala-i-Jangi prison compound in Afghanistan. Two years later, also in Afghanistan, two more members of Special Activities Division died in an ambush while tracking a terror cell. Then, in 2009, came the bombing at Khost, already mentioned, that killed seven Agency officers. In the Terror War, this history teaches, human intelligence— the gold standard—has proved difficult to develop, and dangerous, too. The effort to learn what the other side is doing is getting our own intelligence officers killed, and in large numbers.

The challenge for the Obama Administration, as it continues pursuing not only the Afghan War but the War on Terror, is to discover ways to improve the nation's ability to gather and evaluate intelligence. Without good intelligence, we will blow up plenty of wedding parties, but all too few terrorist leaders.

The Temptation to Torture

Very well: the War on Terror needs good information. Intelligence is needed not only to know where and when to fire missiles, but also to prevent future attacks on America. If electronic intercepts are next to useless, and human sources nearly impossible to cultivate, one must ask what the alternative is. Yet the answer is obvious.

The alternative is to interrogate the other side's people after capture.

An FBI publication describes "the sole purpose of an interrogation" as "[o]btaining information that an individual does not want to provide."[70] It is by all accounts a tricky business. Despite media reports, the stream of claims from self-styled experts, and the collapse of one suspect after another in the back rooms of television programs like *Law and Order*, the fact is that nobody does it particularly well, and there is no secret key to finding the truth. As one experienced interrogator has put it, "human beings are much more proficient at lying than at detecting lies."[71] Getting the truth through interrogation can be rather hit or miss. An otherwise honest and decent person who has committed only this one crime is considered likely to confess.[72] Professional criminals and repeat offenders seem especially tough to crack.[73] So are those who have issued strong denials, even when obviously guilty.[74]

When the Federal Bureau of Investigation ceased its questioning of the so-called Christmas bomber in December 2009, after just fifty minutes, informing him of his rights and letting him summon a lawyer, critics excoriated the Obama Administration for failing to follow its own procedures. (The Department of Justice had adopted rules allowing extended interrogation when the purpose was not bringing charges but obtaining information.) The critics were at best half right. Nobody has ever won a war by treating it as a matter of law enforcement, and the nation is at war. On the other hand, the criticism requires an important leap of faith: the assumption that had the failed bomber been treated as an enemy combatant rather than a criminal suspect, he would have disclosed more information than he did. Nobody knows the answer to that question. True, long interrogations generally provide more information than shorter ones, and interrogations of less than an hour almost always fail.[75] On the other hand, al-Qaeda, by all accounts, works hard at interrogation resistance techniques. The subject is, literally, covered in the training manual: a copy was recovered by the police in a raid in Manchester, England. Moreover, there are, at the moment, serious disputes over how much actionable intelligence has actually been obtained from high-level detainees in the Terror War. Common sense says there must be some. But those who know exactly how much are keeping mum.

Which leads us to the scariest subject of the War on Terror: what we are willing to become in order to protect ourselves. Much has been argued over the last few years about torture, and other coercive efforts at gaining information. Listening to the debate, one is reminded of Michael Walzer's warning, that nations facing existential threat will always do what they believe they must in order to survive, even when it violates rules that everyone knows should never be broken.[76] This, says Walzer, is reality, and to wish it away is childish. The legal scholar Paul W. Kahn, among the most thoughtful writers on torture today, puts the point another way: there may be, he suggests, "a point at which conflict becomes too primitive to be regulated by moral intuition or legal rule."[77] The War on Terror, Kahn suggests, is almost impossible to conceptualize without torture. He is on to something. The purpose of the Terror War, after all, is not to punish but to prevent; and prevention requires information that many of those who possess it will be reluctant to impart. If those who possess the information would rather not part with it, the government will always be tempted, in the lovely old Britishism, to require it out of them. The greater the sense of threat, the greater the temptation.

And so we must face the question squarely: what is it that we dislike about torture? The obvious answer is that we shrink from the intentional infliction of pain on others, as we should. Yet this cannot be the entire story. Missiles fired from Predators and Reapers inflict death, not merely pain; and they also inflict pain, as the penalty for being near the strike, but not quite near enough to be killed. We seem not to shrink from drone attacks. Economic sanctions inflict suffering, and on ordinary individuals, almost never the key supporters of the regime.* We seem not to flinch from them. Prison inflicts pain; indeed, many of those who are incarcerated suffer vicious crimes behind prison walls. We continue to imprison. None of these common yet violent practices provokes the same popular outrage that torture does. Indeed, as Kahn points out, however horrific torture may be, it is difficult to make the case that it is more horrific than war itself.

The key, then, must not be the pain alone. Here Elaine Scarry is most likely correct. What makes true torture objectionable is the combination of the pain itself and the helplessness of the victim. Torture, says Scarry, mimics war: "Whereas the object of war is to kill people, torture usually mimes the killing of people by inflicting pain, the sensory equivalent of death, substituting prolonged mock execution for execution."[78] And although the just war tradition would not agree that the object of war (as against its effect) is to kill people, the analogy is otherwise apt, which helps explain why torture so frequently arises as incident to war: the two are separate practices, but along the same con-

---

*I discuss the efficacy of sanctions in detail in Part III, below.

tinuum. Note, moreover, Scarry's use of the term "prolonged." This aspect distinguishes torture from many other forms of pain. It keeps going. That is the point. You cannot tell yourself, "If I can make it another half hour, I will survive," because you are the mercy of the torturer, who can stretch the half hour into two hours, or ten, or a day or two, or weeks, or months, or whatever your body is able medically to bear. Moreover, the victim as a rule is restrained: strapped or tied or chained somewhere while the torturer goes about his cruel business.[79]

Where the torturer works, our common understanding of life is inverted. One mark of civilization is that the mind controls the body rather than the other way around. The goal of torture is to make the body control the mind. The torturer wants to force the mind to yield its secrets, and will use the body to get them. Scarry refers to this, memorably, as the body becoming voice: we talk not because we decide to but because the pain wracking our body forces us to.[80]

Once again, it is the helplessness of the victim that creates the horror. There is a powerful symbology in the image of the individual facing overwhelming odds who nevertheless possesses the ability to fight back; he may fail, but he will, as we like to say, die trying. But the victim of torture cannot aspire to this relatively noble end. He cannot fight back and, in the end, cannot resist. The victim is always helpless. The torturer always prevails. It may take time—with modern methods, rarely much time—but, in the end, the torturer always prevails. And although it has become common, in much of the antitorture literature, to claim that torture never works, that one gets only the bad information that the victim invents to avoid the pain, the experience of life bears witness to just the opposite. No doubt those who are tortured might repeat in desperation whatever the torturer tells them to say, and, in this way, confess to things that are not true. Thus, aside from its pain and intrusiveness, torture can result in information that is false. I have no idea how often this happens. Perhaps it happens a lot. This is programming, not invention. The victim is not making up a story. The victim is repeating lines he is being fed. Some have even speculated that the torture victim may intentionally lie. As the legal historian John Langbein has suggested, "Terrorists willing to die for their cause would also be willing to plant false tales under torture."[81] And, of course, there will always be those who torture simply because they are sadists, or because they are lazy, or because the fear of being tortured (as against fear of surrendering information) might make a subjugated populace less likely to oppose the state.

But the problem of false confessions would seem especially acute when the object of torture is to obtain exactly that: a confession. If the confession is itself sufficient to justify punishment, there is no check upon the torturer.[82] When, on the other hand, the purpose of the torture is to obtain secrets, an obvious if imperfect external check exists: the torturer can send off investigators to try to discover whether the secrets are true. In other words, there are likely situations in which torture provides actual information, a fact, as Judge Richard Posner has dryly put it, that may help account for its universal application.

And, in recent history, torture has provided information. In a recent German case, the police threatened torture to get a kidnapper to tell them where he had hidden a missing boy. He told them. (The threat came too late: the boy was dead.) Alan Dershowitz reminds us of the French resistance groups broken during World War II because of information obtained through torture. Indeed, the historian John Keegan points to Gestapo torture as a key reason that underground groups in occupied Europe remained weak and unreliable. There are other sad examples. Just before Christmas of 1983, an officer in the Clandestine Services of the Central Intelligence Agency was arrested by the Ethiopian government. He was tortured for more than a month. He gave away actual secrets, and America's intelligence networks in Ethiopia were largely destroyed. (The officer was later repatriated, only to discover that he had become a pariah: his associates in the Agency seemed to think he should have resisted.[83]) It may even be, as some have suggested, that the experience of pain makes it harder, not easier, to lie. A character in one of John le Carré's novels, subjected to torture, is described thus: "It was not that Jim broke exactly; he just he ran out of invention. He couldn't think up any more stories. The truths that he had locked away so deeply were the only things that suggested themselves."

In a way, that is the torturer's final insult, is it not? The torturer controls the body, and its physical responses, and that is horrific and degrading enough. But, in the end, the torturer controls even the mind, ferreting out all that the victim wishes fervently to protect. There is no process in all of human ingenuity quite so intrusive as to pluck what one wants from the confines of a man's mind.

When I use the term "torture," I am speaking, of course, of the infliction of pain, and intentionally so. Elaine Scarry, writing in 1985, defined torture this way: "Torture consists of a primary physical act, the infliction of pain, and a primary verbal act, the interrogation."[84] And although her more recent views seem more open to considering non-painful acts as torture,[85] I think she was right the first time. Posner suggests reserving the word "torture" for "an inflection point, when the coercion changes from the psychological to the physical."[86] And although I suspect that each of us could easily compile a list of nonphysical procedures we would consider torture, certainly we must draw the line somewhere. Classifying everything unpleasant as "torture" makes a mockery of language. We must not redefine terms to the extent that we become unable to reason about distinctions. Threatening to kill a prisoner is horrific, but not as horrific as actually killing him. Holding him in a position that stresses his knees is outrageous, but not as outrageous as breaking his knees. Forcing him to listen to loud and noxious sounds is terrible, but not as terrible as cutting off his ears. When we say that all that is bad is identical, we are not creating useful moral bright lines; we are, rather, establishing our own moral laziness, our inability to admit that even among those things that shock our consciences, there are degrees of shock.

The degrees matter because there are tipping points. Each of us has heard the various hypotheticals—the thermonuclear device hidden in Manhattan, the child about to be raped and murdered—and each of us, if we are honest, has a limit beyond which we would turn a blind eye to the more coercive forms of interrogation. But each of us must also have a conscience that imposes internal limits, which is why degrees are important: I might say, for instance, in order to save the child, I will countenance threatening to cut off the perpetrator's fingers, but not actually cutting them.* Simply to dismiss each of these possibilities under the single term "torture" is to deny both the ability of reason to draw distinctions, and the inevitability that humans will make compromises.

This is not to say that we should give any of this the force of moral or legal legitimacy. Alan Dershowitz, an opponent of torture, has offered the controversial suggestion that since there are circumstances in which we would all approve it, we should legitimize it, developing rules and standards and perhaps even judicial warrants.[87] And even Elaine Scarry, perhaps the most articulate academic critic of torture, has conceded that the

---

*To intercept the obvious rejoinder, if the child who is under threat is my own, I should not have a role in the decision, because my reason will not be the driver of my views.

practice might well be moral in extraordinary circumstances, provided always that the torturer later be forced to make his case to a jury in open court[88]—a proposal similar to Dershowitz's, but with the judicial review after rather than before the fact. (This is what happened in the case from Germany mentioned above.) The trouble, of course, is that by allowing torture even a conversational legitimacy, we guarantee its future use: or, as Jean Bethke Elshtain has put it, "[T]hat which is rightly taboo now becomes just another piece in the armamentarium of the state."[89] That is the point of the law professor Charles Black's famous argument, that there no doubt are situations in which even a judge would permit torture to continue, but we should still prefer the judge who, even as he turned a blind eye, would insist that torture has no place in the legal system.[90]

Black's argument will never persuade an antitorture absolutist. Neither will any of the others. And absolutism is defensible, as long as it is pure. The supposed absolutist who ends his argument by saying, "Besides, I believe we can achieve our just ends without resorting to torture" is not an absolutist at all. His quarrel is not moral but empirical; he is skeptical not of the tool but of its necessity. The suggestion of that common caveat, *I believe we can,* is that, should the assumption turn out to be wrong—should the existential threat be looming, and nothing but torture suffice—the supposed absolutist would say, "Well, in that case, torture away."

The true absolutist is rare. The true absolutist will say, and mean it, "Never resort to torture even when there is no other way. If the bomb is ticking, if the skies are falling, if the nation is on the verge of destruction, we are nevertheless morally better people if we do not torture." This position is, in its way, noble, but it fails to partake of the reality that we have no choice but to rank evils. To say, "I would never torture to prevent mass murder" is indeed admirable; but it is not clear why it is more admirable than to say, "I would never torture except to prevent mass murder."

Moreover, as Posner points out, calling oneself an absolutist does not really answer the principal argument. Even if torture is always wrong, "there is such a thing as a lesser wrong committed to avoid a greater one."[91] This holds true, at least, in some versions of secular philosophy: the orthodoxy of the Christian tradition would forbid the intentional infliction of evil in pursuit of good. And just war theory certainly would not countenance setting out to harm a helpless prisoner—even a helpless prisoner who has done the most terrible things. I suppose that is why I consider myself an absolutist. But it seems to me an error in analysis to suppose that if one does not oppose torture in all circumstances, one must therefore be a monster. Although there may be hidden sadists in any security force, I suspect that most of those who torture on behalf of the United States imagine themselves making just that compromise: committing the lesser wrong to avoid the greater one. Perhaps this tradeoff is unwise. Perhaps the tradeoff is often immoral. But I cannot call it absurd.

OBAMA AND TORTURE

And where does President Obama stand? In his campaign, of course, he condemned in ringing terms the use of torture to obtain information. After taking office, Obama immediately signed Executive Order 13491, described in the press as banning torture. The order, however, does not ban the practice as thoroughly as one might suppose. Its command, which applies to all those "detained in any armed conflict," provides:

> such persons shall in all circumstances be treated humanely and
> shall not be subjected to violence to life and person (including

murder of all kinds, mutilation, cruel treatment, and torture),
nor to outrages upon personal dignity (including humiliating
and degrading treatment).

Now, to begin with, we might all have different views about what
constitutes treatment that is degrading or humiliating. But put
that to one side. The use of torture (of whatever euphemistic
variety) by American interrogators has been by most accounts
relatively rare. The more serious physical risk for prisoners of
the War on Terror has been rendition to countries not particularly squeamish when it comes to method. That is, they have
been tortured not by the United States but by someone else.
There the President's executive order creates a task force,
charged with, among other duties, the following:

> to study and evaluate the practices of transferring individuals
> to other nations in order to ensure that such practices comply
> with the domestic laws, international obligations, and policies
> of the United States and do not result in the transfer of indi-
> viduals to other nations to face torture or otherwise for the pur-
> pose, or with the effect, of undermining or circumventing the
> commitments or obligations of the United States to ensure the
> humane treatment of individuals in its custody or control.

The executive order neither bans nor regulates rendition. It
simply establishes a task force to study the practice. The task
force was supposed to issue a report to the President within 180
days. And report it did, proposing that renditions be continued,
but that the United States monitor the treatment of detainees
once they are shipped abroad.[92] Far from a break with the past,
this practice promises a continuation of the practice of past administrations, who used a similar caveat, with disappointing results. The President is said to have issued classified executive

orders that still allow rendition of suspects to countries that torture, and, according to media reports, the practice may actually
be expanding rather than contracting, for precisely the reason
mentioned above: because intelligence to fight the War on Terror has been so difficult to come by.[93]

Indeed, early in 2010, the media reported that the American
military, along with Pakistani forces, had captured the chief military strategist of the Taliban. He was being interrogated by
American and Pakistani intelligence officers, not on United
States soil, and not in Guantanamo or some secret American
prison, but in Pakistan, a country not noted for its delicacy in
these matters. One wonders whether the interrogators were using what the previous Administration euphemistically called
"enhanced" techniques to gain information. Media reports certainly hinted at the possibility of torture—notwithstanding the
presence of Americans among the interrogators. Nothing in
President Obama's executive order would rule this out. The
only oddity is that so many of the protesters who despised rendition when it was done by the previous Administration have si-
lenced themselves. But in a partisan age, principle seems to
matter less than advantage.[94]

Or perhaps the protesters were wrong. The President's policy
makes a tragic sort of sense, once you concede the importance
of winning the Terror War. Evidently, the Administration has
grown wary of the alternatives. The law-enforcement model, under which the reason to apprehend terror suspects is in order
to punish them and deter others, has limited utility if your goal
is to protect the country. The "pure" Geneva Convention model,
in which enemy combatants may be interred indefinitely, to prevent their return to the battlefield, might seem attractive were
the enemy in danger of running short of troops. But the goal in
the Terror War is information. (Indeed, some of us read Article
17 of the Third Geneva Convention as forbidding one standard

practice of interrogators: the offering of better conditions of confinement—more letters home, a larger cell—in return for information.[95] I hasten to add that this is not the majority view.)

We are left therefore with a conundrum. Signals intelligence is of limited utility in the Terror War, and human sources are difficulty to cultivate and impossible to trust. Interrogation, then, becomes the only means of pursuing the battle. Obama evidently has realized this. Putting aside the question of how to treat those captured on United States soil, there is another glaring matter that the media have somehow managed to ignore. American forces, whether regular military or CIA, are capturing high-valued targets, as they are known, practically every month. These prisoners are no longer being ferried to Guantanamo. The "secret" overseas prisons operated by the Agency have been dismantled. (True, the news media have reported, to little public fanfare, that the Administration may simply build another facility to house terror suspects, well beyond the nation's borders.[96] The Bagram Theater Internment Facility in Afghanistan has reportedly been beefed up for this purpose.[97]) In one case during Obama's first year in office, the military reportedly killed an al-Qaeda leader in a helicopter attack rather than capture him, precisely because there was no place to keep him.[98] Assuming, however, that this is not the usual practice, there must be prisoners. They are being interrogated somewhere. Unless we have built new secret prisons to replace the old ones, the only place left for interrogation is under the authority of other governments. Perhaps the prisoners are even providing useful intelligence. It seems unlikely, however, that all of them are providing it voluntarily.

If this is what the Obama Administration is doing, and the odds favor it, then, in a sense, the President has decided to continue the policy of coercive interrogation. All that has changed is that American hands will no longer be dirtied. This is of course a horrific measure for any government to take. But here is where Kahn's point has weight: once President Obama decided to continue pursuing the War on Terror, he had no choice but to decide, also, to continue to press, and press hard, for information. The point of the Terror War, remember, is less victory than prevention. The goal is to keep America safe from attack. You cannot keep your enemy from striking unless you know his plans. And so the President has decided that he has to ask, sometimes, not gently.

To the devotee of the just war of tradition, the Obama approach is, to say the least, worrisome—certainly as worrisome as was his predecessor's—but the realist will ask whether there is an alternative. Fighting the "root causes" of terrorism has proved rather complex, not least because of the debate over what those root causes are. For instance, the claim that terror begins in poverty and ignorance runs counter to the data indicating that those who plan terror attacks and those who carry them out tend to be middle class and educated.[99] To the extent that terror is a response to the nation's foreign policy (or, for that matter, its domestic policy), one might decide to change course in order to avoid stirring up trouble, but this creates perverse incentives: terror has in common with other activities that once it begins to pay off, more people will engage in it.[100]

One might go in the other direction, hunkering down and hoping to build sufficient walls to shield the nation against attacks, but history teaches the unreliability of this approach. There is a difference, as Thomas Schelling memorably put it, "between fending off assault and making someone afraid to assault you."[101] Athens, by far the predominant military power of its day, was defeated in the Second Peloponnesian War precisely because of its decision to withdraw within its fortifications, daring its enemies to launch assaults. Sparta and its allies dared, and Athens lost. France attempted something similar between the World Wars, also to ill effect. Battles as well as wars are lost this way. During the Civil War, the Battle of Chattanooga nearly ended the same way, for the Union forces under the command of General William S. Rosecrans holed up behind their fortifications rather than striking against the enemy. The city would have been lost, and Tennessee likely with it, had not Rosecrans been reinforced at the last minute. In more recent history, Saddam Hussein's decision, absurd in military terms, to hold his best troops back in a reserve around Baghdad, rather than sending them into the field against the invasion, contributed to the rapid collapse of his regime in 2003. No doubt Saddam would have lost anyway, as the South very likely would have lost the Civil War in any case; but warfare is a string of individual battles, not one vast conflict, and the more battles you win, the better your chances of survival.

When I make this point in class, my students are quick to note that the United States is not in danger of immediate extinction. Fair enough. The historian David Day points out that nations tend to collapse not when they are defeated in war but when they are occupied by the enemy.[102] Moreover, as the economist Barbara Ward noted nearly half a century ago, the United States, whatever it faces, is buoyed in its battles by a belief in its own exceptionalism, its certainty that its institutions, its people, its values somehow combine to build a community dedicated to the specialness of the American way of life.[103] Thus far, war or no war, the American way of life seems to be bearing up relatively well. Such suffering as exists in the land is, for the most part, not the result of external attacks.

In short, although the United States may be facing, in the philosopher Michael Walzer's famous typology, an emergency, it is not facing an existential threat.[104] Much of the hard-edged debate about the proper measures to take in combating terror attacks likely turns on precisely where on the spectrum one believes we fall. Perhaps there are measures short of war available to protect America, but President Obama has made plain that he does not believe this. (Even at a very liberal school like Yale, most of my students agree.) In Obama's rhetoric, like his predecessor's, even the Terror War has been forced upon the nation, making it not only a war of self-defense but a war of last resort, against foes with whom negotiation is impossible; that is, a just war. And in pursuing that just war, the President is prepared to approve many of the very practices for which his predecessor was condemned.

Let us ask, then, why Obama's evident about-face, not only on rendition but on so many other issues? A friend of mine in a position to know reports that the President and his senior staff were "stunned" by the threats spread before them at their first postelection briefings on national security. No doubt there are things that President Obama and his aides know about the world now that the rest of us do not. If the things that they know are frightening enough that a President who ran for office criticizing renditions and secret prisons now acknowledges their grim necessity, perhaps we should all be scared.

Very scared.

Obama and *Jus ad bellum*

Let us take a moment to review. We set out to discover President Obama's views on the morality of war. In this first part of the book, the question has been, more precisely, what counts as a just cause for war. The answer so far is defense of the nation. This priority does not of course separate Obama from any other American leader. What is more intriguing is the breadth the President brings to his understanding of this principle. We have discerned, from the President's words and actions, that in defense of the country, we may:

- fight preventive wars that are not truly forced upon us;
- send Special Forces troops or missiles into countries such as Yemen with which we are not formally at war;
- hunt down and eliminate our "enemies" (as defined by the President) before they have the opportunity to attack us;
- capture those enemies on the battlefield and imprison them indefinitely overseas, beyond the reach of the American judicial system; and,
- in the search for the information needed to prosecute the Terror War, turn some of those captives over to countries willing to use coercive forms of interrogation.

Each of these actions is at least problematic under the just war theory President Obama has invited us to apply to them. Some on the antiwar side seem to be throwing up their hands and asserting that Obama is "as bad" as Bush. This criticism misses the point. Obama might have been the peace candidate, but he is a war President. When he runs for reelection in 2012, his leadership in the wars America is fighting will quite justifiably be central to the popular assessment of his presidency. Like many who have moved from outsider to insider, he has discovered that war is a more complex matter than it appears from a distance. In particular, the prosecution of war while holding to absolutist ethical positions turns out to be impossible; impossible, that is, if your goal is to win. This has always been the hardest truth about war. In the same way that war efficiently destroys lives and property, it effectively explodes moral generalizations. As we have seen, not everything America is doing in pursuit of its security can stand close scrutiny under just war theory. Still, one must be realistic: If a war is a just one, the just side must be permitted to try to win. The notion that it will do so in perfect compliance with abstract rules is a fantasy. Obama, to his credit, has come to understand this.

One might answer of course that if war is so horrible, it is never worth fighting. This is an entirely defensible ethical position, but it is not the position of the just war tradition on which the President relied in Stockholm. The just war tradition asks, first, when it is appropriate to fight a war: the problem known as *jus ad bellum*. President Obama has given us his answer. The second question the tradition asks is how it is appropriate to fight a war: the problem known as *jus in bello*. Let us turn now to the President's answer to that question.

{ II }

NO EQUIVALENCE

President Obama on *Jus in bello*

War, American Style

We like our wars cheap. Cheap in money, yes, but also cheap in blood. Quick, surgical, easy, done by remote: the model for American warfare today is the MQ-1 Predator drone, launched from a ship standing off shore, controlled from a console deep in the bowels of the Central Intelligence Agency, stealthily and accurately seeking its target, and then firing off its two AGM-114 Hellfire missiles, each with its antitank warhead, and, if the damage that results is not sufficient, throwing in a couple of Stingers for good measure. The Predator can stay aloft, hunting targets, for as long as forty hours. The newer and more expensive Reaper drone has an engine eight times as powerful as the Predator's, and heavier armament. In addition to the usual complement of missiles and warheads, the Reaper can carry, for example, the GBU-12 Paveway II, a "smart bomb" designed to deliver a 500-pound warhead within four feet of its target.[1] (The GBU is the weapon in the famous YouTube video of a laser-guided bomb falling in Falluja, Iraq.) The Reaper, among its other capabilities, can be fitted to take off from and land on an aircraft carrier.

A strike by one of these remote-controlled aircraft can cause enormous death and destruction. The Hellfire is a shaped-charge warhead, meaning that the blast is largely channeled in one direction. It can wreck armored vehicles and penetrate bunkers. The Paveway typically carries the MK-82 warhead, powerful enough to level a fair-sized building. As the Obama Administration ratchets sharply upward the use of drone attacks, in Afghanistan and elsewhere, these are the weapons of choice. Since Obama took the reins, the use of Predators and Reapers has become far more common than under his predecessor. This Administration, like the previous one, insists that the drone attacks result in fewer civilian casualties than either conventional bombing or ground assault. Some critics think the civilian casualties are greater than the Administration admits and, as of this writing, several groups had filed Freedom of Information Act requests, seeking to learn the truth.

Civilian casualties matter. So far, we have focused on what constitutes a just cause for war—the *jus ad bellum*. Just war theory also includes the *jus in bello* criteria, governing how a war is to be fought. These are, principally, proportionality and discrimination. Proportionality holds that even a just combatant should do no more damage than the just end reasonably requires. Discrimination holds that one may not intentionally target anyone other than combatants. True, too sharp a distinction between *in bello* and *ad bellum* can tend to distort the Catholic natural law tradition from which they emerge, a tradition in which, as John Finnis puts it, "every choice must satisfy all moral requirements."[2] Nevertheless, the rules of proportionality and discrimination are widely accepted in secular conversations about just war, and both have been adopted, in form, anyway, in international law. Both raise delicate questions not easily answered.

Consider a simple classroom exercise that I use when I teach the ethics of war. Imagine a soldier on a battlefield, carrying his weapon, attacking his enemy. Plainly, one does no violence to *jus in bello* by shooting him. Now suppose the same soldier, not on the battlefield but in a truck on the way to the battlefield. Presumably, the rule is the same. But suppose now he has taken a break, and is eating his lunch. Suppose he is asleep. Suppose he has just learned that his father died, and is on his way home on compassionate leave, boarding a truck to depart the battle-field, although he plans later to return. Suppose he gets home, and is on his way to the funeral, splendid and handsome in his uniform. Suppose he spends the night at his mother's house, but intends to return to war tomorrow. Can we kill him as he sleeps?

One begins to see the difficulty. Michael Walzer refers to such hypotheticals as the problem of the naked soldier.[3] I often have my students read George Orwell's essay "Looking Back on the Spanish War," where he describes taking aim but then fail-ing to fire at a frightened soldier who is pulling up his pants as he flees: "I had come here to shoot at 'Fascists'; but a man who is holding up his trousers isn't a 'Fascist,' he is visibly a fellow-creature, similar to yourself, and you don't feel like shooting at him."[4] Maybe not; but a retreating soldier remains a soldier. In neither the laws nor ethics of war is the act of retreating gener-ally considered to render a soldier hors de combat—as a rule, he must be surrendering or too wounded to fight, otherwise he might return to the battlefield—and so the Fascist who was run-ning away while tugging up his trousers possessed no legal or moral immunity from Orwell's bullet. During the 1991 Gulf War, the Coalition forces repeatedly bombed and strafed the column of Iraqi troops fleeing Kuwait in panic. Thousands of Iraqi soldiers died. Many observers were shocked, but no rule of war was violated: the retreating Iraqis, until they surrendered, remained combatants, subject to attack.[5]

The question of what makes someone a combatant has be-deviled conversations about just war for centuries. The literature is broad and rich. Here, we need dip into that conversation only a little, because President Obama's vision of just war challenges only a single corner of *jus in bello.* The President has rejected calls from many experts to make missiles fired from drones a rarely used last resort.[6] Instead, the Administration has taken the de facto position that it is appropriate to target the leaders of the Taliban, of al-Qaeda, and of various terror organizations, wherever they may be found.[7] One was incinerated by a missile attack as he reclined on the roof of his father-in-law's house, where he was receiving an intravenous drip, for he was gravely ill with diabetes and a kidney ailment. His wife and in-laws died with him. Another was targeted (and evidently missed) during a funeral procession. The most notorious miss was the wedding party blown to bits in the fall of 2008, killing at least thirty civilians, but, evidently, no senior al-Qaeda leaders. Nevertheless, the drones are said to have killed on the order of two dozen high-valued targets.[8] Note, however, that these men were not on the battlefield. They were not even sitting in conference rooms, planning attacks. They were simply found wherever they could be found, and, to use the President's word, exterminated.

Put aside, for the moment, the civilians also killed in the attacks. (We will return to them momentarily.) Suffice to say for the moment that the President, in approving the bombings, was taking sides in one of the thorniest questions under *jus in bello:* is the definition of a combatant based on what a person is doing at the moment, or what he has done recently and may soon do again? Both positions have their partisans. The answer matters in part because any weapon points both ways. When a truck bomb destroyed the Marine barracks in Lebanon in 1983, killing scores of American soldiers in their sleep, the act was described as terrorism. Perhaps it was. Yet the fact that the Marines were off duty did not render them any less combatants. If our

Air Force were to drop a bomb on a barracks full of combatants, the act would certainly fall well within what is permitted by both the law and the ethics of war.

Take another example I use when teaching this material. Suppose that the Taliban, at war with the United States, were to obtain a Predator drone and use it to launch a Hellfire missile at the Pentagon. Or the White House. The specter is a grim one, given recent history. And yet the question is one that must be faced, given our own strategy. The President's position seems to be that we do no violence to *jus in bello* when we target combatants, and their commanders, even when they are not actually engaged in combat. If he is right, then under the usual understanding of the ethics of war, the rule must hold both ways.

The *usual* understanding.

It is surely difficult for an American reader even to consider the possibility of a just attack on our own land. Alas, such an act of scary imagination is precisely what the notion of *jus in bello* requires of us. As a historical matter, the concept emerges not from mere reciprocity—the fear that if we break certain rules, so will the other side—but from Christian charity. "Even in waging war," wrote Augustine, "cherish the spirit of a peacemaker, that, by conquering those whom you attack, you may lead them back to the advantages of peace."[9] The rules of *jus in bello*, says Michael Walzer, "suggest that war is still, somehow, a rule-governed activity, a world of permissions and prohibitions—a moral world, therefore, in the midst of hell."[10] In short, even when one side is fighting a just war and the other not, the same considerations—and the same prohibitions—bind both. Let us grant for the sake of argument that the United States is very right, and the enemy very wrong, both in Afghanistan and in the wider Terror War. That does not mean that every attack by the enemy is itself unjust. Indeed, challenging though the concept may be in a secular age, the *jus in bello* idea calls upon us to contemplate what is referred to in the literature as "moral equivalence"—that is, that on the battlefield, the just side and the unjust side enjoy the same moral status.

Yes, this doctrine of equivalence means exactly what it says: if the Nazis and the Allies meet at the Battle of the Bulge, and one side is horribly wrong to be fighting at all, and the other side is wonderfully right, both are nevertheless bound by the same considerations, the same moral and legal limits on what they ought to do in their effort to win. This traditional understanding drawn from the ethics of war forms the basis for the similar rules in international law. When a war ends, the winning side has no right to punish the other side's soldiers merely for being on the unjust side. Unless they have committed war crimes, they should be repatriated when the war ends.

This approach, however, rests on a shaky foundation, an assumption often known in the literature as "invincible ignorance," another term stemming from Catholic natural law theology. The term refers to a moral ignorance so severe that the individual cannot reasonably escape. That is, even if the ignorant individual tries to learn the truth, he is limited, perhaps by intellect, perhaps by circumstance, in his ability to understand. Thus does the ignorance become invincible. One may not be deemed invincibly ignorant of the natural law, which may be discerned by all with reasonable diligence, but, aside from that exception, the space of possible ignorance is vast.

Long ago, the concept of invincible ignorance was applied to war, leading to an understanding that soldiers on the battlefield are not charged with knowledge of the goals for which the war is fought. The model works something like this: In the distant capital, alone in his palace, the wicked prince makes up his mind to launch an unprovoked attack against a neighbor. He then forces the peasants into his army and marches them off to the front. They do not know why they are there. They do not know who started the war. They are doing what the evil prince has commanded them to do. They remain ignorant of the details; and of the moral questions about the prince's intention. But they should know without being told that some things are forbidden—launching attacks on unarmed civilians, for example—because these are matters of natural law.

What was war like then? As the historians remind us, the soldiers in the earliest wars by and large were peasants, raised in a world of loose governance, accustomed to resolving their own disputes, often through violence.[11] In a sense, marching off to war was a continuation of the way they led their lives, except that they were now fighting for someone else. As a historical matter, the notion of equivalence rests heavily on this model. In this vision soldiers are pawns, moved around the board by the players, their princes who alone know the truth of what is going on. The pawns are merely doing as they are told. They are not analytical or questioning. Their simplicity is protection against blameworthiness.

In international relations, when discussion turns to what has become known as the Law of Armed Conflict, the notion of moral equivalence is hardly mentioned. The secular rules of jus in bello rest more readily on principles of reciprocity (I won't punish your soldiers if you won't punish mine) and perhaps on the virtue of necessity (if soldiers knew they could be punished for fighting on the unjust side, nobody would risk fighting at all). This is why the hypothetical example in which al-Qaeda or the Taliban possesses a Predator drone with its Hellfire missiles carries such force. Under the theory of equivalence, whatever the just side is free to do in prosecuting the war, the unjust side can, too.

But President Obama cannot possibly believe this. Remember the premise of his eulogy for the seven CIA officers slain in the Khost bombing: the task in this war is to eliminate our enemies. Not capture them, or negotiate a peace, but eliminate them. Presumably the President believes that this is a just course of action—he thinks, in other words, that killing the enemy, foot soldiers and leaders alike, is the right thing to do. I very much doubt, however, that he also thinks it the right thing to do when the enemy kills our people.

International lawyers, particularly those who work for the government, are able to offer intriguing but not altogether satisfying explanations for this distinction.[12] But let us here stick with right and wrong, and what President Obama believes. So, let us again suppose for the moment an attack on America using the same technologies that we use in prosecuting our various wars. It is difficult to imagine many Americans, were so horrific an event to occur, nodding sagely and saying, "Well, it's war." Certainly no President could take that attitude. Consider the President's words at the memorial service for the soldiers and others killed in the attack on Fort Hood, Texas, in November of 2009:

> This is a time of war. Yet these Americans did not die on a foreign field of battle. They were killed here, on American soil, in the heart of this great state and the heart of this great American community. This is the fact that makes the tragedy even more painful, even more incomprehensible.

The argument seems to be that being killed "on American soil" is worse, even in time of war, than being killed abroad. On its face, this seems entirely reasonable.

Imagine, however, a memorial service in Afghanistan for Taliban members killed by American attack on their home soil. Suppose a Taliban leader explaining how much greater the tragedy when his fighters are killed at home rather than abroad, say, in the United States. I suspect that most Americans would find the argument incomprehensible. We resonate intuitively with the President's words, but we would reject the same claim on behalf of our foes. Thus we find it perfectly sensible when the President goes on to say, at the Ford Hood service:

> It may be hard to comprehend the twisted logic that led to this tragedy. But this much we do know—no faith justifies these murderous and craven acts; no just and loving God looks upon them with favor. For what he has done, we know that the killer will be met with justice—in this world, and the next.

Again, imagine now the Taliban memorial service, a leader condemning the "twisted logic" behind America's drone attacks, and insisting that God does not look upon the killers with favor. Suppose he goes on to promise that those who have slain on his soil "will be met with justice—in this world, and the next."

Feel the chill?

Feel the difference?

When the President of the United States pronounces these words, we feel comforted and reassured. When the leader of the enemy pronounces them, we feel threatened. The distinction in our response does not rest on our interpretation of arcane questions of international law. The distinction rests on our deep-seated belief in our country. For this reason, it seems fair to say that Obama's broad view of the confines of the Terror War suggests belief not in equivalence but in a rather different proposition, one common to our politics: Attacking America is morally different from being attacked by America.

Well, of course. Once stated, the proposition is obvious. What else would an American leader, or the leader of any state, possibly believe? If you attack us, you're the bad guys. If we attack you, we're the good guys.

Period.

Perhaps the conclusion is what patriotism requires: we love our country, so you dare not attack it. But before we dismiss the sentiment as mere chauvinism or self-love (more on this later), let us consider how very natural it feels, and not only for Americans. Perhaps every society feels the same tribal tug, the us-versus-them that creates different moral categories for those who dare raise their hands to us. In much the same way that a boy will protect his little brother, without asking who started the fight, a country surely registers a sense of entitlement not to be the object of warfare, even when, around the conference table or seminar room, we can assign a perfectly legitimate rationale for an attack. But not every society wields the weaponry of the world's sole remaining superpower, or has interests it is willing to defend in so many corners of the globe.

We like to think of ourselves as peace-loving people. In some ways perhaps we are. We should not forget, however, that the peace we love is purchased at a price. The state, as Paul Kahn reminds us, "has its origins in violence" and "will maintain itself through violence"; a violence, says Kahn, that lies in some sense beyond the reach of law.[13] We can reason together, and should, about when and how to fight, but we should not pretend that war can be avoided. America, like most nations, will use force when it is under threat, but will never see the use of force by others against it as legitimate. President Obama, in rejecting the notion of moral equivalence, is only giving voice to this public sentiment.

Indeed, the moral equivalence of soldiers has lately been subjected to withering criticism, much of it in the military journals,[14] although mainstream philosophers have also had their innings. One might ask, for example, whether it is realistic to contend that in a war of murderous aggression, such as World War II, the Germans really had no idea of the principles behind the regime for which they were fighting. (Remember that each member of the German army had to swear an oath of personal loyalty to Adolf Hitler.)[15] The philosopher Jeff McMahan, who has devoted much of a recent book to questioning the doctrine of moral equivalence, points to a nice hole: if police shoot at crooks, do the crooks possess the moral right to shoot back? No, says McMahan, because the work of the crooks and the work of the police is not morally equivalent. Why, then, assume an equivalence for the work of the good guys and the work of the bad guys in war?[16] Some historians have even suggested that knowledge of the nature of the war actually weakened the will of the German army to resist, and that a crucial factor in the Allied victory was the conviction, strengthened not weakened as the war progressed, that their side were morally in the right.[17] The same might have been true of Confederate soldiers during the Civil War, especially when they came face-to-face with regiments of former slaves, who, according to antebellum cant, had loved their masters. Evidently, they did not, a realization that terrified their onetime owners.[18] And John Keegan, seeking to explain the rapid disintegration of the large Iraqi army in the face of the 2003 invasion, suggests that expectations of how hard troops will fight to defend their homeland must be adjusted when the land in question is governed by a dictator.[19] Michael Walzer puts the point this way: "When soldiers believe themselves to be fighting against aggression, war is no longer a condition to be endured. It is a crime they can resist."[20] If this is so, then placing upon the two sides the construct of ignorance may be a bit of a stretch.

Besides, as military ethicists have pointed out, in the contemporary democracy, there is no such thing as invincible ignorance.[21] American soldiers on duty in Iraq or Afghanistan have available the same sources of information as those back home who fight so bitterly over the wars: the same newspapers, the same websites, the same cable television talk shows. The soldiers know why they are there. They can, if they choose, follow the debate. And, whatever their views on the war, they understand the theory behind it. Their educational level compares favorably with the educational level of the public at large, and the educational level of the officer corps surpasses it. In consequence, say some of the military critics, to base an entire theory of ethics and international law on a presumption about the ignorance of the soldier is both absurd and insulting.

The philosopher David Rodin has crafted a clever case against invincible ignorance.[22] Rodin reminds us that no more than one side in a war can ever be fighting justly, and, in some wars, both sides are fighting unjustly. Therefore, fewer than half of warring parties at any time anywhere in the world are likely to be just. Were we to sample randomly from among all sides fighting all wars, the chances are better than fifty-fifty that we would select an unjust side. A soldier who is not certain of the justice of the war should not rely on his government's own assessment, says Rodin, because "he can know with certainty that there is at least a 50 per cent chance that he is fighting on the unjust side."[23]

Jeff McMahan puts the point more strongly. He suggests that the notion of moral equivalence discourages soldiers from taking independent moral stock of the war they are fighting. He argues that the development of better tools to force soldiers to consider the justice of their cause "could provide a basis for holding them accountable for their participation in unjust wars—accountable perhaps in law but certainly to their own consciences."[24] One sees the argument elsewhere, too: were soldiers accountable for the morality of a war, they might make more effort to work out its ethics. In other words, if we want soldiers to be morally serious, the moral equivalence doctrine gets the incentives wrong.

Taken seriously, this argument makes more difficult that staple of antiwar protest, "I oppose the war but I support the troops." Not impossible, just more difficult. One may oppose a war on the ground that it is unjust, in which case it is an act of mass murder, or one may oppose a war on the ground that, although possibly just, it is imprudent: a sensible and reflective contention that is rarely heard, perhaps because it does not make for clever slogans on bumper stickers. If the war is unjust, an act of mass murder, then why does one support the troops who are doing the murder? Presumably, because they have been forced or duped into battle—they are just following orders—in short, their ignorance is invincible. But if one tosses out the invincible ignorance argument, as many thoughtful people in and out of the military advise, then we are left with the assumption that American troops, at least, know exactly what they are doing, know it at least as well as the critics and perhaps better. There is no secret font of information kept from those at the front. Consequently, if one really believes that an American war is a crime, all the troops should stand in the dock.

Good Guys versus Bad Guys

But nobody believes this. We believe what I mentioned a few pages ago seems to serve as the basis of President Obama's ethic of war: Attacking America is morally different from being attacked by America. Let us call this the American Proviso. The American Proviso would seem to be the ideal path out of this jus in bello thicket, a path that does not require us to accept the justness of the Predator drone operated by al-Qaeda or the Taliban, and also does not require us to stand our troops in the dock. The Obama Administration, if one takes seriously its words and actions, must accept the American Proviso, even though, for reasons of international politics, it can hardly say so. The Proviso is, perhaps, a living monument to the worrisome wisdom of Oliver Wendell Holmes Jr.: "I think that the sacredness of life is a purely municipal ideal of no validity outside the jurisdiction."[25] In other words, no matter how passionately we may speak of the value of life at home, we rarely mean it abroad. The sacredness of life stops at the water's edge.

So, let us follow the Proviso for a moment. The moral equivalence argument holds that whatever the ethics of war allows us to do in war, our adversaries can do as well. The American Proviso says this is not so. On the contrary. If one accepts the Proviso, then the reason that there is no moral equivalence between "our" forces and "their" forces is that "we" are better than "they" are. Even the critics of the Terror War or the Afghan War or the Iraq War seem to accept the Proviso, at least implicitly, for it has long been a staple of antiwar argument that whatever other countries may do, however the other side may behave, America has an obligation to act differently. The underlying assumption would seem to be that we must behave in a way that is . . . morally superior! The doctrine of moral equivalence, in Holmes's term, becomes a purely municipal ideal.

How does the Proviso then keep us out of the thicket? The path mirrors a similar controversial argument under international law, and would go something like this:

> Yes, of course, under the ethics of war, our enemy can use whatever means against us we can use against them. But this applies only to enemies who are actual combatants under the rules. If our enemies are not combatants, then they have no right to fight us at all. They are not simply forbidden from using weapons of mass destruction or Predator drones, they are forbidden from doing battle in the first place. In consequence, anything they do on the battlefield is a violation of the rules of

war, and, and, as unlawful combatants, they are liable to be shot (or blown to bits by missiles) wherever they may be found.

This was the approximate position of the Bush Administration, not in the war against the Iraqi military, but in fighting the subsequent insurgency, and in battling al-Qaeda and the Taliban. Critics were livid. The term "unlawful combatant," they contended, had been all but invented by Bush's people out of whole cloth, to justify a whole range of abuses, from targeted assassinations to torture.

The term has an instructive provenance. The Supreme Court famously applied it in 1942, sustaining the trial by military commission of accused German saboteurs.[26] Under international law, an unlawful combatant lacks belligerent rights; that is, he cannot wage lawful war. Many international lawyers take this precise view in justifying the evident double standard in America's current wars. More useful for our purposes is the role of the concept in the ethics of war. Jeff McMahan has argued that unlawful combatants should not be presumed to have the same right to wage war as lawful combatants, and that the doctrine of moral equivalence should not apply when one side is, as a matter of morality, plainly in the wrong.[27] If we follow this logic, then every act of war by a side plainly wrong is unjust. Thus, there is a sharp moral difference between a strike by the good guys against the bad guys and a strike by the bad guys against the good guys. The first is morally permissible; the second is not.

My point is not to defend the Bush approach, or the Proviso itself, but to suggest that the Obama approach, sub silentio, must be more or less congruent. Nothing else can explain the Administration's evident view that every attack on our forces during the present war is an act of terrorism, whereas every attack that we launch is justified, or the determination to kill the leaders of the enemy wherever they may be found. True, in his Nobel Address, Obama seemed to argue the opposite:

> America—in fact, no nation—can insist that others follow the rules of the road if we refuse to follow them ourselves. For when we don't, our actions appear arbitrary and undercut the legitimacy of future interventions, no matter how justified.

But the President's actions do not bear this out, and were the Taliban indeed to use a Predator to launch missiles at a target within the United States, Obama would surely be swift to condemn the attack as an act of terrorism, not an act of war. The needs of domestic politics aside, the simplest explanation for the distinction is that the military scholarship criticizing the doctrine of invincible ignorance has carried the day. The enemy cannot do the same things that we do because the enemy's forces are not morally equivalent to ours. Especially in the War on Terror, we take the view that those on the other side are perfectly aware of what they are doing. We will not allow them to claim invincible ignorance if accused for their unlawful acts. Thus they should not fight at all, but, if they do, they deserve what they get.

Perhaps this is a scary conclusion. Perhaps the Proviso seems hubristic, a throwback to the days of America's imperial ambitions. But I believe that it captures the attitude of American policymakers, not just in this Administration or its predecessor, but over a good many years. We want to believe that we are special. The historian Deborah Madsen has persuasively shown how a strong belief in exceptionalism has dominated every era of American history, so much so that even dissenting and critical movements have always adopted rhetoric proposing that America is (and ought to be) different from the rest of the world.[28] Maybe we are wrong. Maybe America is not special at all. But anybody who is elected President is likely to believe we are.

By now the reader is surely wondering what would happen if the whole world behaved this way, if every country considering war decided that its enemies were less morally worthy and, therefore, entitled to less respect on the battlefield. After all, no country, when attacked, shakes its collective head and says, "Oh, well, at least the enemy is fighting by the rules." No army decides to accept more casualties to spare the other side's troops. When I teach the ethics of war, I ask my students how many of them, entrusted with command of an army fighting a just war, would risk the loss of extra soldiers on their side to reduce the risk to the soldiers of the enemy; then I ask the same question, only with civilians as the casualties.

In both cases the answer is close to zero.

One of the most philosophically intriguing lines in any Hollywood production in recent decades occurs in the film *True Lies*, when Arnold Schwarzenegger, upon being unmasked as an undercover operative for American intelligence, is asked by his astonished and furious wife (Jamie Lee Curtis) if he has ever killed anyone. "Yes," says Arnold. "But they were all bad." This is how we Americans have always liked to think of war, and how we like to think of it now, too: the good guys are out there killing the bad guys. And this is, in a sense, the subtext of President Obama's insistence on getting the terrorists before they get us. They are bad guys, the President is telling us. We are only killing the bad guys.

ASSASSINATION

Fair enough. We are killing the bad guys. President Obama may have inherited the wars he is fighting, but he is killing the bad guys all the same. In particular, he is seeking out the leaders and bombing them remotely. So, let us give the policy its rightful name: assassination. The word is an unpleasant one, to be sure. For most of human history, however, assassination of the other side's leaders was seen as an appropriate tool of warfare.[29] Then it wasn't.[30] Perhaps this was part of a larger trend, identified by the historian John Keegan, of separating the business of war making from the business of governing. No matter how mighty the American military, we are a long way from being a warrior society. History knows many such societies, cultures in which able-bodied men, particularly those of wealth or ambition, were all expected to be prepared to fight at any time. Since the rise of the nation-state in the seventeenth century, the warrior societies have vanished.[31] No longer does the prince lead troops upon the battlefield. Keegan argues that the ancients would have found this separation decadent. Maybe so. Until a few centuries ago, it was precisely prowess as a warrior that qualified one to rule.[32] Assassination might lead to vengeance, but it was not considered dishonorable. As a warrior, the ruler took the same risks as everyone else. But the wheel of history turned. As the rulers have grown increasingly remote from the battle itself, the world has grown increasingly troubled at the idea that the leaders might be targets. And so, today, the people who make the decisions on war no longer take the risks of war.

The Geneva Conventions, although they ban murder, do not define it. And they do not mention assassination at all.[33] The plain language of Article 23b of the 1907 Hague Regulations prohibits "assassination, proscription, or outlawry of an enemy, or putting a price upon an enemy's head, as well as offering a reward for an enemy 'dead or alive,'" but, as far as I can tell, hardly anybody takes it seriously. In recent years, the United States has made a regular practice of putting bounties on enemy leaders. True, we do not say we want them dead; but if a bounty leads to a location, we are as likely to send in the Hellfire or Paveway as we are to land Special Forces.

Here international law and the ethics of war converge. Just war theory allows the targeting not only of combatants but also of those who are in the military chain of command. This would suggest that as long as the head of government can give orders to the military, it is not necessarily immoral to try to kill him. Thus, in the words of one scholar, "the targeting of military or political leaders" may be "a morally legitimate tool of war" when "justified as a preventive use of force against the initiator or controlling force of unjust aggression."[34] Assassination may even be morally attractive when doing so might actually shorten the war, thus saving life.[35] Any number of theorists have tried to apply this logic to the War on Terror.[36] The Obama Administration plainly believes the same.

To be sure, the Administration does not like the word "assassination." In a speech to the American Society of International Law in March of 2010, Harold Koh, legal adviser to the State Department, offered a justification for killing the leaders of al-Qaeda and the Taliban. Koh's argument matters in assessing the view of the Obama Administration because his office carries the principal responsibility of establishing the legality of the foreign policy of the United States. Although Koh, to be sure, was speaking of international law, not ethics, the just war theorist nevertheless will find his language familiar:

> But individuals who are part of such an armed group are belligerents and, therefore, lawful targets under international law. During World War II, for example, American aviators tracked and shot down the airplane carrying the architect of the Japanese attack on Pearl Harbor, who was also the leader of enemy forces in the Battle of Midway. This was a lawful operation then, and would be if conducted today. Indeed, targeting particular individuals serves to narrow the focus when force is employed and to avoid broader harm to civilians and civilian objects.[37]

Note the twin claims: first, that one may target those who lead the enemy forces, at moments when they do not happen to be engaged in military action; and, second, that targeting the leaders with guided weapons actually reduces civilian casualties.

Next, Koh responded to a common argument that the drone attacks should be likened to execution, that we are in effect carrying out the sentence of death without bothering with a trial. Said Koh: "[A] state that is engaged in an armed conflict or in legitimate self-defense is not required to provide targets with legal process before the state may use lethal force."

Finally, he contended that drone attacks should not be considered assassinations in the first place: "[U]nder domestic law, the use of lawful weapons systems—consistent with the applicable laws of war—for precision targeting of specific high-level belligerent leaders when acting in self-defense or during an armed conflict is not unlawful, and hence does not constitute 'assassination.'"

I have known Harold Koh a long time, and count him as a dear friend, but on this last point he is perhaps trying too hard to thread the needle. Since the days of President Gerald R. Ford, assassination has been banned by executive order, and Koh is trying to explain why the President he serves is not violating those executive orders. This seems to me a quite unnecessary exercise. In the first place, none of the orders in question ever quite get around to defining what assassination is.[38] More to the point, no President can bind a future President. If Obama chooses to assassinate the leaders of the enemy, that is, as a legal matter, his own affair.

We can construct, by combining Obama's arguments with Koh's, a complete explanation of the policy of what I think is still best labeled assassination. According to the President, the United States has the right to "eliminate" its enemies before they can do harm to its interests. There is no point in reasoning with them, says the President, because some evils cannot be reasoned with. It is appropriate, says the legal adviser, to use missile strikes to get the leaders, even when they are away from the battlefield, because we are acting in self-defense (or as part of an armed conflict), and, therefore, the "targets" (that is, the leaders) are not entitled to warning or trial.

It is important to note how few actual limits this argument places upon presidential prerogative.[39] Let the President believe that he is acting to defend the nation, and he can evidently target anyone in the world. The Obama Administration evidently takes the view that even American citizens, if they stir up attacks against the nation, are legitimate targets.[40] As of this writing, the only American citizen known to be on the Administration's assassination list is Anwar al-Awlaki, the radical imam linked to at least two 2009 attacks, the shootings at Fort Hood in November, and the attempted Christmas bombing of an airliner. He was likely connected as well to the attempted bombing of cargo planes headed for the United States in the fall of 2010. At the time of these events, Awlaki was believed to be in Yemen. But suppose he happened to show up in Paris. Or New York City. By the logic of the Administration's argument, he would be every bit as legitimate a target for killing, American citizen or not.

Thus the discretion of the commander in chief to assassinate enemies turns out to be breathtakingly broad—broader, from what I can tell, than was ever claimed by President George W. Bush, who as far as is known never targeted American citizens. One is reminded of Lincoln's repeated reference to the "broader powers conferred by the Constitution" upon the commander in chief, who in times of emergency, thought Lincoln, could do what he thought necessary for defense of the country.[41] (Ironically, it was left to Jefferson Davis, president of the self-styled Confederate States of America, to complain that

Lincoln was usurping the powers of Congress in his unilateral prosecution of the young war.[42] But even Lincoln, whose "broader powers" sometimes led to the arrest of antiwar journalists and speakers, shrank from asserting a right to kill the leaders of the rebellion wherever found.

The best analogy to the Obama Administration's claim, as several observers have noted, is to the treatment of pirates. There the traditional answer of both international law and morality remains, in essence, the same one offered by Cicero two thousand years ago: "[A] pirate is not included in the number of lawful enemies, but is the common foe of all the world."[43] "The common foe of all the world"—*hostis humani generis*—was reserved traditionally for those whose conduct was subject to punishment, even capital punishment, no matter what the rationale or cause. If a pirate cannot lawfully fight, then none of his belligerent acts are ever legitimate. He is a criminal, who can be killed whenever and wherever found. The Bush Administration was much criticized for seeming to lump the nation's enemies automatically into the category, but this would seem to be the position of the Obama Administration as well: that unlawful combatants include terrorists generally, and the Taliban as well: at the moment, toward everyone warring against America. They are unlawful combatants who can be killed where found.[44]

The argument usually presented for treating the terrorist like the pirate or brigand is that, like them, he does not fight for a public authority; that is, he is not answerable to a sovereign. A just war, remember, traditionally requires the leadership of a sovereign. In the Middle Ages, a public war between sovereigns was considered bellum hostile; the only sort of war the church would endorse. The pirate and the brigand fought not for the sovereign but for the self.[45] The terrorist, then, is similarly viewed as answering to no sovereign. So is the Taliban, it seems, now that it holds no formal power. This is the position of the Obama as well as the Bush Administration. The key question is who gets to decide which enemy falls into which category.

The answer, evidently, is that we do. More to the point, when the nation is at war, the executive decides who is *hostis humani generis,* and so liable to be killed wherever found. The only check on this authority would seem to be the President's own good faith. I leave to others the propriety of such a claim as a matter of international law. My concern here is with the ethics of war. As a matter of just war theory, one would hope to see so broad a claim of authority used sparingly. In the particular case of assassination, one would want to see, at minimum, a persuasive argument for military necessity, an argument that cannot be persuasive unless the policy is likely to be successful, a hotly debated point.

Indeed, a part of the debate among military analysts centers on what precisely constitutes success. Critics of the drone strikes claim that every missile attack makes it easier for our adversaries to recruit the next terrorist. Supporters argue, to the contrary, that targeting leaders will make it harder for the terror groups to recruit and train members, or to plan and execute attacks. This was the position of the Bush Administration. Others worry that this strategy of decapitation might simply destroy the chain of command while scattering the resources used for the attacks; in other words, that attacks may be less coordinated and even less competent, but that there might be more of them. If this second proposition proves true, then the argument must be restated in a form suggesting that the Obama Administration, like its predecessor, is willing to accept a certain number of poorly planned and executed attacks, in exchange for preventing a smaller number of cleverly planned and far more damaging ones.[46] This trade-off might satisfy the requirement that the missile strikes be necessary, but a trade-off of this sort should at least be articulated publicly, perhaps as part of a major presidential address on war policy.

Alas, Presidents tend to give major addresses only on issues that already engage the popular attention. The drone strikes kill only distant strangers, with no immediate cost in American lives and, as a result, warrant hardly a mention on the evening news. Perhaps the attacks are indeed necessary. Perhaps all those who make war on us should be killed wherever they are found. If so, perhaps the President should more firmly lay out that case to the American people. He should tell us that we are different. That our lives are worth more than other people's.

I doubt that we would be hard to persuade.

AGAIN EQUIVALENCE

Let us assume, for the sake of argument, that we are justified in targeting enemy leaders for assassination. (Yes, as we have seen, the Administration does not like this word, but, to paraphrase one of my wisest professors, you can call it Thucydides or you can call it bananas, but it's assassination all the same.) So, as I said, let us assume that the assassinations are justified. (And also that, under the Proviso, similar attacks against our own leaders would be unjustified.) Still, if we are going to launch these attacks, we must then address the problem of civilian casualties directly. Those leaders we target, when found, are rarely alone. They are surrounded by others, usually noncombatants, many of whom will inevitably die when the Hellfire missile or Paveway bomb strikes. To be sure, hiding among noncombatants is itself a tactic, adopted in the hope that the United States will hesitate. Some might argue, therefore, that it is the fault of those who hide, not those who attack them, that innocents must die.[47]

But this answer may be too glib. That the bad guys are hiding among the innocent does not automatically give us permission to kill the innocent in order to catch the bad guys. Judith Jarvis Thomson, in perhaps the leading philosophical study of self-defense, puts the point this way: "The fact that it is villains who, in the course of fighting an unjust war against your side, have so arranged things that you can save your life only by killing a person does not by itself make it permissible to kill the person."[48] Defenders of the assassinations, notwithstanding the harm to civilians, generally take refuge in the doctrine of double effect, because the attack is never intended to kill the innocents, but only the terrorist leader hiding among them.

The doctrine of double effect is actually defined in different ways by different philosophers. It is often misstated. It stems from Catholic theology, and the struggle to bring into practical effect the orthodox Christian principle that one may never act on the intention to do wrong. Ending the life of another is wrong. Plainly, we often act in ways that end the lives of others, as when we engage in acts of self-defense. Does this mean that self-defense is wrong? The doctrine of double effect holds that when an act has two effects, one intended and one incidental, we may commit the act as long as the intended end is justified, and as long as the good that we therefore create greatly outweighs the harm of the unintended effect. The key point is that we must never intend the bad effect. Thus, for example, in the case of self-defense, the doctrine of double effect would hold that I may defend myself with as much force as may be necessary. In Augustine's words, "Let necessity, therefore, and not your will, slay the enemy who fights against you."[49] I may never intend to kill my attacker, but, if there is no other way to defend myself, the attacker's death may be justified as an unintended by-product of my justifiable decision to defend myself. If, however, I do intend the death of my attacker, the doctrine of double effect does not apply.

In truth of course we can explain very little of life this way. For example, large swaths of our criminal law are inconsistent with the doctrine.[50] Efforts to apply double effect to international law have had equally mixed success.[51] Nevertheless, although Thomson calls it "a very odd idea . . . that a person's intentions play a role in fixing what he may or may not do,"[52] the doctrine is well established in Catholic theology, and has played an important role, too, in secular thinking, which is what here concerns us. So let us, for a moment, pursue our Predator and Reaper example through this doctrine.

Take again the case of the terrorist leader, known to be plotting against the United States. The only opportunity to get him is at his sister's wedding. Firing our missiles at the procession, we will certainly kill the terrorist, but we will also kill thirty or forty innocents. Killing the terrorist leader is the intended "good" outcome. Killing the other members of the procession is the unintended "bad" outcome. Thus it may be argued that we are able to justify the killing of the innocents, as long as we do not intend to kill them, and as long as their deaths are a significantly smaller harm than the harm we are seeking to prevent.[53]

Examples such as this are common to the literature. It is useful to realize, however, that they are not, in a pure sense, cases of double effect. The double effect doctrine was not developed as a way of balancing cases of small-evil versus big-evil. It evolved, rather, to solve the particular problem of causing a death when one really means to pursue some other, entirely moral, end. In the case of drone strikes against the terrorist leader, the entire point is to kill him. Thus, we do indeed intend the very thing that Augustine and the later theologians who developed the theory never permitted us to intend: his death. The traditional doctrine of double effect therefore does not apply.[54]

When we use our drones, death is precisely what we intend. President Obama, like President Bush before him, has made this objective crystal clear. During his campaign for the Democratic nomination, Obama gave a major foreign policy address at the Woodrow Wilson Institute in Washington, DC. Said then-Senator Obama:

> Beyond Pakistan, there is a core of terrorists—probably in the tens of thousands—who have made their choice to attack America. So the second step in my strategy will be to build our capacity and our partnerships to track down, capture or kill terrorists around the world, and to deny them the world's most dangerous weapons. I will not hesitate to use military force to take out terrorists who pose a direct threat to America. This requires a broader set of capabilities, as outlined in the Army and Marine Corps's new counter-insurgency manual. I will ensure that our military becomes more stealth[y], agile, and lethal in its ability to capture or kill terrorists.

The words could hardly be less equivocal. Capture or kill terrorists, said the Senator, outlining the policy he planned to follow. Take out terrorists. These are statements of intention, and the intention is to take life. This is not double effect. This is a decision to kill.

Killing, of course, is what one does in war. We do not live in a world of pure moral abstraction. We live in a world of human weakness, expressed through politics. Politics can be as violent as anything else. No doubt there seems something detached, even old-fashioned, about insisting that we must never intend the death of anyone else, but must kill, as Augustine said, only by necessity, never by will.[55] For most Americans, the drone attacks on terrorist leaders do not seem the occasion for serious moral analysis. In this sense, President Obama, like his predecessor, has accurately read the public spirit. There are people out there who mean us ill, and most Americans want them eliminated. Questions of philosophy seem abstruse and unimportant, perhaps even a bit old-fashioned, in the face of our fears. We want the threat to go away. We want it kept overseas. In adopting the Bush policy of striking first, of getting them before they can get us, President Obama is trying to give us what we want.

TERROR

One reason the rhetoric of war seems, in the modern age, so old-fashioned is because it is. The just war tradition evolved in an era when it was widely understood that the moral problem involved in war is the killing. Nowadays, with our thought blurred by materialism, we tend to behave as if the moral problem involved in war is the dying. One is reminded of the point made by Anthony Kronman, in his fine monograph on contemporary higher education: "Other living things die, but only we are tormented or inspired by the knowledge that we will."[56] That knowledge has always been with us. As Kronman points out, it often inspires. But lately it seems instead to torment.

That torment is reflected in the peculiar agony of the movement in America that goes by the name "antiwar," even though at times it isn't. A broad opposition to warfare can stem from a principled opposition to killing and violence, and often does. Yet our major "antiwar" demonstrations tend to be painfully selective. Yes, the carnage in Iraq in the early part of the war was horrific, but considerably less horrific than in almost any other large-scale war, and easily dwarfed by the millions—yes, millions—dying in the civil war in the Democratic Republic of the Congo at about the same time. But those deaths seemed less important to most who called themselves antiwar. One cannot help but wonder whether, whatever its noble aspirations, the movement turns out to be narrowly chauvinistic, adopting the nationalist view that the lives that matter most are the lives of those who live here. Certainly that view is defensible; necessarily, it is the view of the political leadership, including, as we have seen, the Obama Administration; but it is hardly antiwar. I am not sure, however, that those critics are correct who refer to this position as isolationist. Rather, I suspect that this instinctive resistance to war reflects the existential horror of death itself; a fear that is very Western, and nowadays very American, but carries little moral content. Talal Asad, in his controversial study of suicide bombers, argues that one reason the West is so susceptible to the terror the bomber causes is precisely that we value our own lives so highly.[57] One can conceptualize the Terror War as pitting people who are not afraid to die against people who are. Possibly that imbalance will mean that the people who want very much not to die will fight all the harder to avoid what they fear. But, here again, the understandable reaction to fear is not at all what the fathers of just war theory had in mind. Their appeal was to reason, not emotion, and they understood, correctly, that the true moral burden the warrior takes on is not his willingness to die for his society but his willingness to kill for it.

Killing is the central moral problem of war. Nothing should be simpler. The killing in war is unlike the killing in any other human activity. It is organized, efficient, vast, and authorized by the state. Because we are human, we naturally worry about the dying. Because we are moral animals, we should worry about the killing. So should the suicide bomber. When motivated, supposedly, by religion, the bomber is like Melville's backwoodsman, who dwells among the works of God, but is not imbued by them with a godly mind. Perhaps the early Christians were wrong, and God does indeed command the slaughter of innocents, but the Western tradition is otherwise. Indeed, it was the slaughter of innocents in the New World—the massacres by the Spaniards of the native people—that led the theologians at Barcelona, in the sixteenth century, to revise and systematize the ethics of war, precisely in order to keep innocents from harm.

President Obama, in his Nobel Address, seemed to condemn all killing in the name of God:

> These extremists are not the first to kill in the name of God; the cruelties of the Crusades are amply recorded. But they remind us that no Holy War can ever be a just war. For if you truly believe that you are carrying out divine will, then there is no need for restraint—no need to spare the pregnant mother, or the medic, or the Red Cross worker, or even a person of one's own faith.

The argument might seem rhetorically attractive, but, if seriously meant, ironically would serve as a rejection of the very just war tradition on which he says he is relying. Yes, history teaches that terrible things have been done in the name of God, by Christians, Jews, and Muslims alike. On the other hand, if a believer in any of these traditions takes the faith seriously, it would be a grievous wrong to kill if you were going against God's will. Forget the suicide bomber. Consider an American soldier who is a Christian. Assume that he is fighting justly, targeting only enemy troops on the battlefield. He cannot possibly accept the President's admonition never to kill in God's name, else he would not be able to kill at all.

I am not offering a defense of the suicide bomber, who in plying his murderous craft seeks out and kills noncombatants by design. Here the President seems to confuse cause and effect. The Nobel Address suggests that wars fought in God's name would have no limits, that anything would be permissible. But it is precisely to limit what can justly be done in war that the Christian theologians developed the criteria of *jus in bello*. The reason that the suicide bomber is wrong is not that he does what he does for God; it is that what he does is immoral. Exploding a bomb in the middle of a shopping mall is evil if the bomber thinks God wills it; but it is just as evil if the bomber is an atheist who believes he is arousing the sleeping consciousness of the proletariat and bringing us closer to world revolution.

All killing is morally problematic. But not all killing raises the *same* moral problem. It is the very state that kills in war, one must understand, that we in ordinary course expect to protect us from violence. In war, that state is instead committing violence, and on a massive scale. At the same time, it is the commission of violence that protects us from violence. The police go armed; our soldiers, more so. The world of laws, whether national or international, survives because it is enforced on dissenters at the point of the gun. But war is not law enforcement. War is not, contra Hegel, a continuation of the dialectic, the battle over abstract ideas. War is the work of a more primitive urge, an aspect of humanity older than the state but also necessary to its existence: the determination to kill them before they kill you.

Yet war is also about sacrifice.[58] Those who fight, risk. And they risk on behalf of others. Ideally, when a country is at war, its people sacrifice at home, too. Indeed, it is a fair criticism of both President Obama and President Bush that each insisted on the necessity of fighting abroad but neither called for any serious sacrifice at home. By not asking the people of the United States to do anything, however small—no extra war taxes, for instance, and no draft—our war leaders created a sharp discontinuity between the experience of war abroad and the experience of war at home. Presumably both Obama and Bush decided that the American people would not willingly make sacrifices in support of the war, and this calculation might well have been correct. But when the war has no home front, it is far easier for the people and their representatives to claim to support it. Although every casualty is a tragedy, the bald fact is that the rate at which American service members have died in Iraq and Afghanistan is vanishingly small compared to every other large-scale war the nation has fought. This is not Vietnam, where every family in America knew someone who was killed.

The subtext of Professor Asad's argument about the suicide bombers is that when one is willing to kill but not to sacrifice, a dangerous inequality arises. There is some scholarship today taking the position that there is a vague unfairness in using weapons technology so advanced that only the other side's forces are at risk: as I tell my students, the image of "war" that drew the attention of the early Christian writers involved a terrible destruction on both sides. Asad's point is different. He thinks the contemporary challenge is an inequality not in means but in fears. He scoffs at our efforts to reduce suicide bombers to individuals acting out of some rational impulse: anger over Iraq, anger over support for Israel, anger over modernity, anger over some other American act. This, according Asad, is an effort to manage the world by imagining that everyone is basically the same. "[W]e ask for an explanation in terms of motive," he writes, "only when we are suspicious of what the action means."[59]

Here Asad is offering a double criticism: On the one hand, we do not understand the violence of the suicide bomber because, in our Western minds, the bomber's violence is at some fundamental level different than our own. On the other hand, we are trying to impose on the bomber our own fear of death. "He must have been very upset indeed to die this way," we think, because, when we are upset, we, too, kill, but only from a safe distance. Asad seems to see the fact that the bomber frightens us as a measure of our decadence, or perhaps our narrow-mindedness. He is not defending the suicide bombers. He is accusing the West, in effect, of overreacting, of creating differences (say, between the suicide bomber and missile strikes) in order to excuse our own policies.

Well, maybe. Perhaps my students are brainwashed Westerners, but they always argue that suicide bombing is indeed different, not because the bomber kills himself, but because he seeks out civilians, in zones that are softly defended and easy to hit, refusing even to attempt to draw the distinctions that the ethics of war demand. Augustine, remember, argued that if one kills in war one must do so out of reluctant necessity, not out of desire. In his *Reply to Faustus,* Augustine warned that among the true evils of war are "revengeful cruelty" and "fierce and implacable enmity."[60] The bomber who seeks out soft targets is guilty of both; and if moved by a fury over American policy, he is guiltier still. I am old enough to remember the seventies, and the arguments in campus coffeehouses over whether the fact of accepting America's benefits would justify the decision, when the rest of the world at last rebelled, to treat all of us—men, women, and children alike—as if we were in the front lines. Our urtexts back then were the works of Franz Fanon, asserting the belief in the cleansing power of violence, the only path to creating true revolutionary consciousness. By killing, wrote Fanon, the oppressed became conscious of themselves as powerful. The argument was always frightening in its unyielding militant sophistry; but it remains the logic, even today, of the bomber.[61]

As to the bomber's willingness to die, perhaps the supposed retreat of religious faith, especially among our chattering classes, does indeed create a greater fear of death than in the past, but I am skeptical that this fear is transferable to our military forces, where acts of enormous heroism continue to take place.[62] And although I am sensitive to the claim that we could reduce or eliminate suicide attacks by changing our policies, the argument is a non sequitur. The fact that a man is willing to die for a cause, said Oscar Wilde, does not make the cause right; and the same is true of a man's willingness to take along a few dozen or a few hundred victims as he does it. Opposition to a policy, however fierce, is not evidence that the policy is wrong.

Let us be clear: The suicide bomber is not a just warrior. He is not a warrior at all. He is a war criminal. He targets noncombatants, a violation of the Geneva Conventions, and he refuses to fight in uniform, and therefore is not a legitimate combatant under Geneva in any case.[63] Ironically, he violates the international law of war for the same reason that his existence is itself so frightening. Talal Asad puts the point this way:

> The bomber appears as it were in disguise; he appears anonymously, like any member of the public going about his normal business. An object of great danger, he is unrecognized until it is too late. Signs taken innocently are other than they appear.[64]

The terror bomber, then, is aptly named. Wearing no uniform, offering no means of identification, he brings the battle into the schools and buses and plazas of a society trained to think of war as something fought by other people, far away. He creates fear, and the fear engenders the search for blame that is one of the least attractive characteristics of our politics. Our complacency is shattered, so we rush to figure out whose fault it is. Is the right too hard-line in foreign affairs? Is the left too soft? Has the President failed, or his minions, or the Congress? Should we sack the Secretary of This or the Director of That? Surely there is blame to be placed somewhere.

Indeed there is. And the Obama Administration, after some early stumbles, seems to have settled on the answer.

The fault rests, entirely, with the bomber.

Targeting Civilians

The suicide bomber is a special case of a larger problem. He exemplifies what the literature has come to call "asymmetric warfare": war in which one side follows the rules and the other does not. Here we begin to see why the principles of *jus in bello,* adopted almost wholesale by international law, are not necessarily efficient. There are virtues, to be sure, in reciprocity—I will limit the conduct of my own forces as long as you will limit the conduct of yours—and, among those ostensibly committed to the rules, the fear of tit-for-tat may create a useful deterrent. But in asymmetric warfare the inefficiency of doing the right thing becomes deadly. When one side is constrained by jus in bello and the other is not, the rational action for those willing to flout the rules is to mix with noncombatants. Once the mingling is complete, the forces restrained by a fear of harming noncombatants (or restrained by a concern about public outrage) are likely, as one observer has succinctly put it, to "hesitate before shooting."[65]

True enough. And fair as well: the just warrior should hesitate before shooting when civilians are in the line of fire. But hesitation is not necessarily inaction. We see this worked out in American war-fighting doctrine. On the question of interrogation tactics, President Obama has pointed to the *Army Field Manual* as morally authoritative, so it is worth taking a moment to see what the *Manual* has to say about civilians. According to paragraph 25 of the *Manual,* "[I]t is a generally recognized rule of international law that civilians must not be made the object of attack directed exclusively against them."[66] On the other hand, paragraphs 39 and 40 permit "bombardment" even of "towns, villages, dwellings, or buildings," as long as they are "defended," a word defined in turn to include, among other things, "[a] place which is occupied by a combatant military force or through which such a force is passing."[67] The *Manual* allows bombardment of towns occupied by combatants, including aerial bombardment, until the town surrenders, provided only that the American commander must "do all in his power to warn the authorities" that the bombardment is about to commence.[68]

Just war theory teaches the same lesson. Here (unlike in the drone example above), the doctrine of double effect does indeed apply. In fact, it applies twice. You have the right to attack your enemy. Killing him is a side effect. (Yes, that is a stretch, but it is the stretch natural law has long made.) And you have the right to pursue him even into an inhabited area. If attacking him there is a necessity, you have the right to do it, as long as you do not intend the deaths of the civilians surrounding him.[69] (Thus, just war theory cannot countenance, for example, the fire bombing of the German cities in World War II,* or the dropping of the atomic bombs, especially the second.) You should take all reasonable measures to assure the safety of noncombatants, but ultimately just war theory takes the position that it is the one hiding among the civilians, not the one pursuing, who has put them at risk. The answer that in the previous section we labeled "glib" turns out to be correct.

And before the reader rises up with a howl of fury, it is useful to note that the Geneva and Hague conventions also allow the bombardment of the town where the enemy is hiding. Nothing in the traditional law of war or the modern law of armed conflict prohibits attacking civilian targets when combatants are housed there. Indeed, under Geneva, even a building clearly marked as a hospital becomes a military target once armed combatants decide to hide within. For this reason, the law of war has traditionally been understood to mean that it is those who would hide among civilians, not those who attack them,

---

*Michael Walser's fascinating defense of the fire bombings is discussed below.

who are committing a war crime. This approach, although nowadays widely ignored, is quite sensible if one actually wants to protect noncombatants. If the mere act of hiding among civilians means one is liable to prosecution and punishment under the laws of war, then one is less likely to hide there.

Indeed, that thesis helps explain why no American administration, Republican or Democratic, has made a serious effort to have the Senate ratify Additional Protocol I of the Geneva Conventions. Protocol I, adopted in 1977 and ratified by most countries in the world, is meant to remedy a number of perceived shortcomings in the law of war, holdovers from the era when legitimate violence was waged only between sovereign powers. By the 1970s the news was thick with resistance and guerilla movements of one sort or another. Protocol I, among other things, seeks to confer most of the rights of combatants upon those who do not fight in uniform—a break with at least two centuries of understanding.[70] The reason for the proposed change was ostensibly to protect such irregular organizations as the Palestine Liberation Organization, which back in the 1970s was still largely engaged in military struggle. But there was then, and is now, nothing but a tactical choice to prevent any guerilla group from donning its own distinctive uniforms. Even suicide bombers could wear them. Of course, if the bombers wore uniforms, they would be unable to mingle with civilians and would thus have trouble reaching soft targets, but that is precisely the point.

It is difficult to imagine President Obama as a fan of Protocol I. The language he has used in condemning the irregulars fighting against American forces in Iraq and Afghanistan has been strident but firm. (Remember the Proviso.) He has left no wiggle room. He wants them dead. Obama's press secretary, Robert Gibbs, has referred to Osama bin Laden as "nothing but a cowardly, murderous thug and terrorist." Obama's Secretary of State has referred to the targeting of innocents as "cowardly, not courageous." The language used by Obama's attorney general, Eric Holder, in condemning Khalid Sheik Mohammed, supposed mastermind of the 9/11 bombings, does not propose anything like the normal course of treatment for prisoners of war; and Holder's words about Osama bin Laden, whom he has promised will be killed rather than captured, are hardly what the drafters of Protocol I had in mind. The evident view of the Administration is that there is a kind of combatant who should not be treated like others and, by extension, should not be on the battlefield to begin with. At the moment, the nation's enemies fall into that category. To take a word used by any number of Administration figures but not, as far as I have been able to discover, by the President, the secret bombers who hide in a crowd are "cowardly."

But what can one seriously expect? The philosopher Jeff McMahan refers to Protocol I as "a virtual invitation to engage in distortion and abuse."[71] McMahan has in mind language in the protocol that he sees as all but inviting attacks on civilians. Perhaps he is right. But the protection for combatants not wearing uniforms issues the same invitation. The reason that the Geneva Conventions and their predecessors have long limited combatant rights to those who fight in uniform is to protect noncombatants. The uniform requirement allows soldiers to see who is a combatant and who is not. A group that refuses to wear uniforms is, by that act alone, knowingly placing civilians at risk. To be sure, since the middle of the twentieth century, guerilla movements have been engaged in precisely this act, thus blurring the distinction between combatant and noncombatant.[72] Perhaps the blurring is sometimes necessary in order for a just guerilla movement to succeed. But let us be very clear: when there is no way to distinguish combatants from noncombatants, more noncombatants will die. Thus, here again, the theory of requiring a uniform is to protect civilians through deterrence: if you know that the price of protection under Geneva is to fight in uniform, goes the argument, you are more likely to wear one.[73]

Another way of putting the point is this: if you fight in war without wearing a uniform, you are unprotected by the provisions of the Geneva Conventions that apply to combatants. If captured, you are not entitled to its protections, because you have violated the law of war. The fear of what might result from remaining outside the Geneva Conventions is supposed to provide sufficient deterrent. Historically, soldiers caught fighting without wearing uniforms were often executed on the spot. Indeed, this was common practice as recently as the Second World War.[74] Nothing in the traditional reading of Hague or Geneva forbids this.[75] Such treatment is less likely today, at least if one is captured by the United States. (The Taliban have been known to execute even American soldiers who were wearing uniforms when captured.) But even if summary execution is improbable, the possibility that one will not be treated fully in accord with the requirements of Geneva is supposed to make one wear the uniform.

The principal objection to the requirement to wear a uniform runs something like this: the military uniform nowadays has the function of camouflaging the soldier, not distinguishing him.[76] But this is beside the point. Certainly the soldier in uniform will hide from the enemy. He will hide, however, in the desert, or in the jungle: that is what the camouflage is for. (This is especially true with modern digital camouflage, where the pattern is broken up into pixels instead of splotches.) The camouflage would not aid him in hiding among noncombatants. On the contrary. A man in combat dress in the middle of a town would stand out, as he should. The purpose of the uniform requirement is not to make the *soldier* easy to spot; it is to make the *civilian* easy to spot. The rule helps make clear, in the midst of battle, whom *not* to shoot. If both sides follow the rules, a soldier can safely ignore those in civilian clothes, confident that they mean him no harm. If the soldier prefers to hide among the innocent, thus increasing the risk to their lives, it is not unreasonable to treat him as a criminal.

At this point some of my students usually object, pointing out that one can well imagine an oppressed people, rising up against a murderous government or occupying force. Surely, my students say, such an entity should have the right to resist, despite the fact that its members wear no uniforms and indeed are not an organized fighting force. The answer is yes, of course, one wants the truly oppressed to be able to resist. Here, however, one must resist the temptation to give legal status to the resisters for the same reason that we concluded earlier we must resist the temptation to give legal status to the torturer: Once the legal exception exists, everybody will claim to be covered by it. Instead of crafting legal categories, we should be willing to do moral reasoning. We should support resistance movements not when they have met a legal test but when we think, based on all the facts, that they are morally right. This of course means that we must go to the trouble of informing ourselves and reaching reasoned opinions, rather than reducing every conflict to the size of a bumper sticker, but the payoff for that hard work is a better world. In the meantime, if we really believe in the paramount importance of protecting civilians, we should leave the international rules as they stand. If you want to fight legally, you have to be identifiable as a fighter.

The Obama Administration, following the lead of its predecessor, seems to have extended this reasoning well past any question of whether or not one wears a uniform. Criminality seems implicit in the very notion of making war against America. When I refer to criminality, I do not have in mind trials for war crimes; I have in mind the notion that the criminal, who does not follow the rules of the battlefield, is not protected by them either. Of course, this argument is necessarily controversial. It may even be wrong. But there seems little doubt that the Obama Administration believes it. Certainly it is difficult to uncover another rationale for its continued insistence on treating those captured on the battlefield as wrongdoers.

When We Break the Rules

And yet America, too, does wrong, and we do wrong in every war. No President dares admit this painful truth, but there is no avoiding it. War is horrible. Always. This point the media tend lazily to miss. When Americans are fighting abroad, reporters have no trouble spotting outrages. Of course. How could they not? If you look for wrongs, you will find them. Honest reporters should not cover them up. But they should act less surprised, and perhaps even give the public some context. Outrages happen in every war. In war, civilians die, usually in large numbers. Prisoners of war are mistreated, even in the most just of wars. Consider the "greatest generation." A controversy has swirled for years over the supposed mistreatment of German prisoners by the Allies during World War II. More than one official commission looked into the matter. Nobody thought the Allies were blameless; nobody thought the wrongdoing was other than intermittent. Then, in 1989, the Canadian novelist James Bacque published a best-seller, *Other Losses*, claiming widespread mistreatment of German prisoners, often with the connivance of higher-ups in the chain of command, maybe all the way to Supreme Allied Commander Dwight Eisenhower. Bacque put the number of deaths in Allied prisoner-of-war camps at 800,000 to 1 million.

As history, Bacque's book was bunk. Scholars considered his reading of the sources weak.[77] The numbers of deaths he cited have turned out to be absurd exaggerations, often based on comically bad arithmetic.[78] But even the doubters admit that widespread abuse occurred. For example, the military historian Albert E. Cowdrey, a sharp critic of Bacque, nevertheless concludes that up to 56,000 German prisoners of war may have died in the Allied camps, although the true number, he says, is most likely smaller.[79] (The United States has always admitted that about 15,000 died.) Cowdrey suggests more scholarly study, adding that the results would likely "offer a sobering corrective to any remaining illusion that in World War II all the humanity was on one side."[80] After all, 50,000 may not be 800,000, but it is still a soberingly large number.[81] I hasten to add that the fact that some terrible things were done by some Allied forces does not reduce the vast moral gulf between the two sides. Indeed, it is estimated that more than 3 million Soviet prisoners died in German hands, and at least 1 million German prisoners in Soviet hands. The number who died at the hands of the Japanese has never been adequately counted, but torture, beatings, decapitations, and other mass killings of prisoners in their hands are well documented, and at least one-quarter of American servicemen captured in the Pacific died in captivity.[82]

In short, whatever problems may have occurred in American camps, other countries involved in the war mistreated prisoners of war by design. Yes, there remains considerable truth in Orwell's dictum: "[A]trocities are believed in or disbelieved in solely on the grounds of political predilection."[83] (Indeed, we might explain much of what passes for contemporary political debate by reference to precisely this principle.) But here the facts are plainly on America's side.

Nevertheless, the treatment of prisoners matters. Prisoners of war are removed from the battlefield, but this is detention, not punishment. They may no longer be targeted because they are no longer combatants: they no longer possess the legitimate authority to kill, and therefore may not be killed.[84] Nowadays, the treatment of prisoners of war is governed by the Geneva Conventions, at least if the prisoners have been fighting on behalf of a belligerent who adheres to its terms. Much of the dispute over what to do with those captured in the Terror War arises precisely because they are, by and large, not fighting according to the rules. Even if, as some believe, the Geneva Conventions by their terms therefore do not apply, the ethics of war do. Suppose we are persuaded that the United States has no legal obligation to grant to prisoners taken in the Terror War the dignity and protections against physical harm articulated in the Conventions. That supposition does not conclude the moral question. Indeed, here is precisely the point. The just war tradition, remember, distinguishes sharply between *jus ad bellum,* the justification for the war, and *jus in bello,* the means by which the war is conducted. It has long been understood that a just war should never be conducted in unjust ways. The Geneva Conventions tell us, at best, the limits of what we are required or forbidden to do; they do not tell us what we should or shouldn't do. This I take to be the point of President Obama's choice to invoke just war theory rather than international law in his Nobel Address. He was interested not in what is legally ordained but what is morally ordained.

But we should press this abstract principle a bit. Even the most just of wars will at best adhere to the rules imperfectly. What we must accept, if we are ever to be a mature nation, is that every war, however just, will include the commission of manifold injustices. Back during the Civil War, General William Tecumseh Sherman, the conqueror of Atlanta, lamented the damage his forces did as they marched through the South, but added that the "disorder" was inevitable: "You cannot help yourself, and the only possible remedy is to stop war."[85] Exactly. You may seek to do without war, but, if ever you do have war, you must accept its horrors. Says Walzer: "We don't call war hell because it is fought without restraint. It is more nearly right to say that, when certain restraints are passed, the hellishness of war drives us to break with every remaining restraint in order to win."[86] One can hardly imagine a different result. After all, as John Keegan has wryly put it, "For killing to be gentlemanly, it must take place between gentlemen."[87] But there are no gentlemen on the battlefield.

This perhaps is the principal lesson of Steven Spielberg's magnificent film *Saving Private Ryan*. Although touted, justifiably, as a celebration of the achievements of the greatest generation, the film also suggests the difficulty, in the heat and fear and anger of battle, of adhering perfectly to the rules of *jus in bello*. In one memorable scene, we see the aftermath of a battle over a fortified German position on D-Day. The Germans have killed dozens of the attacking Americans. At last the position is overrun. The Germans give up. Some flee. Some surrender. We see a fleeing German shot in the back. We see two with their hands in the air, trying to surrender, who are also killed. Captain Miller (played by Tom Hanks) watches, seems about to act, then turns away.

What are we to make of this scene? That the American soldiers are terrible people who have committed a heinous crime? I think not. The point is more subtle, and therefore often lost in the black-or-white shouting matches of contemporary politics. In war, says Walzer, there is often "a kind of killing frenzy that begins in combat and ends in murder." There may even be a sort of "temporary insanity": "a frenzy of fear such that the soldier cannot recognize the moment when he is no longer in danger."[88] The point is that, in war, decent people fighting for the just side will at times do terrible things. To pretend that their emotions will never get the better of them is childish. To seek somehow to bring them all to justice is again to confuse cause and effect. The war itself is the cause—not some defect in the nature of a few wayward soldiers, but the war itself. That was Sherman's point: "You cannot help yourself." You try. You do your best. You train your people, you hammer home the rules, and, if you really care about what happens in the battle, you raise your children to believe the same propositions. If you are serious, you might even build your society around self-discipline and self-denial, even in the face of horror and fear. But, in the end, no matter what, your efforts will be imperfect.[89] If you fight a war, terrible things will happen. If you do not want terrible things to happen, do not fight any wars, but bear in mind the risk that the rest of the world might not mind doing terrible things quite as much as you do.

Nor are civilians immune from this mistreatment. One interesting just war question arose during the culminating battle of the Iraq War, the Allied assault on Baghdad. The Republican Guard, the best trained and best equipped Iraqi divisions, were deployed outside the city limits, between the advancing invaders and the remnants of the government. Had the Republican Guard retreated into the city, the war would doubtless have been prolonged. The American command, as John Keegan reminds us, has bad memories of urban warfare.[90] The decision to bomb Baghdad so heavily was aimed in part at deterring that retreat, by persuading the Republican Guard units that surrendering in place would be preferable to being destroyed by American air attacks. The strategy was successful: the Republican Guard never withdrew to the city. But the population of Baghdad suffered.

In that case, of course, the civilian suffering was in effect part of the planning; and, given that the city of Baghdad was defended, the bombardment was permissible as a matter of international law. The just war theorist, however, would at least raise questions, for the expected civilian deaths were not incidental to a successful attack on military forces; rather, they were designed to keep the military forces in place. But one must not be naive; at some point one must concede Michael Walzer's point that if a war can indeed be just, the just side must be allowed to try to win.

Questions of a different sort arise when civilians are harmed through the same frenzy that often leads to seeming injustices on the battlefield. Consider another Civil War example. A black regiment arrived at a Virginia plantation, where the master had recently whipped a number of female slaves. The black soldiers, upon hearing the tale, tied the master to a tree, and a soldier who had formerly been one of his slaves whipped him until he bled. Then the women he had beaten were allowed to whip him, too.[91] At the distance of a century and a half, most of us probably view the punishment as poetic justice. From the point of view of the ethics of war, however, the whipping is impossible to justify, especially without trial. Remember that the former master was a civilian. Indeed, once the motive for the whipping is understood to be revenge, the action of the soldiers fits precisely one of Elaine Scarry's sad, elegant descriptions of torture: "converting the other person's pain into his own power."[92] The point is that what Walzer describes as the temporary insanity of battle can seize those with whose causes we agree. One has weapons, one has fellow soldiers, one has all that is needed to use force to expunge the anger and pain of whatever wrong has been done. During the Second World War, as the theologian Donald Shriver has noted, the Allies slowly came to the view that the enemy was not merely the German army, but "a whole national people."[93] This attitude, suggests Shriver, made the principle of discrimination considerably less important in the public mind, enabling, for example, the fire bombings of the German cities. Take another example involving black troops in the Civil War. A white man was hanged after defending, in the hearing of black soldiers, the massacre of captured black troops at Fort Pillow, then threatening to cut one of the soldiers' throats himself. As a formal matter, he was hanged for the threat. As a practical matter, he was hanged for his gloating.[94]

Horrifying—but so often a part of war. Every war. There is a tendency, nowadays, to endow the Geneva Conventions, and other traditions that have guided warfare, with a talismanic quality, a suggestion that by violating them or even interpreting them loosely rather than strictly, you accept moral doom upon the entire project of your nation, now and forever. If this is what we think, we had better grow up. There is a lovely scene in Gore Vidal's novel *Lincoln* where the sixteenth President, asked by Secretary of State William Seward what he would tell his son should Congress ever impeach him for his violations of law, replies that at least he would have saved the Capitol, so that they would have a place to impeach him. Lincoln's most criticized wartime decision was probably the suspension of habeas corpus. Defending the decision later, he famously asked: "Are all the laws, *but one,* to go unexecuted, and the government itself go to pieces, lest that one be violated?"[95]

Game theorists would point out that violations of the rules can be rational, even necessary to victory. The tit-for-tat strategy, proposing that you follow the rules until your opponent decides not to, is often the wisest course of play.[96] Interestingly, the Geneva Conventions take a similar view: the people of states that do not abide by their provisions are, for the most part, not protected by their provisions. The Conventions are not handed down from on high. They make no claim to universality.[97] They are treaties, in which different nations agree to follow those rules when they fight each other. They nowhere promise to follow them at any other time.

The restriction would doubtless chafe the absolutist, but it actually makes a good deal of sense. The idea is to encourage compliance with the rules, by making the costs of noncompliance too high—in short, to deter breaches. As a practical matter, the strategy can actually work. Consider another example from the Civil War. An often-forgotten provision of the Emancipation Proclamation welcomed freed slaves as Union soldiers.[98] In response, the Confederacy declared that any former slaves who became officers in the Union army, would, upon capture, face trial for insurrection, the punishment for which was death. Lincoln retaliated at once, ordering that for every former slave executed by the Confederacy, one captive Confederate officer would be executed by the Union.[99] The rules of war, even as understood at the time, would have condemned Lincoln's tit-for-tat strategy. Many a modern game theorist would approve it. Indeed, Lincoln's prompt announcement seems to have had a partial deterrent effect, because the Confederacy never officially sentenced any black Union officers to execution. On the other hand, black troops, whether or not former slaves, were routinely brutalized upon capture.[100] The Confederate military refused to include them in prisoner exchanges.[101] Often the Southern armies slaughtered black troops outright, whether on the battlefield or behind prison walls. No Confederate soldiers were ever punished for these war crimes.[102] Lincoln threatened retaliation and even murder trials several times but never acted, and the slaughters continued.[103] Frederick Douglass argued repeatedly for a harder line.[104] One wonders whether Lincoln should have done more, whether, had he executed a Confederate officer in retaliation for every massacre, official or not, of black soldiers, the South might have stayed its hand.

Such an action on the President's part, as I have suggested, would most certainly have violated the rules of war. It would also very likely have saved a good many lives. The absolutist would have condemned Lincoln's patent violations of law; but the black soldiers whose lives were saved most probably would have cheered.

CRITICISM AT A DISTANCE

This is not to say that violating the rules of *in bello,* or the strictures of international law, is justifiable. Sometimes excusable, maybe—but not justifiable. Over the years America has relied upon its unspoken Proviso as a justification for many things. But the Proviso does not justify everything.

Consider again the aforementioned scene from *Saving Private Ryan,* in which German soldiers are shot while attempting to surrender. Few would have blamed the fictitious Captain Miller had he ordered his men arrested. But he did not. A few minutes later, we see one of the men who had killed a prisoner weeping uncontrollably. We are never told why, but the tears seem appropriate to the horror, and to the tension. It is a tribute to Spielberg that we are so carried along by the pace of battle that we do not so much forgive Miller's soldiers their transgression as forget that it ever occurred. We participate in the frenzy. We accept the complexities of the battlefield, the fear, the anger, the pain. And the irony, too: later in the film, Miller's men want to execute another prisoner, a machine gunner who has just killed one of their comrades. Captain Miller instead orders him released, for they are on a mission and cannot take him along. The prisoner promises to turn himself in to American military police. (In the traditional custom of war, this was known as "parole.") Instead, the German returns to the battle, where he kills several of Miller's men. We are left to wonder, should the German have been killed in the first place? Or was it proper instead for Captain Miller in effect to sacrifice the life of his own soldiers in order to protect the man who would take their lives?

My students and I engage in lively debate on the question, but perhaps only one who has been to war can offer a complete answer. Frank Haskell, a survivor of Gettysburg, had this to say about those who were not there and criticized the conduct of those who were: "It is very pleasant for these people, no doubt, at safe distances from guns, in the enjoyment of a lucrative office . . . where mud and flooding storms, and utter weariness never penetrate, to discourse of battles and how campaigns should be conducted and armies of the enemy destroyed."[105] The war affects your point of view. To a point, Haskell is right. I have not been in battle, and I suspect that few of my readers have. Neither have most political or academic or media observers or critics. At the same time, if civilian control over the military means anything, it means that the views of those not present still count. What we should learn from Haskell, as from other veterans who have made the same point, is to be modest rather than hubristic in our criticism.

Let me be clear. I am not saying—emphatically not saying— that only those who have experienced combat are entitled to an opinion. If we believe our democratic pretensions, we should not seek to muzzle each other by so celebrating expertise that crucial moral and political decisions become the purview of a small elite, whether soldiers or sermonizers or scientists. We should criticize freely, and those with the most power should take the most hits. Indeed, dissent remains the life's blood of any democracy, a proposition routinely neglected by those holding the reins of power at any given moment.[106] Nevertheless, obligatory or not, our criticisms should be restrained, modest, always conscious of the possibility that insiders see something that outsiders do not; that a point of view informed with more knowledge or experience than our own might turn out to be the better one.

President Obama has made the transition from outsider to insider. His war policies, and the reasoning behind them, have come more and more to resemble those of his predecessor. Although there are those on the right who look at our warlike President and accuse him of cynicism, and there are those on the left who look at the same President and accuse him of betrayal, I think the truth is different. For it is a painful fact known to all of us, but too often forgotten, that deciding is a more difficult matter than criticizing. It might even be that Obama the insider has realized what Obama the outsider did not: whatever the mistakes of his predecessor, President Bush acted out of a belief in the urgency of the threat facing the nation. The threat was neither invented nor imagined, but is instead out there in the world. The plotting against America continues. If you pay attention, you can hardly miss the fresh headlines every month or so about another conspiracy blocked by federal authorities.

So the nation is at war. Genuinely at war, against enemies who mean to do America harm. We might argue vehemently about the underlying issues, but there would be no American troops in Afghanistan, and probably none in Iraq, had the towers not come down on September 11. Still, now that we are fighting, Obama, like Bush, has evidently come around to the view that victory will require measures that at best skirt the edges of what is morally justifiable: those drone attacks, for example, or the rendition of prisoners. Presumably, in the sober precincts of a country at peace, the nation's leaders might make a different set of choices. Faced with an emergency, we often reason differently. One result is that we often reach moral conclusions very different from those on which we would settle were we to reflect at leisure.[107] This is what Lincoln did when he suspended habeas corpus. And although Obama has steered clear of serious restrictions on personal freedom at home, he has plainly come to the view that the emergency abroad justifies extraordinary measures.

Of course, once we openly acknowledge what we all know to be true, the risk is that a government will declare what Michael Walzer calls "supreme emergency" where none actually exists.[108] When the supreme emergency exists, says Walzer, ordinary moral considerations might be overridden. Not suspended, but overridden. Indeed, "They have to be overridden precisely because they have not been suspended."[109] His case is both descriptive and normative. He believes that states do behave this way and that, in certain cases, they are justified in doing so.

I do not mean to suggest that President Obama has explicitly endorsed Walzer's notion, although President Bush arguably did. Nevertheless, Obama's words and actions as war leader suggest that he does indeed believe that we face an emergency, and that in times of emergency the rules are different. Walzer's theory has been understandably controversial among philosophers and legal scholars.[110] It has also garnered a great deal of attention in military circles, where the reaction has been, let us say, uneasy. So, for example, Martin Cook, a professor of philosophy at the Air Force Academy, warns that even if we accept that in war some terrible things might happen, we should leave in place the possibility of punishment for the perpetrators, as a deterrent, and also as a reminder.[111] And the military ethicist Alex J. Bellamy, analyzing the same case from which Walzer proceeds—the bombing of German cities by the Royal Air Force during the Second World War—points out that, as a practical matter, governments do not admit that they have broken the rules. Their choice to obfuscate or flat-out lie, even to their own people, suggests a concern that there is little popular support for an emergency ethics.[112]

I am not sure, however, that the critics have Walzer quite corralled. His prediction that governments under threat will act in ways that violate the accepted rules is well borne out by history. And, as we shall see, the people often go along with whatever is required to protect them. Walzer argues that this places enormous pressure on the selection of political leadership: one wants the nation to be led by those with the wisdom neither to panic nor to mislead about the nature of the threat we face.[113] In other words, the worse things get, the more the nation requires leaders who will be loath to decide that an emergency exists. Many of those who voted for President Obama probably believed, in Walzer's terms, that the previous Administration had been too quick to find existential threats to the nation. The new broom, they must have hoped, would sweep away the old arguments. As we have seen, that is not quite what happened. Instead, Barack Obama, like his predecessor, has come to the view that the best available strategy is preventive war, a policy of striking at the terrorists before they can attack. This, remember, is the President's vision of a just war: fighting in defense of your country, you may take what measures you deem appropriate. And the only limit on propriety seems to be the President's own sense of ethics. From the point of view of just war theory, such a conclusion is worrisome. Nevertheless, now that we have had consecutive Presidents who reason along these lines, we should accept that things may be like this for a while.

OBAMA AND SHAPING THE PEACE

And what about the other half of the Bush Doctrine? Not the idea of fighting the nation's enemies on their home ground, and stopping them before they can bring their plans to fruition, but the idea of using America's might—economic, diplomatic, and military—to spread democracy abroad? That aspect, it seems, President Obama finds more worrisome. During his presidential campaign, he excoriated the Bush Doctrine, and even accused one of his primary opponents, in what evidently was meant as a telling criticism—of endorsing it. Much of the media attacked the Bush Doctrine as well, although rarely pausing to spell it out. In truth, many different ideas have been labeled the Bush Doctrine. Let us take a moment and consider what Bush himself thought his doctrine was.

President Bush announced the doctrine that has come to bear his name in his 2002 commencement address at West Point. They key language:

> Our nation's cause has always been larger than our nation's defense. We fight as we always fight, for a just peace. A peace that favors human liberty. We will defend the peace against threats from terrorists and tyrants. We will preserve the peace by building good relations among the great powers. And we will extend the peace by encouraging free and open societies on every continent.

And he continued: "Building this just peace is America's opportunity and America's duty."

The key to the doctrine is not the method but the goal: "encouraging free and open societies on every continent." Of course, when the most powerful nation in the world announces what it plans to encourage, everybody pays attention. In this case, paying attention was appropriate. At first blush, President Obama's decision to reject this prong of the Bush Doctrine might seem curious. After all, the spreading of democracy and freedom abroad sounds at first blush more laudable than tracking terrorists to their hideouts, and hitting them before they hit you first. Encouraging the spread of free and open societies was an ambitious goal, and in most ways a morally attractive one. Unfortunately, Bush's presidency, and thus his doctrine, will be forever marred by their association with the unpopular war in Iraq. Certainly they go together in the national imagination. To many Americans, to many people around the world, thoughts of the Bush Doctrine spark images of imposing democracy by force.

But when viewed in isolation, apart from the matter of any particular war, the doctrine possesses a lovely aura of nonviolence, of hope, even of transcendence. It is consistent with the notion at the heart of the Augustinian just war tradition: the use of power to achieve justice and good order. Moreover, it is in keeping with a trend in just war thinking, for a growing number of theorists believe that we should give more attention than we do to the problem of *jus post bellum* (literally, "justice after war") or *jus ad pacem* (in simple terms, "just peace").

There is a sense in which the idea of just peace is fundamental to the idea of just war. Augustine, in laying the groundwork for the notion of fighting in a just cause, has this to say: "He, then, who prefers what is right to what is wrong, and what is well-ordered to what is perverted, sees that the peace of unjust men is not worthy to be called peace in comparison with the peace of the just."[114] Aquinas, in formulating more fully the principles of just war, relies on Augustine's insistence that war be waged only "with the object of securing peace, of punishing evildoers, and of uplifting the good."[115] To the fathers of the doctrine, the pursuit of peace was the only just cause for war.

To be sure, Augustine and Aquinas and other Catholic thinkers had in mind a peace consisting of order in accordance with God's will. This is not the place to join battle on whether living according to God's will or the will of some secular philosopher ought to be the more appealing. For present purposes, the minimum lesson we take from the Catholic tradition is that the leader who decides to fight a war should have in mind a clear picture of the more-just peace that is to follow. The leader should be able to articulate that vision, and willing, too, to prosecute the war until the vision is attained. In this sense, a principle of just peace might require a just case for ending the war, just as there must be a just case for starting it.[116]

For Obama, the most striking illustration of this dilemma is presented by the Iraq War. As a longtime opponent of the war, Obama promised repeatedly during the campaign that he would wind it down. As President, he is doing so, at a slightly faster pace than his predecessor negotiated, but on basically the same model.[117] The challenge is to articulate the reason for the withdrawal. It matters whether the United States is quitting Iraq because its mission has been accomplished or because we should not have been there in the first place. If the first is true, if, in effect, America won the war, then perhaps we need not worry about whether there exists a just case for exit. If this is what the President believes, he should certainly say so.

If on the other hand the war continues, not yet won, then it is not obvious that we ought to leave just because we should never have gone. When Colin Powell, then Secretary of State, warned President Bush on the eve of the Iraq invasion, "You broke it, you bought it," he was predicting that additional challenges would arise subsequent to a successful invasion. Powell was right, and, at this writing, many of the challenges remain. The notion of *jus ad pacem* suggests that America must be cautious indeed in turning over its responsibilities to the Iraqi government. With the best of intentions, we broke the country. We have to fix it, if we are able, to make it better than before. Here even those among my students who are most vehemently against the war tend to agree.

And yet there is a problem. Michael Walzer, in supporting what he calls "just settlements," has warned that a just war should be modest in its goals.[118] The just end of a just war, says Walzer, should generally involve the undoing of the evil that sparked the conflict, but not the creation of a new international order.[119] Even as academic thought has turned increasingly to the problem of just peace, many scholars have maintained that an American vision of just peace will tend to accord not with the needs of the many (as Augustine also suggested), but rather with the best interests of the United States. This is precisely what the more thoughtful critics of the Bush Doctrine accused President Bush of doing: seeking to create a regime of peace consistent with American interests. And the charge is at least half right. Whatever the idealism of his vision, Bush was always careful to specify that the spread of democracy abroad is also in America's own security interest. On the other hand, if we Americans believe the words of our own founding documents, the spread of freedom and democracy to other people must be counted as a good.

Walzer, writing back in the post-Vietnam era, cautioned against the "Democratic idealism" that "sometimes prolongs wars"; that is, the effort to build something better, so that whatever threat to peace arose before will not arise again.[120] As another ethicist noted during Vietnam, the United States had the choice of sending more troops or fewer, of withdrawing at once or gradually, but the one thing it could not possibly do was guarantee peace.[121] Here is a point often misunderstood in the overly simplistic media whirl, where bumper sticker slogans pass for argument. Peace does not just happen. Peace is created, and sometimes the creation is bloody. When the Civil War began, nobody was quite sure what peace would look like, but, certainly, there came a time when returning to the status quo ante was impossible. Lincoln had to visualize peace, and work for it. Only when the war became fierce did Lincoln come to accept that any real peace had to include the end of slavery. This demand the South refused, and so the war continued. Of course, Lincoln could have envisioned peace as simply the withdrawal of Union forces from the South, but that would have been a false peace, a mere temporary absence of formal battle.

Sometimes, the same moral imperatives that drive the just war must drive the creation of order and justice afterward.[122] If you begin a just war to obtain a just goal, then peace short of that goal might render the war unjust: death and destruction to no apparent end. President Obama has said many times that he believes the Afghan War to be a defensive war of necessity.

He therefore owes us an explanation of what form of just peace would accord with the war's just goals. He views the Iraq War as unjust. But it is a war nevertheless, and there, too, the President should lay out for us a vision of what form of peace he envisions. For just as the wrongful driver must make whole the victim of an accident, so should the wrongful invader do what it can to make up for his wrong.[123]

So the morality of ending a war raises issues of some complexity. There are weighty arguments on all sides. President Obama has articulated more than once his goals in pursuing war. In his Nobel Address, however, he also granted us a sketch of his vision of what would constitute a well-ordered peace: "Only a just peace based on the inherent rights and dignity of every individual can truly be lasting." Obama rejected what he called the "stark choice between the narrow pursuit of interests or an endless campaign to impose our values around the world," presumably the Bush Doctrine. Earlier, in his autobiography, Obama had offered an analogous criticism: "I agree with George W. Bush when in his second inaugural address he proclaimed a universal desire to be free. But there are few examples in history in which the freedom men and women crave is delivered through outside intervention."[124] Obama, in the Nobel Address, continued in a vein somewhat closer to what he had criticized:

> I believe that peace is unstable where citizens are denied the right to speak freely or worship as they please; choose their own leaders or assemble without fear. Pent-up grievances fester, and the suppression of tribal and religious identity can lead to violence. We also know that the opposite is true. Only when Europe became free did it finally find peace. America has never fought a war against a democracy, and our closest friends are

governments that protect the rights of their citizens. No matter how callously defined, neither America's interests—nor the world's—are served by the denial of human aspirations.

Finally, said Obama, a just peace "must encompass economic security and opportunity." Why? Because "true peace is not just freedom from fear, but freedom from want." He summarized his vision this way: "Agreements among nations. Strong institutions. Support for human rights. Investments in development." As critics have noted, the President did not say how this just peace was to be attained. But at least he told us where he thinks the world ought to be going.

True, President Obama has made clear his preference for diplomacy rather than force. So have his predecessors, including President Bush. And although this book is about the President's view on war, not his views on foreign policy generally, it is nevertheless worth reminding the reader of Obama's view that conversation has limits, that there are evils one must fight. Thus, two months after his Nobel speech, President Obama expressed his frustration with the limits of dialogue: "We have bent over backwards to say to the Islamic Republic of Iran that we are willing to have a constructive conversation about how they can align themselves with international norms and rules and re-enter as full members of the international community." The Iranian government, he added, has so far made a different choice.[125]

Notice the two key assumptions fueling the President's disappointment: first, that "constructive conversation" is a goal that other nations also wish to pursue, and, second, that the point of the conversation would be to persuade Iran to "align" itself with "international norms." Immediately one should see the problem. One weakness of the Bush Doctrine, said many thoughtful critics, was its idealism ("romanticism" might have been a better word), because it conceptualized a world in which people, and countries, can be moved by ideas rather than interests. The entire realist school of foreign policy rests on the notion that the Enlightenment thinkers were right on the subject of international relations, that countries are moved by their interests and not by verbal appeals.[126] In the case of Iran, this would mean that conversation in and of itself serves no particular purpose. Countries, say the realists, are not persuaded to do the right thing. They are shown how doing the right thing is in their self-interest; that is to say, how doing the right thing will leave them better off than not doing the right thing.

And sometimes—if you take the President's words at face value—sometimes, whether you like it or not, you have to fight. Some evils, as Obama said in his Nobel Address, cannot be resolved through dialogue. Some evils are not amenable to persuasion. They must be combated instead by force of arms. We should hope those evils are few. As the world's superpower, however, we must at least debate the matter seriously. Odd though it may sound, the world needs us, and, at times, needs us to fight. Nevertheless, the President should never forget that war rarely accomplishes its objectives except imperfectly. As the church historian Robert Bainton has noted, commenting on the pre–Pearl Harbor support among some Christians for American entry into World War II: "To be sure, the war might not establish democracy, liberty, and a just and enduring peace. The only thing war can ever do is to restrain outrageous villainy and give a chance to build again."[127]

But suppose the outrageous villainy is committed by someone who has done your country no wrong? Suppose, as has often happened, that a regime decides to murder a significant subset of its population? No claim of self-defense is available. Yet President Obama, in his Nobel Address, implied the possibility that justice may permit another country to intervene militarily to stop the killing. Let us turn next to that challenge.

THE RIGHTS AND DIGNITY
OF STRANGERS

President Obama on *Jus ad Pacem*

DEFENSE OF OTHERS

A few years ago I had dinner in Aspen, Colorado, with a group of thoughtful, progressive individuals who professed heartfelt concern about the state of the world beyond our borders. I raised the subject of Darfur, a region in southern Sudan, where, at this writing, government-armed militias continue their long campaign of negotiating and ignoring cease-fires, then attacking the villages and refugee camps of the dark-skinned Christians they seem determined to destroy, using rape, pillage, and finally murder to drive them from their homes. My dinner companions were, to say the least, disturbed; as I described some of the horrors that led the Committee on Conscience of the United States Holocaust Memorial Museum to issue its first ever warning of a "genocide emergency," they grew agitated.[1] Yes, they agreed, the situation was terrible. But my friends had no idea what the solution might be. Their only certainty was that America should send no troops to protect the victims. "It's so far away," said one. "There's nothing we can really do."

Well, yes. Darfur is indeed far away from the United States, as most of the world's most violent trouble spots turn out to

be. And, as it turns out, the modern ethics of war and international law both offer much the same response. If a threat appears against your own country, your options for repelling it
are broad. If instead the threat is against someone else—particularly when, as is all too common, another country's governing clique is targeting some portion of its own people—then
neither international law nor the ethics of war offers much assistance to the stunned outsider who wants to intervene. On
the contrary: when another country offers no threat to your
own, the theory of just and unjust wars is wary of allowing you
to attack; and although the murky mishmash known as international law pretends to honor the Genocide Convention,
which commits the signatories to preventing genocide, the pre-
vailing custom, as we shall see, is that the one form of prevention that might actually work—military intervention—is all but
forbidden.

This episode comes to mind as I reflect on a relatively unre-
marked portion of President Obama's Nobel Prize acceptance
address. Military force, said the President, "can be justified on
humanitarian grounds, as it was in the Balkans, or in other
places that have been scarred by war." He added: "Inaction tears
at our conscience and can lead to more costly intervention
later."

All of this is true—and if the President turns out to mean it,
he will demonstrate a radically different understanding of *jus
ad bellum* than is captured in the actions of recent American
leaders. Samantha Power, in her book *A Problem from Hell: America in the Age of Genocide,* contends that the United States has
never sent troops to end a genocide. (The standoff bombing
during the Bosnian crisis occurred, let us say, rather late in the
slaughter.) One of the saddest moments in the book comes
near the end, when Power tells the story of how George W.
Bush, at the start of his Administration, was handed a list of re-

cent atrocities around the world where his predecessors had failed to intervene. (The list is a long one.) Bush wrote across the memorandum, in red ink, "NOT ON MY WATCH"—and then proceeded to behave like all the others.[2] Yet we should not be too critical. Such a failure represents realism, not hypocrisy. American leaders know that their nation has little stomach for war in the first place, and is unlikely to be excited at the thought of sending armed forces to places in the world where no American interest is at stake.

We take for granted the existence of a right of self-defense, and the right applies not only to persons but also to the states into which they organize themselves.[3] Saint Ambrose, along with his disciple, Saint Augustine, argued that the morality of defending others is higher than the morality of defending oneself. The common analogy is to a man walking in the wilderness who spots another under unjust attack. The stroller is free to intervene.[4] Augustine, among others, would argue that he is obliged to do so. Passing the point whether the two were wrong about individuals, is it possible that they were right about states? Certainly a growing number of scholars seem to think so. In the academy, the post–World War II consensus focusing on sovereignty and stability as crucial to preserving international order has broken down. Sovereignty is the virtual wall a country builds around itself. Under international law, a state was traditionally left undisturbed as long as it does not do any damage outside the wall. Inside the wall, countries were traditionally left to their own devices. Perhaps the consensus was a mistake: a necessary mistake, but still a mistake.

Certainly one has the impression that Obama thinks so. During his presidential campaign, he promised that he would "respond forcefully to all genocides." He renewed that pledge in 2009, on the fifteenth anniversary of the Rwandan genocide, in which the Hutu majority massacred as many as a million

Tutsi. But now his language was more tepid, with no mention of a forceful response: "We must renew our commitment and redouble our efforts to prevent mass atrocities and genocide." In his December 2009 Nobel Address he chose a middle ground, noting the possibility of humanitarian intervention without actually calling it an obligation:

> [T]he purpose of military action extends beyond self-defense or the defense of one nation against an aggressor. More and more, we all confront difficult questions about how to prevent the slaughter of civilians by their own government, or to stop a civil war whose violence and suffering can engulf an entire region.
> I believe that force can be justified on humanitarian grounds, as it was in the Balkans, or in other places that have been scarred by war. Inaction tears at our conscience and can lead to more costly intervention later. That's why all responsible nations must embrace the role that militaries with a clear mandate can play to keep the peace.

Here the President has chosen his words with care. He says only that force "can be justified" to protect strangers from harm, not that it is in any sense obligatory. This is in keeping with the caution traditionally expressed by international lawyers, as well as by American presidents—a caution that has in almost every case become simply an excuse for inaction.

In recent history the most famous moment of inaction was the aforementioned genocide in Rwanda. The slaughter began in the spring of 1994, and, over a course of a bit more than three months, led to the death of one out of every five residents of the country. Although the popular image of the attacks is that they were carried out entirely by the Hutu militias, particularly the *Interahamwe* ("We Stand Together"), subsequent evidence has made clear that the planning involved the highest councils of the government. The killings started slow and gained momentum. All over the country Tutsi were hacked to death. With machetes. Some were shot, but the machetes were the public face of the genocide. The West was appalled. The West was outraged. The West condemned and counseled and called upon. But the West never lifted a finger to stop the killing. The United Nations at this time had peacekeepers on the ground in Rwanda. Their commander warned that the genocide was in the offing. Human Rights Watch coldly records the response: "U. N. troops . . . tried for a few hours to keep the peace, then withdrew to their posts—as ordered by superiors in New York—leaving the local population at the mercy of assailants."[5] The killing continued unabated, in full view of the world. One of the killers later described the task as "almost pleasantly easy."[6] If close to a million dead proved not sufficient to get the leaders of the West to do more than wring their hands, it is difficult to imagine what would be.

Perhaps Barack Obama will be no different from other Western leaders. Perhaps his fine words about taking up arms to prevent the suffering of others will prove to be just talk. Perhaps, given history, this is the way it pays to bet. But let us imagine for a moment the opposite. Let us consider the possibility that the President means what he says—not only in his Nobel Address, but in his autobiography, where he wrote: "War might be hell and still be the right thing to do."[7] Thus we are presented squarely with the ethical question, a variant of what lawyers call the slippery slope: when to do it. Perhaps there are some evils which, for a time, we must live with. Certainly there are also horrors so great that it may be appropriate, even obligatory, for other countries to use force to stop them. The slippery slope problem arises because of what one of my Yale colleagues likes to call "the temptation to empire": once we begin sending troops to right terrible wrongs, we might easily wind up using force to reshape large parts of the world to our liking.

This is not the place to review all aspects of the argument. A few examples should suffice to show its breadth and complexity. Thus, some scholars argue that, to avoid overreaching, we should limit from the outset any discussion of the legitimacy of humanitarian intervention to the situation in which the intervenor is trying to correct "widespread deprivations of internationally recognized human rights."[8] The various international conventions on human rights create, in the words of Michael Reisman, "a template of domestic governance."[9] Many theorists would limit intervention to situations already covered by the Genocide Convention, in order to free potential intervenors from the need to work through their own moral standards.

Michael Walzer, whose book *Just and Unjust Wars* remains after more than thirty years the leading text on these questions, prefers a more fluid definition. The time to step in, says Walzer, is when "a government turns savagely upon its own people."[10] He quotes with approval the language of Thomas Franck and Nigel Rodley, that the determination to intervene "belongs in the realm not of law but of moral choice, which nations, like individuals, must sometimes make."[11] And when is this moral choice justified? When one is responding to activities "that shock the moral conscience of mankind."[12]

True, in more recent work, Walzer has explained that his advice is not meant to be mandatory, but he has nevertheless stuck by his preference for a standard that rests on moral rather than legal reasoning.[13] He has cautioned, too, that potential intervenors must "ask what the costs of intervention will be for the people being rescued, for the rescuers, and for everyone else."[14] This is a useful reminder of the fact that there are genuine costs to intervention: one is fighting a *war,* for goodness sake. And the war must meet all the usual tests that we have discussed.

Thus, even when a humanitarian crisis provides the causa, the military option must be a last resort, and stand a reasonable hope of success. Even then, one sovereign state is invading another that has done it no wrong. The *causa* that leads to the attack has been committed by a sovereign against its own people. Thus humanitarian war differs from defensive war—even preemptive defensive war—in that there is no way to disguise the fact that the state going to the defense of the people of another is the aggressor. The state that is attacked neither struck first at its attacker, nor had any plans to do so.[15]

For just this reason, one must avoid temptation. Many a tyrant bent on expansion has announced that he is invading the country next door because its government is doing such terrible things. And of course, all through history, the temptation to remake the lives and circumstances of others has been a constant. Here one thinks of V. S. Naipul's suggestion that there exists a constant human yearning for an undeveloped land to shape into our ideal; and that we are perfectly happy to assume away the inhabitants in order to demonstrate that the land in question is indeed empty.[16] Now we see why the right intention criterion matters. I mentioned back in Part I that secular just war thinking has largely ignored the requirement in Aquinas that the war be pursued only with rightful intention. But in the case of a humanitarian war, the intention actually matters. The singular characteristic of the war for a truly humanitarian cause is that the state waging war has no interest in the outcome other than to prevent a great horror from continuing. Thus, John Howard Yoder, one of the great constructive critics of modern just war theory, strives to distinguish the humanitarian intervention in what he considered its original sense—"military operations undertaken in the interest of the people of a country against their own government"—from a later sense of "efforts to stabilize crises . . . especially where efforts to serve refugees were being compromised by continuing military violence and banditry."[17] Let us adopt this narrow definition, excluding, despite their overlap, such well-intentioned altruistic interventions as peacekeeping and nation-building, which tend as a rule to present operations more difficult to evaluate and considerably longer in duration.[18] And, for most theorists, the duration matters. Michael Reisman has put the point this way: "Humanitarian intervention is a short-term initiative, aimed only at stopping massive and ongoing human rights violations. Once the violations cease, it is no longer justified."[19] And the notion that one can and should fight to protect human rights has certainly gained adherents.[20]

Critics warn, however, that if violation of human rights becomes the standard for intervention, we may wind up going to war to promote causes more controversial than shocking. To take one example, a number of scholars over the years have come to regard the establishment of liberal democracy as an appropriate goal of multi-lateral policy.[21] Under the Bush Administration, the United States was active in trying to persuade the world that democracy itself is a human right. Might we then go to war to reshape tyrannical nations into democracies?[22] Indeed, a broad range of state conduct might be implicated: for example, France's decision to prohibit the wearing of religious apparel in its public schools, including head scarves for Muslim girls, could be said to violate a core concept of religious liberty protected by Article 18 of the Universal Declaration of Human Rights.[23] The relentless secularism of the French schools might indeed amount to a systematic violation of human rights, even if not all observers would agree that it meets Walzer's "shocked" test.[24]

One might avoid these pitfalls by using a variant of Obama's answer. In his Nobel Address, remember, the President asserted, flatly, that there exist forces in the world sufficiently evil that they must be combatted by force of arms. That word *evil*, which caused such tumult when used by Obama's predecessor, turns out to play a potentially crucial role in helping us to make distinctions. Suppose that the critics are right that France is violating the fundamental human rights of Muslim girls and their families. That does not mean that France is evil. France is acting out of a determination to secularize its society—a determination that is profoundly mistaken and even in some ways prejudiced, but is not actually evil. And, if we take Obama seriously, it is only that which is evil that we should consider resisting with military force.

Alas, President Obama has not offered a standard for determining which evils need combatting by force. Even with respect to concrete examples he remained circumspect in his Nobel Address, mentioning two specific instances that would justify the use of force: "to prevent the slaughter of civilians by their own government, or to stop a civil war whose violence and suffering can engulf an entire region." Those key words—"prevent" and "stop"—suggest a preference for taking action before a genocide or other horror begins. This is a perfectly sensible place to start. But what do you do once things heat up?

Some scholars believe that intervention to protect the oppressed at some point becomes obligatory, or nearly so—that a state possessing the means to do so might sometimes have a moral duty to go to the aid of the suffering people of another.[25] Actually this was a common argument in the early iterations of Western just war thinking. It was central to Martin Luther's case against most rebellions. Luther famously preached obedience to constituted authority. What, then, to do when those in power turned out to be brutal oppressors? Luther argued that in such a case overthrowing the tyrant was the job not of the people but of another prince—that is, the country next door.[26] There exist circumstances of humanitarian tragedy so clear and compelling that, in Elshtain's phrasing, "an *ad bellum* tripwire has been crossed."[27] Some scholars draw analogies to the criminal law, where I certainly have the right to use violent force to defend another person against threats to life and limb.[28] (Remember again the hypothetical walk through the forest.) And although many scholars warn that sending your soldiers across the border when there is no threat to yourself threatens the very concept of sovereignty, others contend that if sovereignty makes humanitarian interventions more difficult, then sovereignty itself needs rethinking.[29] For example, we could consider a country that systematically kills off large numbers of people no longer a sovereign, but a lawless brigand; and, as we have seen, the brigand can be killed wherever found.[30]

The Genocide Convention is often read to require rather than permit intervention by the contracting parties to end genocidal slaughter beyond their borders. True, as Fletcher and Ohlin point out, hardly anybody takes seriously these days the notion that the Convention might mandate a rescue.[31] But that change in interpretation is likely the result not of some legal insight unavailable in the past, but of the politics of the present day: nations with the power to intervene want not to intervene, and therefore will read the convention that way. This tendency reduces or perhaps eliminates the deterrent effect of potential intervention. If a regime is contemplating slaughter, the belief that punishment is unlikely will make the slaughter more likely to occur.[32]

True, there is always the possibility that the leaders of a genocidal movement might be hauled in front of either the International Criminal Court or a special tribunal, such as the one set up to try Rwandan war crimes. Perhaps these possibilities do indeed reduce what might otherwise be a higher rate of officially sanctioned state murder. But they do not reduce it to zero. Consider once more the crisis in Darfur, labeled a genocide by almost everyone except the United Nations. Tens of thousands have died. Hundreds of thousands have been displaced. The

United Nations so far has preferred to treat the problem as a civil war, and the West prefers to negotiate cease fires. The government of Sudan routinely breaches them, and more die. The International Criminal Court has authorized an arrest warrant for Omar al-Bashir—at this writing the president of Sudan—but only for war crimes, not for genocide. Certainly the threat of prosecution seems to have had little if any deterrent effect. Would the serious possibility of military intervention by a Western power make a difference? Possibly not. What worries many human rights advocates is that, once again, nobody with the power to stop the killing will even try. And yet it is difficult to see how Darfur could fail to meet the President's description of an event to which one might justifiably respond with force: "to prevent the slaughter of civilians by their own government, or to stop a civil war whose violence and suffering can engulf an entire region." Indeed, even under Walzer's test, what is happening in Darfur and in Congo and elsewhere in Africa at this writing is enough to shock anyone; and without military intervention from the West, tens of thousands will continue to die.[33]

Still, what matters just now for America and the world is not what the "right" standard is. What matters is what President Obama's standard is. Assuming that his words about humanitarian intervention were not just words, he will sooner or later—probably sooner—have to make a decision about whether to risk American lives to save the lives of strangers. Perhaps, as one cease fire after another collapses in Darfur, that decision is already upon him.

THE CASE FOR PRUDENCE

Yet there is a risk both ways. If you hide behind sovereignty and sanctions, thousands die. If you intervene, you are starting a war—and, as we have seen, the consequences of war are impossible to predict. This is the lesson of Clint Eastwood's exquisite 1992 film *Unforgiven*. To somewhat oversimplify the plot, the peace of a frontier town in the old West is broken when a ranch hand assaults a prostitute at the local brothel, badly cutting her face. To the dismay of the woman's coworkers, the sheriff (Gene Hackman) imposes a minor punishment on the assailant and his friend, requiring them to turn over some prize ponies to the brothel owner, who seems perfectly happy with the deal. Incensed, the women pool their savings to hire a gunslinger (Eastwood) to take revenge upon the ranch hands. But, having summoned him, they find that they cannot control him. The machinery of justice-as-vengeance, once loosed upon the town, is not subject to rules, or to recall. The moral of the story is that some terrible ills must, in an exercise of prudential judgment, be allowed to stand, because the remedy may be worse; or that, if we decide to make right what has been left wrong, we must accept the likelihood that the real costs to real people will be greater than we expected.[34]

But prudence is an imperfect muse. If world leaders begin celebrating military action to protect people from their own governments, the temptation will grow for the unscrupulous and the ambitious to join the party. Not just nature but the state of nature abhors a vacuum. And one can imagine at once a set of standard, ready-made explanations. Every state possessing territorial ambitions may begin to find faults—*causae*—in their neighbors. The bad old days before World War II taught the world to respect territorial integrity could return. Yes, the world might have looked the other way when Vietnam overthrew the Khmer Rouge on humanitarian grounds, but what would the world have done had Saddam Hussein in 1991 justified his invasion of Kuwait by pointing to a fundamental lack of respect for human rights on the part of the monarchy? Probably the same thing it did do: cheer the American-led war to kick him out. If so, his effort at justification would have been rejected, on the simple ground that everyone knew he was lying. But if that is the reason that the world would have disbelieved him, then the right intention criterion discarded long ago by Grotius has reappeared, as it were, at the back door: whatever words Saddam might have spoken, his intention would have been thought to be something other than peace.

Thus we can posit at least a prudential check on the freedom of the neighbors of the contested state to declare it failed and so install a new regime. The world might refuse to allow the intervention. We speak here not of the processes of positive international law but of the suasion, or the threats, of the international community. Just war theory has nothing at all to say about whether to go ahead in the face of international uproar, with the tantalizing exception that just war theory prohibits war that lacks a reasonable possibility of success. A war can be just though all the world condemns it. A war can be unjust though all the world endorses it.

Of course the process might not work. The world could not prevent the Soviet invasion of Afghanistan in 1979. The world could not prevent the Anglo-American invasion of Iraq in 2003.[35] But the Soviet action could hardly be labeled a war for humanitarian purposes. As for Iraq, when the war began, supporters cited a variety of justifications. In time, the language of humanitarian intervention became commonplace: the trouble turned out to be Saddam Hussein's vicious treatment of his own people. Even if one finds this explanation persuasive, there are obvious risks when the justification for a war can change freely as the war progresses.[36]

I would not want to say that such a change in rationale is never justified. Consider two American wars that are taken axiomatically as good wars: the Civil War and the Second World

War. The Civil War for all intents and purposes overthrew the institution of slavery, the second vanquished the Nazi menace. But of course, although many Northerners supported the war because they opposed slavery, many others believed only in fighting for the Union. Lincoln himself, at least in the war's early stages, remained cagey on whether slavery itself was sufficient *casus belli.* Yet as the war ground on, Lincoln slowly embraced the forced abolition of slavery, first as a military necessity, later as a moral imperative. In short, the justification changed. In the case of World War II, for all that we would like to believe that the Allies always had in view the ending of the murder of millions of Jews, not one nation seems to have entered the fray with that objective in mind. Nevertheless, as the horrors of the Nazi regime became clear, the Allies fought all the harder. Perhaps, then, the *causa* that justifies a war may indeed evolve. We must be cautious, however, lest we simply wind up searching for justifications for a war that is really being fought for gain.

On the other hand, if our enthusiasm might make it difficult to find a stopping point, an overabundance of caution might make it equally hard to find a starting point. It is possible to act too soon to end humanitarian tragedy, but it is usual to act too late. Samantha Power, in *A Problem from Hell,* points out that the United States, far from being too adventuresome, has *never* intervened to stop a genocide absent a compelling national interest. Even the Kosovo bombing was arguably too little, and too late. Power points out that policymakers consistently find ways to justify inaction, at least to themselves: perhaps the most common, says Power, is to insist that the information is less clear than it seems, and that what appears to everyone else to be a slaughter is, on closer inspection, some other beast.[37]

So, yes, prudence will likely curb potential humanitarian excesses by the United States, and by other countries as well. If Power is correct, then prudence will likely curb us sufficiently that just war theory will scarcely be needed to tell us when to intervene to put an end to oppression and tragedy: we are not going to do it. When then-Senator Obama wrote in *The Audacity of Hope* that outside military intervention has rarely delivered freedom to a people,[38] he thus overlooked the irony that hardly anyone in the world has ever bothered to try. The truth is, our reluctance to act turns just war theory inside out. For although just war theory evolved to solve the problem of when, if ever, the believing Christian could make an exception to the rule against taking a human life, the church fathers, unlike the early secularists, believed there were times when one nation was *obligated* to attack another to defend the innocent. The world today, led by America, evidently does not.

In assessing President Obama's suggestion of a willingness to use force to end great horrors, then, we must consider this history. Presidents almost always speak as though they are willing to do whatever is necessary. And then they don't. To my Aspen dinner partners, this dichotomy was untroubling: these events that happen so far away are not our business. That is very much our habit—turning away from suffering abroad, hoping, perhaps, that somebody else will solve the problem. In particular, we seem to do our best to stay away from the seeming epidemic of violence on the African continent.[39]

And Africa has indeed in recent years suffered an avalanche of horror—slaughters in Darfur and the Congo and Rwanda and Chad and elsewhere—more, sadly, than most of us can keep up with. Some observers consider what has been going on for the past decade and a half the African World War, a conflict that has engulfed perhaps a dozen countries, leaving millions of casualties, as the West obsesses about smaller conflicts. The Middle East, the Persian Gulf, southern Asia—these, we seem to think, are the real wars. Africa fails to capture our attention. Now and then there are special envoys or emergency meetings or grave pronouncements, but there is never real action. In the Sudan, a long succession of far-too-rosy peace agreements and far-too-tiny peacekeeping forces have failed to bring peace. Outside the door of my office hangs a cartoon, where, as bodies pile up in Darfur, a figure representing the United Nations stands on the sidelines and says, "Call me when you have some Europeans."

A few years ago, I sat on a panel with a British journalist who had spent a great deal of time reporting Africa's wars. Asked why Westerners seemed not to care, he suggested that when we read the stories of the latest African horror, we shudder with revulsion and say to ourselves, "Who could live that way?" By asking the question, we sort ourselves and those who are warring into distinct categories: people who could live that way and people (like ourselves) who could not. Without meaning to, the journalist went on, we decide that Africans are fundamentally a different kind of human being than we are. We thus lose the empathetic connection necessary to stir us to action.

He was exaggerating, of course. I do not for a moment imagine that my Aspen dinner partners considered Africans subhuman. Their instinct—that some conflicts are too far away to matter—is widely shared. Here we are perhaps trapped by the confines of secular philosophy, where a threat to the self is seen as justification for a great deal of violence. But threats to others call for lesser measures. Thus the *New York Times,* a few years ago, editorialized about the Sudan, and said this: "The United Nations has described the carnage in Darfur as the world's biggest humanitarian crisis but continues to prove itself completely useless at doing anything to stop it. In the Security Council, China protects Sudan."[40] Powerful words. But what was the solution? The best the *Times* editors could come up with was replacing the African Union peacekeepers with a United Nations force, to whom the United States would supply reconnaissance and air support. The assumption, still, is that even if ground troops prove necessary, it is somebody else's job to provide them.

Which leads us to the problem: *There isn't anybody else.* Seriously.

How America is Different

Like it or not, the United States remains the world's police-man. President Bush, although the fact may be difficult to re-member, campaigned in 2000 on the idea that the United States should be more "modest" in its foreign policy goals. Events changed his mind. President Obama sounded similar themes. And events seem to have caught up with him. "As for whether the U.S. is willing to carry on with the task of keeping peace in the world," writes the historian Paul Johnson, "it really has no alternative." President Obama, says Johnson, "will dis-cover through bitter experience" what his equally optimistic predecessors learned: "that he has to be the lawman, that he must keep the world-town safe."[41]

To understand why this is so, let us begin by distinguishing peacekeeping from warfighting, for the two are easily confused. Peacekeepers are supposed to do precisely what the name im-plies, enforce a peace already negotiated. All over the world are countries willing to send brave soldiers willing to do that difficult and dangerous job. This generosity contributes to a more stable world. But a force of peacekeepers can do its job only when a peace is in effect. The peace might be shaky, but the peace must exist. It is not the job of the peacekeepers to create it.

Consider that last point again: Peacekeepers can only keep the peace. Once stated, it becomes obvious. Peacekeepers can-not stop a slaughter. They cannot impose a peace when another country prefers to fight. That is a job for warriors: the point the *Times* overlooked. If you are trying to put forceful end to a genocide, you will likely need not a peacekeeping force but a warfighting force. Think about it. You are no longer being invited in to monitor the work the diplomats have done. You are in effect mounting an invasion where you are likely to meet resistance. For an invasion, you need an army. You need an army that can project force over a long distance, landing troops, supplying them, replenishing them, for what might be an extended period. Only a handful of nations any longer possess armed forces that can take significant military action half a world away.

Suppose, then, for the sake of argument, that we care about the horrors other governments do to their people, and that we care enough to use force to halt the horror. If we insist on not sending our own troops, what alternatives are available? An obvious answer—the immediate one my students come up with—is to assemble a coalition, combining the armed forces of several different countries into a single fighting force. Indeed, casual followers of things military might imagine that getting soldiers together on the battlefield is a simple matter: 5,000 of ours plus 5,000 of theirs creates an integrated fighting army of 10,000 soldiers. Nothing could be further from the truth. Imagine a basketball team that starts two professionals, a college journeyman, and two high school kids, and you begin to see the problem. Training matters. Experience matters. Not only the amount, but the type. Different countries spend different amounts of resources on logistics and training and weapons. They fight according to different military doctrines.

To take just one example, American Army doctrine teaches to attack into an ambush. This might seem a minor point, but it is a major one, especially in modern asymmetrical warfare. The instinct of most of us, if ambushed, is to flee. Most armies in the world train their forces to withdraw under ambush, or to hunker down and call for help. The United States is among the few nations still serious about teaching troops to move directly toward the ambush rather than away. Attacking into the ambush is a long-standing precept of American military doctrine. (John Kerry's Silver Star was awarded for attacking into an ambush.) As one experienced soldier has put it: "Never away, always into it. Believe me, only highly trained and disciplined troops will do that."[42] The idea is that attacking the ambushers is a surprise, a sort of counter-ambush that might shift the initiative your way.[43] A withdrawal under fire is a difficult and dangerous maneuver. Even if you are outgunned, pressing forward against every instinct often turns out to offer better chances of escape than retreating.[44] Training of this sort is the stuff of months and years, not days and weeks. If American troops are fighting alongside troops from another country with different training—perhaps counting on them to guard the flank—and an ambush occurs, it is easy to see how disaster would ensue were the other troops to flee, leaving the American flank unguarded. And examples of doctrinal differences are endless.

Fighting forces are not fungible. To suggest otherwise is not supportive of the troops but contemptuous of the military as profession and as science. If you replace a battalion of American Marines with a battalion of soldiers from another NATO member, you are likely facing a significant downgrade in quality. If you replace the NATO battalion with a battalion from a developing country, the loss will be even worse. Not all troops are trained in the same way, or with the same skill. Not all bring the same level of professionalism. Even NATO—with the key exception of Great Britain—does not train its forces to the level of the Americans. A staggering forty-one cents of every defense dollar spent in the world is spent on the United States military.

The United States trains better because it has more money to spend, more space to practice in, more installations, more weapons (including retired stock), and better educated soldiers than any country in the world. Nobody else is even close.[45] We spend more than anyone on weapons systems, and maintain them better.[46] And because America's armed forces rotate constantly around the world, and often do battle, they have reached levels of efficiency unmatched by their rivals—or their allies.

On top of all this, the United States military makes use of the digital battlefield in a way that would baffle all but a handful of armies in the world. For example, American soldiers are issued the Defense Advanced Global Positioning System Receiver, or DAGR, a form of GPS that is lightweight and accurate and virtually unjammable. But at over two thousand dollars a unit, the DAGR is too pricey for most military forces. Some use civilian GPS systems. Many use no positioning system at all. American forces, ground or air, can be guided to the point of attack by the Vehicle and Dismount Exploitation Radar, or VADER, a detection device sufficiently sensitive to spot an individual planting a roadside bomb—from a hovering UAV five miles up. Down on the ground, they can monitor the VADER's cameras in real time. And although some experts believe that the long-time technological advantage of the American military has slipped a bit,[47] there are still few nations in the world able to muster anything like the American digital battlefield, with its comprehensive linked systems and equipment. One consequence of the more advanced American military technology and training is that it becomes ever-harder for other countries to fight alongside our troops.

Under President Obama, the development of new weapons systems continue apace. In some cases it has accelerated. The Air Force has successfully tested the X-37B, the so-called "space plane," which looks like a shuttle, behaves like a UAV, and has a mission nobody will disclose. The Air Force is also developing a smart missile that can be launched from the United States and strike any spot on the face of the planet in less than an hour. The military is developing directed energy weapons, the stuff of science fiction, powerful lasers and microwaves able to destroy missiles, wreck electronic systems, or even kill the enemy from a distance with what amounts to a death ray—or, at the proper settings, to incapacitate people without killing them. The Office of Naval Research, as part of its "Swamp Works" program, is designing an intelligent torpedo with a computer brain that will be able to tell the difference between the signature of a passing enemy ship and the variety of countermeasures now routinely deployed to fool its less-educated cousins. We are developing smarter combat robots, better systems to indicate to commanders the position in realtime of every soldier on the battlefield and the condition of his weapons, and camouflage so advanced that it will render the wearer invisible to most detection systems. Future warfare will feature an ever greater use of "smart" weaponry: smart bullets that can be guided to the target the way we now guide missiles, for instance, or smart dust, wireless sensors, each the size of the grain of sand or smaller, to transmit signals, track the enemy, and, potentially, guide those smart bullets. There are even smart anti-missile defense systems, like Israel's Iron Dome, which detects an incoming missile attack, then calculates the landing spot, so that a warhead is not wasted shooting the intruder down if it is only going to strike desert anyway.

And then there is cyberspace, the lone area of technology where we may not after all be leading the world—many experts believe that prize goes to the People's Republic of China—but we are doing what we can to catch up. At this writing, the

Obama Administration is pushing ahead with the Comprehensive National Cybersecurity Initiative, the controversial internet monitoring and protection measure developed by the Bush Administration. A 2010 report from the International Institute of Strategic Studies warned that the world right now is about as prepared to defend against cyber attacks as it was prepared to defend against nuclear attacks at the dawn of the Cold War.[48] The United States has recently created a Cyber Command within the Pentagon. And, if Richard Clarke's sources are to be believed, the United States has already taken the offensive, planting "logic bombs" deep inside the computer infrastructure of other countries, programs that will, upon command, shut down or destroy large parts of their networks.[49]

The President's endorsement of all this research in military technology is entirely rational; indeed, indispensable. Maintaining a technological edge has long been vital to the American theory of deterrence.[50] Being better armed really does make a difference. No less an authority than Nikita Krushchev noted, writing of America's superiority over the Soviets in atomic weapons after World War II, "This situation weighed heavily on Stalin. He understood that he had to be careful not to be dragged into a war."[51] A recent example of how the technological gulf matters is Israel's 2007 bombing of a Syrian facility believed to be designed for making fuel for nuclear weapons. The facility was guarded with the Pantsir-S1 surface-to-air missile system, the most advanced Russian antiaircraft technology. Missiles fired from the Pantsir can strike a target five miles in the air. Russia uses the same technology to protect its own crucial military installations. Nevertheless, Israel apparently blinded the Pantsir so that the attack was not detected. To this day, neither the Russians nor the Syrians have evidently figured out how.

This is not to say that the President has green lighted everything the military wants. The Administration eliminated, for example, the Army's cherished Future Combat Systems program. Critics argued that the program was aimed at preparing for large-scale conventional wars unlikely to be fought. Maybe they were right, and one cannot have everything. On the other hand, if such a conflict were to arise, it would be best to be prepared. Moreover, the Obama Administration seems determined to cut the size of the military budget in real terms, presumably in order to free up money for other priorities. At this writing, the Administration is pushing to reduce the number of Navy carrier battle groups from eleven to nine—and even at eleven, the number was below the level of readiness most experts consider necessary. There has also been recent controversy over increased military wages and benefits, with the Defense Department warning that troops will soon be paid so much that procurement and maintenance might suffer. The obvious solution is to increase pay without requiring that the money come from other programs— except, of course, that resources are limited, and, again, choices must be made.

Still, one can go too far. Some Administration officials have suggested that the military's share of the budget, as a percentage of GDP, is too high. The Administration's budget projections show a steadily shrinking share. One cannot have everything, but how one fights and wins with less is a tricky question. Merely ending the wars we are currently fighting does not solve the problem—even assuming that the War on Terror has a conceivable end. There will be other wars. There are always other wars. We presumably want to avoid the Athenian solution to which I adverted earlier: the notion that if you are powerful enough, you can withdraw behind your borders with your fine weaponry and nobody will dare touch you. History teaches that great nations who choose that strategy rarely stay great.

THE LACK OF ALTERNATIVE

One reason the President is green lighting so many forms of military research is likely his desire to reduce the nation's stockpile of nuclear warheads. This seems an eminently sensible idea: certainly the United States can continue to deter attack with an arsenal limited to 800 or even 400 warheads. The President's pledge not to upgrade the nuclear arsenal is more worrisome. The Pentagon does not want to increase the number of nuclear warheads, but it does want to improve the quality of the ones it has, mainly the B-61 and other relics of the Cold War, a stockpile long untested and thought by most experts to be deteriorating. The decision not to upgrade the nuclear arsenal is a matter for executive decision; there is no binding law or treaty forbidding it. I suspect that in time, the President will change his mind.

In the meantime, the problem remains. We reached this point in our analysis, remember, by considering who should act in the face of genocide and other horrific slaughters. The answer is, if the United States does not do it, nobody will. Given the vast gulf in technology and training, it is unrealistic to imagine American soldiers fighting side-by-side with the forces of other nations to prevent those evils so great that, to borrow Walzer's phrase, they shock our consciences. And yet we are unwilling to commit serious ground forces to stop horrors that nobody else is able to control. What, then, are the other possibilities—apart from doing nothing?

Some observers seek refuge in pleasant fantasies: that an independent United Nations military force, or perhaps a world government, might solve the genocide problem. These grand and magical solutions seem unlikely to help. Consider first the independent United Nations deterrent.[52] The practical and logistical problems, as many observers have pointed out, seem insuperable.[53] Assuming, however, that these challenges could be met, there is little reason to expect any practical effect. Although one wants to take seriously the role of the United Nations in preventing such outrages, it is difficult to do so. Parse the history how you will: the fact remains that in 1998, a mixed international force under United Nations command essentially stood by and allowed wanton slaughter of perhaps as many as a million Rwandans. In the summer of 1995, Dutch peacekeepers under United Nations command allowed Serbian forces to overrun the "safe zone" city of Srbenica, barely firing a shot. The result was the largest massacre in Europe since World War II. True, the failure to act did not necessarily represent fecklessness or cowardice. Many observers have pointed out ways in which the structure of the organization makes the application of violent force on behalf of its members all but impossible. Diplomacy failed to halt the killings. In Bosnia, it was American air power, in conjunction with a reluctant NATO, that finally put an end to the violence. In Rwanda, the United Nations did not even try, despite repeated pleas from their commanders on the ground for permission to intervene.

Well, of course. No army can operate when it has fifteen commanders-in-chief, all of whom must be consulted before each major decision. As one supporter of humanitarian interventions has put it, "The Security Council might be one of the most ossified political bodies on earth."[54] There is no reason to think that the command of a military force would bring about any sudden de-ossification.[55] Happily, the United Nations now has a full-time office working on the problem of genocide, at least trying to keep the issue alive and before the world. But it is difficult to imagine that the organization's leadership, however composed, suddenly growing bold and decisive in the application of force against genocide. Indeed, at this writing, as the crisis in Darfur goes through its annual worsening, the Security Council cannot even reach agreement on relatively mild sanctions against the regime in Khartoum. The principal opposition comes from Sudan's major trading partners—particularly China. The Obama Administration has mysteriously chosen to tone down rather than ratchet up its criticism of Sudan. Once again, as in Rwanda and the Congo, the world—America included—and, certainly, the United Nations—as much as says: "A few thousand dead Africans, what's the difference?"

As to the single world government, it seems unlikely to be any wiser than a single local or national government. Suppose there is but one government, and that government decides to commit genocide itself: to whom do the sufferers then appeal? Or suppose the single existing government chooses to turn a blind eye to some corner of the globe where people are being wiped out. That is what the world tends to do today. But at least now, with many governments to choose from, there is the chance, however small, that one of them might be moved to intervene. As Michael Walzer has wryly noted, as long as there is a risk of fire, it is best to have more than one fire department.

Another possibility is that we might contract out the violence sometimes needed to block a greater violence, hiring mercenaries to do the good work of protecting people other than ourselves.[56] That way, we can wear with pride the mantle of those who do what is right in the world, without ever risking the early shroud so often worn by those who do it dangerously. This approach of course gives the lie to Samuel Huntington's famous argument, in *The Soldier and the State,* that a democracy whose people are unwilling to fight their own battles may find itself in serious difficulties, not least because of the radical separation that develops between military and civilian culture; but also because a country whose voters rarely need to count casualties from among their own loved ones will wind up making war too recklessly.[57] Huntington was pleading with the nation to retain, on democratic grounds, the military draft; but the argument applies, with still greater force, to the contracting out of the hard work to others. Indeed, an independent United Nations force, comprising soldiers motivated by neither patriotism nor national interest, would be in effect a mercenary army. In war, a nation's soldiers will undergo enormous suffering and even risk their lives in a great cause—especially the defense of their country—but mercenaries famously will not.

Perhaps they can be moved by a great cause. But, while we await the far-off day when the miracle occurs, perhaps we, too, can be so moved. President Obama's Nobel Address proposes that we will one day have to use force to stop a horror that does not involve our own national interest. One is reminded here of Augustine, who long ago proposed that to justify violence (in the rare cases where justification was possible) one must be moved by something other than self-interest. What one had to avoid, said Augustine, was acting out of *libido*, meaning an inordinate affection. For Augustine, even self-defense was generally motivated by *libido*: the individual defending himself loved himself enough to commit violence against someone else. This choice Augustine found troubling. After all, we were not to love this life so much as the next. Doing violence to preserve that which we should not love in the first place was then a clear instance of self-interest.

We need not find Augustine entirely persuasive on the issue of self-defense to understand how *libido* can blind us to the needs of others. One wishes, urgently, for the Heavenly Kingdom, where true peace reigns. In this broken world, however, what the stranger sometimes needs is neither our sympathy nor our warm wishes, but the force of our arms.

NATIONAL WILL

Of course, we cannot send our military everywhere, spending blood and treasure to rescue the suffering. So we choose not to send our military anywhere, except in defense of our own interests. Some recent studies suggest that the American public will accept relatively large numbers of casualties as long as the nation seems to be winning the war: it is not combat deaths, but combat deaths in vain, that people evidently mind. If the proposition is correct, the news media will bear the grave responsibility of providing actual information, a perhaps impossibly distant cry from their usual choice between two dread roles: a mindless cheerleading at the opening of hostilities, or a cynical focus on American deaths once things inevitably grow dicey. This matters for two reasons. First, the refusal of the media to spend much time on issues other than American casualties makes it all but impossible for political decision makers (even assuming that the will exists) to harness public sentiment to send American armed forces to aid non-Americans. Second, as Jean Bethke Elshtain notes, the fear that we might lose American lives has led to a choice in most situations of stand-off bombing instead, with the unhappy result that the public has become "rather inured to the routinization of use of American bombing in foreign policy situations." Thus a presidential decision to send bombers but not troops "scarcely registers on the [public's] radar screen."[58] The ability to fight a war without using troops creates what Michael Walzer calls "a new and dangerous inequality."[59]

Let us consider the second problem first. Although there are, to be sure, a handful of activists who seem to grieve less for American dead than for those America kills, most people seem to be the other way around. When we send young people into harm's way, the media pay attention. When our contribution is not our blood, but rather our bombs and missiles, the media shrug. In this sense we are, like every nation on earth. One might call this attitude narcissistic, or even chauvinistic, and in my weaker moments I have called it both. In truth, we are merely being patriotic. We love our country. Nothing could be simpler.

We love our country, and we value the lives of Americans above the lives of non-Americans. As we have seen, President Obama's theory of war certainly shares these characteristics. Politically, this priority is uncontroversial, as perhaps it should be.

And yet, from the standpoint of the ethics of war, we must raise certain questions. Consider the use of standoff bombing— for example, in Kosovo in 1999, when some 38,000 bombing runs by NATO aircraft resulted in zero casualties from enemy fire. When we bomb safely, the casualties are others, and also other. The just war tradition has long condemned massive bombing campaigns because of the impossibility that they can obey rules of proportionality.[60] Perhaps we accept a bombing campaign for the same reason the tradition is concerned about it: the bombing kills only strangers.

But bombing rarely resolves a humanitarian crisis, not least because air power cannot hold a piece of ground. The bombing in Kosovo is often described as a victory because it forced the Serbs to the bargaining table, and apparently ended their ethnic cleansing, but it also killed many noncombatants, and did only a little to disturb the murderous gains the Serbs had made. Perhaps that was not the point. Perhaps killers must at times be allowed their spoils. We live in an imperfect world and lack either the power or the wisdom to perfect it. Still, if you are in the hating business, it is not a bad trade to create flooding genocidal horror, give up a few leaders for prosecution, and keep everything else you have won.

President Obama's Nobel remarks, as we have seen, imply a commitment to do more—to use military force, when required, to prevent the most vicious crimes of a regime against its own people. As of this writing, that commitment has yet to be tested. Past Presidents have expressed a similar intention, in the abstract, to place American forces in the path of killers, only to discover that the political capital needed to sustain such activity has been squandered on other battles. At the conclusion of his controversial monograph on the origins of war, the historian Donald Kagan muses on whether liberal democracies of the present day possess the stomach to go to war when they must, given that they are, in his words, "devoted to and increasingly shaped by an ethical system that is commercial, individualistic, libertarian, and hedonistic, at the other end of the spectrum from the agricultural republics of antiquity, with their respect for the power and glory of states and the sacrifices these require."[61] He suggests that a reluctance to fight has led, as a historical matter, to a decline in power and prestige, in a world in which war not peace is the common human condition.

If Kagan is right—if the modern democracies are reluctant to fight even when their own position in the world is at stake—then it is surely unrealistic to expect them to sacrifice life and livelihood for the suffering people of another state. Recent history teaches that nobody else will either, and that the world's solemn commitment to prevent abuses of human rights, up to and including genocide, does not include a serious commitment to take any risk to ensure that the tyrants do not flourish.

THE ILLUSION OF SANCTIONS

In the West, the most frequently mentioned alternative to war to stop oppression is economic sanctions. My students propose them all the time. The Obama Administration, like its predecessors, displays a strong preference for sanctions over military action, and a strong belief in their efficacy. Pick a problem area—Iran, Korea, Sudan—and the chances are you will find President Obama negotiating with other countries to impose, or improve, a regime of economic sanctions. This long-standing American preference is in political terms entirely understandable, because it purports to resolve international crises yet puts no American lives at risk, but the preference for sanctions is, from the standpoint of ethics, quite puzzling. As the philosopher Richard Norman points out, the preference for sanctions is hardly a preference for non-violence; it simply displaces the violence from the regulator onto the regulated:

> We should also be clear about the moral status of sanctions. They are not nice. Like war, they are a coercive threat. They involve the deliberate infliction of suffering in order to pressure people into compliance. Like war, they inflict suffering on people who are "innocent" in the sense that they are not individually responsible for the actions which sanctions are intended to oppose.[62]

This is a point insufficiently appreciated. Sanctions involve violence and the threat of violence. They apply force against violators—sometimes deadly force. And their entire purpose is to keep a particular country from receiving products for which it is willing and able to pay—including, sometimes, products that represent necessities.

Actually, we should know this already, from our own history. America has faced sanctions in living memory: the oil embargo imposed by OAPEC* in October of 1973 after the United States resupplied the Israeli military during the Yom Kippur War. Nobody died. Our economy is now, and was then, far too dynamic to be stifled. And yet the results were palpable. Expensive. Not nice. The boycott caused a shortage. Spot oil prices shot up. Domestic prices followed. The shortage created the infamous

---

*OAPEC is the Organization of Arab Petroleum Exporting Countries, and included, at the time of the boycott, the Arab members of OPEC, and several Arabic states that produced oil and were not OPEC members

long lines at service stations. The government implemented gasoline rationing. And there was more. As the website of the Department of Energy drolly puts it: "A year of bad news was punctuated in December, when the President announced that because of the energy crisis the lights on the national Christmas tree would not be turned on."[63] How serious was the crisis? So serious that, according to recent news reports, the Nixon Administration seriously contemplated the possibility of launching a military assault to take control of the Mideast oil fields.[64] Hardly surprising: the boycott led to what one scholar called "the most gigantic reallocation of income in history."[65] The embargo ended in March of 1974, after the United States promised to press for peace between Israel and Syria. But the boycott, despite the hardships it caused, was at best a limited political success. True, Israel withdrew from the Golan Heights two months after the boycott ended, but many observers believe that plan was already in the works, meaning that OAPEC members accepted what was in essence a face-saving exchange. This would make sense if, as seems likely, the embargo harmed the producers more than it did the consumers. Indeed, studies have suggested that although initially the embargo placed considerable pressure on the West, OAPEC finally capitulated because "market conditions and commercial objectives so required."[66]

America—or part of America, anyway—had faced the equivalent of sanctions long before: during the Civil War. Sherman's march from Atlanta to the sea has become the stuff of legend, in North and South alike, because of the swath of destruction his army cut as it moved. Crops were burned, livestock killed, homes destroyed, train rails torn up and sometimes melted down. This was not, however, wanton cruelty, and Sherman was not the only Northern general to pursue it. It was, rather, a strategy, one also attempted by the Confederacy, but less successfully—a strategy aimed at depriving the opposing side of the resources it would need to continue the war. No working farms would mean no food for the troops. No mills would mean no uniforms. In a sense, although operating as it were from the inside out, Sherman's army was pursuing a strategy of economic sanctions. The only difference is that his march laid bare the truth that, in the modern world, we like to hide: sanctions are violent, and do genuine harm to innocents. The fact that we may not see their effects on the ground does not mean that the effects are not there. Sanctions tend to distribute their effects downward.

What does it mean to say that the effects are distributed downward? Consider a recent example. During the period when mandatory United Nations sanctions applied to Iraq, it was common for Western critics to point to the number of people who died as a result of not receiving sufficient food or medicine. Actually the sanctions excepted food or medicine, and the casualty figures released by the Iraqi government to demonstrate the harm done by the sanctions were surely exaggerated: by several measures, the median caloric intake of Iraqis actually increased during the sanctions. Nevertheless, the critics had a point. The Iraqi government claimed that the sanctions led to the deaths of between 1.5 million and 1.7 million children. Some opponents of the war (Ramsey Clark comes to mind) accepted these numbers at face value. But even more skeptical Westerners (*Reason* magazine, for example) conceded that the number of children dead from the ripple effects of the sanctions was likely in six figures.

For the sake of argument, let us take, as a conservative estimate, half of the lower figure: 50,000 children dead from the sanctions on Iraq. What would we think of a war, even a just one, that killed only children, and, by the time it ended, had killed 50,000 of them? Surely we would think there had been a massive violation of *jus in bello*. We might even scream for war crimes trials. But it is difficult to see how else sanctions can work. If we imagine a wicked regime, the last people the regime will allow to suffer will be its own supporters. In other words, the regime actually has an incentive to make sure that the effects of the sanctions fall upon the poor and oppressed, the outcasts of its society.[67] Thus every call for sanctions should be tempered by a recognition of what sanctions do, and to whom—that they are, in Norman's words, not nice. When we target a wicked regime with our weapons, we are fighting its military. When we target a wicked regime with sanctions, we are fighting the poor, and the suffering, and the children. That is the fact we must bear in mind the next time we choose to treat an agreement on sanctions as a victory.

There are no magic bullets in international affairs. If facts matter, sanctions have a poor history.[68] Effective administration of a regime of sanctions presents a formidable collective action challenge: countries you think are on your side lie and cheat.[69] And history has demonstrated that target nations sufficiently clever can find ways of circumventing them. Norman cites the example of the futile sanctions on Italy after the invasion of Ethiopia in 1935. Sanctions failed to prevent North Korea from developing nuclear weapons and ballistic missiles to deliver them. Sanctions failed to stop the rearmament of the Nazi regime between the World Wars. And—again from the other side of the ledger—sanctions from the Arab world failed to shake American support for Israel.[70]

It is easy to see why sanctions tend to fail. The reason they are imposed is to make it difficult to complete transactions that would otherwise be profitable. Suppose you are trying to sell arms to Country A in defiance of sanctions. You have to factor into your decision the risk of being caught. If you are caught, the chances are you will lose your cargo and pay a fine. The amount of the loss, discounted by the likelihood of being caught, will often be small enough to make a large transaction worthwhile. You will want to be compensated for your risk, so you will charge more for whatever you are shipping. But at the right price, you might still make the attempt. A sanctions regime tends to drive up the prices of forbidden commodities, not make transactions impossible. Again, consider the American Civil War. At the beginning of the war, the South blockaded Washington, and no goods could arrive via the Potomac River. The blockade failed. For the next several years, the Union blockaded Southern ports. The price at which cotton was sold within the South fell dramatically, because of the risk of transporting it through the blockade. But it was often still transported, with enormous profits to be made at the other end—sometimes England, sometimes New England—where scarcity had driven the prices higher. (In *Gone With the Wind*, Rhett Butler earned his wartime fortune as a blockade runner.)

Another way of considering the point is by analogy. Sanctions on, say, military equipment are like the war on drugs. If there is a willing buyer and a willing seller, the best the sanctions can do is drive up the price of the goods. Increasing the price is not trivial, but it is not the same as a ban—especially if the buyer is willing to pay. In the war on drugs, the addict may bankrupt his family (if middle class) or turn to crime (if not) to obtain the resources needed to buy the more expensive commodity. Note how the suffering is then imposed on others (the family, the victim of the crime). In the case of sanctions, one would expect the willing buyer to try to impose the increased costs on others. This is what happens when, as we have seen, the regime obtains the resources to get what it wants by allowing the economic condition of those at the bottom to deteriorate further.[71] In other words, even "targeted" or "smart" sanctions cause suffering among ordinary people, and, for a determined regime, a good deal of it. Naturally one might therefore hope for a revolution, but if making the poor's condition worse is a just way to overthrow the powerful, one might simply bomb the poor neighborhoods directly, hoping that their residents will rise up, not against the outsider who dropped the bomb, but against their own government. The absurdity of this proposition helps illustrate what is wrong with the theory that sanctions will cause those who are suffering to rebel. (The same argument applies, mutatis mutandis, to the claim that sanctions will cause the middle class to rise.)

The truth is, sanctions don't work very well. The empirical work on this is firm and consistent. The *highest* estimate in the serious scholarship is that they succeed in no more than one-third of the cases where they are imposed.[72] A more conservative estimate may be closer to five percent—that is, one in twenty.[73] Recent work in game theory helps explain why the record is so dismal. The purpose for which A institutes a regime of sanctions against B is to deter a particular course of conduct by B—that is, to change B's behavior. When A threatens sanctions, there are two possibilities. First, B might not believe that A will carry out the threat, in which case B's behavior will not change. Now, suppose B believes that A is serious. B then decides whether the sanctions will do so much harm that its behavior will have to change. If so, B will change its course without sanctions. If not, B will accept the sanctions, and also not change its behavior. In other words, sanctions by their nature can only rarely work; almost always, if B will change its behavior because of sanctions, it will change its behavior when the threat of sanctions seems credible.[74]

All of this assumes that a threat of sanctions is even credible. Often, it is not. Scholars of public choice theory have argued for years that sanctions are generally applied not for reasons of international policy but to satisfy domestic political considerations; and, in particular, that states will tend not to impose or apply sanctions in ways that harm domestic economic interests. Studies of the available data seem to bear this out.[75] Again, consider the 1973 Arab oil embargo, which, as we have seen, likely ended simply because the producing states who had imposed the boycott wanted to increase their revenues.

Another reason sanctions fail is that they are costly at home. They tend to create a competitive disadvantage for the domestic firms of the sanctioning nation, resulting in either political pressure to change or reopen trade, or outright cheating. One of the reasons the sanctions on Iraq failed so miserably was that Iraqi crude, valued for its lightness, remained in demand on the world market. Sanctions might drive up the price, but they will not keep the goods from market. Recent news reports suggest that the United States government has awarded tens of billions of dollars to domestic companies that are doing business with Iran, even as the Administration places pressure on other countries to stop the same commerce.[76] This is not mere hypocrisy. It is the rational pursuit of self-interest. It is also another reason sanctions tend to fail.

During the period of sanctions on Iraq, Saddam Hussein earned an estimated $21 billion in illegal profit by manipulating the Oil-for-Food Program. Small wonder. I mentioned earlier the peculiar myth about that the American oil companies instigated the Iraq war. The image is of Father Martinez, the crooked priest in Willa Cather's classic novel *Death Comes for the Archbishop,* who roused the Taos Indians to revolt, then stepped aside and took the profits, allowing his confreres to die. The war made Martinez "quite the richest man in the parish," says Cather— and she describes in detail the ostentation in which he lived.

But the analogy fails. True, Iraqi crude is especially desirable, because it is so light and so low in sulfur—meaning that it is easier to get it out of the ground, and easier to refine into valuable products, such as gasoline or aviation fuel. But war drives crude prices higher. In the long run, firms that make their money from refined products need prices lower. The sanctions on Iraq limited the supply of light crude on the market, driving prices higher—although not as high as a war. A rational oil company, therefore, would oppose sanctions, preferring to maximize its profits by reducing the price of the light crude it needs to make its products. This is why many of the firms accused of helping Saddam Hussein to cheat on the sanctions were connected to the refining industry; and why they were never supporters of the sanctions in the first place.[77] (Despite the conspiracy theories, the results of the war bore out the fears of the American oil industry: the big winners were refiners from other countries—mostly countries not involved in the war.[78])

Plainly, then, it becomes difficult to build coalitions around sanctions when the countries whose cooperation you require stand to lose serious revenue. But the difficulty turns out to be scarcely greater when the states you hope to recruit have nothing at stake. So, for example, despite repeated efforts, none of the last few Administrations have succeeded in putting teeth into sanctions on the entirely isolated nation of North Korea, even after it kicked out the United Nations nuclear inspectors. In an op-ed in the *Washington Post* early in the Obama Administration, Henry Kissinger put the problem succinctly. Writing of the importance of preventing North Korea from obtaining nuclear arms, Kissinger wrote: "If the United States, China, Japan, South Korea and Russia cannot achieve this vis-à-vis a country with next to no impact on international trade and no resources needed by anyone, the phrase 'world community' will become empty."[79]

Sanctions, in short, are difficult to achieve, nearly impossible to enforce, and ineffective over the long run. They inflict suffering on another country's people instead of its rulers, typically targeting those who are already worst off: in other words, sanctions are cruel. No sanctions have ever stopped a genocide. Nevertheless, most Western observers seem to view sanctions, in

Norman's words, as "morally preferable to war," perhaps because the degree of suffering and killing they demand appears to be less.[80] Name a humanitarian crisis, or a regime seeking weapons of mass destruction, and the Western powers will get together, argue as the crisis goes on, finally agreeing on sanctions, which in all likelihood will hardly alter the target country's behavior a whit; and therefore go back to the table for tougher sanctions, and so forth and so on.

We call a decision to impose sanctions a great victory, and perhaps in some sense it is.[81] On the other hand, the preference also involves an act of sanitizing, and what we are sanitizing is our own souls. We impose sanctions and try not to think about how violently warlike they are. To be crude, we prefer a world in which our bullets starve children to one in which our bullets kill soldiers. Sanctions are directed at the undifferentiated population of the nation whose commerce is blockaded. Few regimes will begin by letting their strongest supporters suffer. The hope must therefore be that the people will, in time, rise up; or that supplies will grow so thin that even the building blocks of power will in time turn against the regime. But few if any police states have been overthrown by a revolution entirely internal.

One could argue, therefore, that sanctions, because they work so poorly, violate the rules of *jus ad bellum,* which require a reasonable likelihood of success. They also, by their very nature, tend to violate the rules of *jus in bello.* Sanctions target noncombatants: that is their design. But setting out to war with the intention of harming noncombatants violates the very first ethical precept of how one ought to fight. If you intentionally bomb a civilian hospital because you think you will thus topple the regime, you are violating both the law and ethics of war.[82] It is not entirely clear why intentionally starving the population is morally preferable.

To avoid this problem, we tend to seek what are known as targeted sanctions, preventing only the transfer, for instance, of militarily critical technologies, as they are known in the argot; and, like most missiles fired from far away, the targeted sanctions often miss their targets. But cheating remains relatively easy. The successful effort by the Saddam Hussein regime to circumvent the military sanctions on Iraq by using the Oil-for-Food program as his vehicle are well documented. So perhaps sanctions are even worse than I have suggested. If they work, they target the population, which the ethics of war prohibits. If they fail, the failures are rarely repaired—or even considered newsworthy. Rather, imposing sanctions has become, more and more, a way of pretending to do something about a problem in the world while allowing us to turn our attention to the far more pressing business of screaming at each other over each percentage point by which the capital gains tax is adjusted one way or the other. If the sanctions work, meaning that civilians suffer and die, we are nevertheless complacent; and if they fail, and military technology slips through the net, we are equally complacent. The only way of interpreting this bizarre indifference is that we do not actually care whether the sanctions succeed or not. The real function of the sanctions is to salve our consciences. And, if we paid attention to their actual effects on actual people, they might not do even that much.

There is something politically sensible but morally scary in the proposition that we are more willing to fight for ourselves than for others, an eerie enhancement of the accident of Americanness, a flaunting of our preponderance on the face of the planet, transitory though it necessarily is. Augustine, who thought self-love the worst reason to do violence, would have been appalled. Opponents of the Iraq War often point out, correctly, that the United States hurts its position in the world when it uses its power in the teeth of international opposition. On

the other hand, we hardly help our position—morally, anyway—
when we insist that the principal purpose of our power is to defend those who, by accident, are born here. This, perhaps, is
the point of the theologian Paul Ramsey's famous Vietnam-era
challenge to opponents of the war to ask themselves how they
thought American power should be deployed in the world: to
produce, in other words, a positive program, not just a negative
one.[83] President Obama, in his Nobel Address, strongly implied
that this positive program might include the use of military
force to defend the helpless, even when America has no interest
at stake. To be sure, most of his recent predecessors have said
something similar. All those who care about human suffering
abroad should hope that this time, we have a President who
means it.

THE ALLURE OF PACIFISM

The remaining possibility we have not yet mentioned is pacifism. I will confess that for much of my life I have tended in that
direction myself, in the sense that I believe the state must have
a powerful reason indeed to use violence or force against a human being. In both my Christian and secular selves, I worry
about how easy we find it to justify coercion. (This applies to
law here at home, too: one cannot consistently be a pacifist
abroad and yet demand lots of domestic laws. Laws are enforced
on dissenters at the point of a gun. The more laws, the more
force you are using.)

In the actual practice of ethical citizenship, however, pacifism is often of limited utility.[84] The theory of just and unjust
wars is a better fit. Here we might reflect once more on the example of walking in the woods. If attacked by robbers, you
might say, were you a pacifist, that you refuse to raise your hand

against another, even in your own defense. Others might find your sacrifice admirable even if they disagreed with it. Indeed, part of why we so marvel at the examples of nonviolent resistance offered by Gandhi and King is that we doubt our own capacity to emulate them.

Yet there is an important moral distinction between being set upon by robbers and refusing to raise a hand in your own defense, and seeing a stranger being set upon by robbers and refusing to raise a hand in his defense. Augustine used a similar example to argue that we owe to others a larger obligation than we owe to ourselves, a distinction that has always been important in the orthodox Christian approach to the problem of just war. It is no accident that Aquinas's discussion of war falls within his chapter on charity—that is, *caritas,* or Christian love—because he, like most of the church fathers, saw war principally not as a means to defend one's self, but as a sacrifice one makes for others. Thus, after reminding the reader to be prepared "if necessary, to refrain from resistance or self-defense," Aquinas goes on to say: "Nevertheless, it is necessary sometimes for a man to act otherwise for the common good, or for the good of those with whom he is fighting."[85]

The distinction between self-defense and the common good was crucial to the church fathers. Thus, for Augustine, part of what justified violence (in the rare cases where justification was possible) was that the one being violent was acting out of something other than self-interest. Remember Augustine's point, that we must beware of acting out of *libido,* or inordinate self-love. Certainly Augustine believed in the defense of the state in which one happened to live. He thought an aggressor should be driven out. The soldier who defended his own state was acting out of a larger interest than the interest in his own life.[86] The same absence of libido might justify as well the soldier who defends against aggression not his own people, but someone else's.

A decision to intervene in the affairs of another country is no doubt in the end a matter of politics. But the arguments for it are moral. Not every form of government is equal. One thinks here of Reinhold Niebuhr: "Pacifism either tempts us to make no judgments at all, or to give an undue preference to tyranny in comparison with the momentary anarchy which is necessary to overcome tyranny."[87] Niebuhr points to the tendency of many pacifists to hubris, because of the belief that they have found the one true solution to the brokenness of man, whereas (in Christian terms, and one would hope in the terms of secular morality as well) none of us can ever be sure. Whatever the attraction of pacifism when you alone are under threat, there is less virtue in being pacifist when called upon to defend someone else.

In a world where people are being slaughtered for their race or their ethnicity or their religion, this is a challenge that matters. One might argue that the correct moral response of the oppressed is to refuse to take up arms against the oppressor. Often this proposition is offered as a generalization from the experience of the resistance movement led by Gandhi in India, or by King in the United States. Both cases, however, involved responses to an oppressor which turned out to have some sense of ethical limits. There were, in both cases, free populations to whom an appeal could be made, who might come to understand the argument expressed through the action of the nonviolent resisters. But here we come upon the problem. "Nonviolent defense," as Michael Walzer notes, "depends on noncombatant immunity."[88] If you face a foe willing to massacre you, not in tens or hundreds but in tens or hundreds of thousands, the nonviolent resistance is likely to fail. This is particularly true when there is no free population to which one might appeal,

as in Nazi Germany; or when the free population is itself delighted at the slaughter, as in Rwanda.[89] Oftentimes, pacifists
will respond to crises like the one in Darfur by answering that
it was not their ideology that created the mess, so it is not their
ideology that needs to fix it. This is a pure non sequitur. The
slaughter in Darfur is a result of neither pacifism nor liberalism
nor conservatism nor Western democracy. It is not the fault of
Obama, or Bush, or American capitalism. But a moral individual who cares about others still has to decide what the people
in Darfur ought to do about the slaughter; or whether anybody
else should help. "It's not my fault" is perhaps the worst reason
in the world for doing nothing.

Genocide has always been difficult for genuine pacifists.
Consider the Holocaust. Gandhi, the great apostle of nonviolence, argued that "the whole of Jewry" could be saved, if the
Jews would only pray for their oppressors: this on the eve of the
Second World War, a time when the Nazi attitude toward the
Jews was perfectly plain to the world. Gandhi added: "The German Jews will score a lasting victory over the German Gentiles,
in the sense that they will have converted the latter to an appre-
ciation of human dignity."[90]

At least Gandhi was being consistent. He argued for his principle, rather than pretending that he need have nothing to say
about the war. Thus George Orwell, in an admiring essay about
Gandhi, challenged other supporters of nonviolence to follow
Gandhi's example:

> Nor did he, like most Western pacifists, specialize in avoiding
> awkward questions. In relation to the late war [World War II],
> one question that every pacifist had a clear obligation to answer
> was: "What about the Jews? Are you prepared to see them ex-
> terminated? If not, how do you propose to save them without

resorting to war?" I must say that I have never heard, from any Western pacifist, an honest answer to this question, although I have heard plenty of evasions. . . ."[91]

And yet the example was in other ways problematic. Gandhi did not merely call for nonviolent rather than violent resistance to Hitler. He evidently believed there was merit in Germany's claim to lands lost in the First World War, even though he regretted that Hitler had turned to war to attain justice.[92] And Gandhi praised the Nazi leader, arguing that future generations would honor his bravery and genius.[93] True, he also insisted that Hitler's actions were "monstrous and unbecoming of human dignity."[94] Yet the praise can hardly be ignored. Probably it was necessary, and not only as a tactic. Gandhi had to believe there was something human and reachable in the worst of dictators, because absent that conscience, nonviolence could never have its desired effect. This core conception is essential to any pacifism that is not mere pose. Anybody can claim to be a pacifist but politically or intellectually serious pacifism is mature enough to accept the consequences. This was Orwell's point, and explains why what I have just said is no knock on Gandhi. Had he not been the man who would say those things about the greatest war criminal known to modern history, he would not have been able to accomplish the things he did. A thoroughgoing pacifist, one who lives his ideals, will always seek the route of activism that spares the lives of actual human beings.

As we have seen, President Obama, if we take him at his word, does not agree. Obama believes that there are evils with which it is not possible to negotiate. No doubt he admires the great pacifists, and he praised Gandhi in his Nobel Address: "I know there's nothing weak—nothing passive—nothing naïve—in the creed and lives of Gandhi and King." But, in the end, this was all only by way of rejecting Gandhi's example. Again, consider the President's words:

> But as a head of state sworn to protect and defend my nation, I cannot be guided by their examples alone. I face the world as it is, and cannot stand idle in the face of threats to the American people. For make no mistake: Evil does exist in the world. A non-violent movement could not have halted Hitler's armies. Negotiations cannot convince al Qaeda's leaders to lay down their arms. To say that force may sometimes be necessary is not a call to cynicism—it is a recognition of history; the imperfections of man and the limits of reason.

Gandhi could not possibly endorse any of this. It would violate his vision of human nature, and of human responsibility. Obama, however, has a different view of both, which may be another way of saying that his transformation into a warrior President is as complete as that of his predecessors.

Obama's Challenge

Let me return to the dinner in Aspen that opened our discussion. The reader will recall that I raised the subject of the genocide in Darfur, and was told by others at the table that someone should do something. From context and intonation, it was plain that "someone" did not mean America. I should not be too hard on my dining partners. No doubt they were simply exhausted, as most Americans are, by the nation's military adventures abroad. Indeed, it often seems to me that the worst thing about the Iraq and Afghan wars is precisely that they have reinforced the American wariness over the use of force, thus making it more difficult for this President, or any President, to persuade us to go to war over a real rather than a hypothetical humanitarian crisis. If, as I argued in Part I, the invasions of Afghanistan and Iraq were both judgment calls, wars of prudence, then we might have been wiser to take into account in our prudential calculation the possibility that we would sate the national appetite for battle, leaving no public will to support the use of force to save the lives of strangers. Perhaps President Bush was right to fight both wars; perhaps, as President Obama argues, Bush was right only about Afghanistan; or perhaps he was right about neither. Whatever might be the answer, one unspoken cost of our wars is the cost to those being slaughtered in other corners of the globe. They need a policeman to protect them, but the only one who could do it is overextended, exhausted, and running out of money.

Yet we must not forget the promises we have made to the world. After World War II, led by the United States, the West swore to stop genocide. We even drafted and signed the genocide convention, announcing our determination never to allow anything so horrible to happen again. There is an eerie disconnection in the way that we celebrate agreements to reduce nuclear arms, calling them contributions to world peace, while all across the globe people are being slaughtered by less sophisticated weapons. In Rwanda the weapon of choice was the machete, and it was used to perpetrate what Samantha Power calls the most rapid killing of human beings in the twentieth century, apart from the atomic bombing in 1945. Preventing another Rwanda, by force if necessary, would be a step toward peace. Until we are willing to take it, we should be wary of self-congratulation.

Otherwise, we risk becoming people who show how much we care by wringing our hands in public. We are uncommonly skilled at examining the carcass after it is dead, castigating "the world," whoever that is, for failing to act. One philosopher has proposed that we need an ethics of remembering,[95] perhaps because there is so much horror to forget. The essayist and poet Diane Ackerman has warned that we have become, courtesy of the media, "helpless viewers of other people's pain"[96]—that we are trained, by the news cycle itself, to see horror as inevitable, and to accept that there is nothing we can do. Elaine Scarry has made an analogous point about war itself: once a conflict ends, she says, we tend to forget just how horrible the battle truly was, remembering the victors (and the losers) more than we remember the injuries done.[97] Our ability to transcend, through an emotional blankness, news of war is itself a challenge to our claim to be moral beings; our ability to place genocide beyond our serious notice is worse. The Nobel laureate Elie Wiesel has warned that our indifference is often "equal to evil." He adds: "But indifference to disease, indifference to famine, indifference to dictators, somehow it's here and we accept it."[98] Michael Walzer, in his essay on "The Politics of Rescue," decries the Western tendency "to wait until the tyrants, the zealots, and the bigots have done their filthy work and then rush food and medicine to the ragged survivors."[99] But to do otherwise would require us to pay close attention, and if we pay close attention we might feel obliged to act, even at the cost of blood and treasure: Wiesel says that if we noticed the evil in the world, "We would have to take a plane, go there and do something."[100] Here is where the dissonance arises: most of us, I suspect, know perfectly well that the world's sole superpower has a moral obligation to act. We also know that we never will. We will, instead, allow the horrors to occur, lamenting them all the way, proud of the way we have displayed our agony by wringing our hands. Then we turn the channel, searching for some more important matter, like who will be the next Senator from East Podunk. Writes Ackerman: "There's no remedy for such colossal guilt except to tune it out, and we do, as we gradually become numb to the suffering of others."[101]

Perhaps I seem cynical. But, as Norman Mailer once put it, cynicism has its own virtues. One of those virtues is that cynicism teaches us to be wary of easy answers—as Mailer says, to distrust the neat patterns into which facts tend to fall. After all, we are not *entirely* numb. What Walzer criticizes is also admirably altruistic: we *do* send help to the survivors. Whether disaster or genocide strikes, America leads the way in providing humanitarian aid. (Let us note, in passing, that the Obama Administration seems to have abandoned its terrible coinage of "man-made disasters" as a euphemism for terror attacks.) Indeed, even in a world in which the United States does not set itself the task of protecting the weak against slaughter, one can easily list missions that would require a large and well-trained military. When generous donations follow horrific disaster, it is the United States Air Force that flies in the food. The American military delivered the lion's share of the relief following the devastating Asian tsunami in 2004. The United States Coast Guard brought in the first supplies after the horrific earthquake in Haiti in 2010. The United States Navy keeps the sea lanes open—the true *Pax Americana*—including, for instance, rescuing ships in distress and taking the lead in hunting down pirates. These services, in turn, lower the cost of commerce around the world.

All of this is heroic. All of it is part of what makes America the most admired nation on the planet. A few years ago, I read a newspaper story in which a Japanese business leader, asked about his nation's rise from defeated aggressor to economic superpower over just a few decades, pointed out his office window at an American aircraft carrier at anchor off the harbor. That, he said, is what it means to be a superpower. America is indeed a superpower, and is, in economic terms, the most generous nation in the history of the planet. We do all of these things, too, because they are, in Augustinian terms, our moral duty: we do them because we can. And yet, if we take President

Obama at his word, he might respond, yes, these are important achievements. But they are not enough. Our obligation to help the suffering is not limited to arriving once the disaster has struck. Some disasters must be stopped by force; and sometimes we are the only ones who can do it. Of course President Obama, should he ever deliver an address explaining why we are going to the aid of the helpless, would say all of this with his special brand of eloquence; given the state of the world, I hope one day soon to hear that speech.

And how will we respond, should this President or the next one ask us to make a great sacrifice on behalf of strangers? I hope that we would answer with the generosity of spirit that has helped build America into the greatest nation on earth. But I worry. Our preference for the comfortable life is understandably great; our knowledge of the suffering of others is often thin. We should be modest about what our military power can do, but we should never fall into the cynical trap of imagining that it can do nothing. Around the world, tyrants slaughter their people. We persuade ourselves that some other form of confrontation—diplomacy, jawboning, sanctions—will do all that is practical, and perhaps all that is necessary, to relieve their suffering. We may not be right, but at least we are happy.

{ IV }

THE AMERICAN PROVISO

President Obama on *Pacem in terris*

The Middle Ground

The election of Barack Obama, according to his critics and admirers alike, ushered in a new era in American foreign policy. Perhaps it did. But it did not usher in a new era in American warfare. Under Obama, we fight in much the same way that we did under his predecessor—for similar reasons, with similar justifications. Strip away the soaring rhetoric and you begin to discover what probably we should have known from the start: Presidents do what they think they must. This is the entire point of the American Proviso. Presidents do what they think they must. Here at home we may worry about law, or ethics, or what the world will think. The old saw is true: the office of the Presidency transforms its occupant, at least with respect to his views about war. Whatever he may think he thinks before taking office, the press of events swiftly remakes his opinions. In time of war this is particularly true. No peace candidate has ever become a peace President.

This, perhaps, is the import of Lincoln's dictum that a man who intends to fight a war has an obligation to win the support of the troops: "I would rather be defeated with the soldier vote behind me than to be elected without it."[1] He made the comment in the summer of 1864, in the thick of the Civil War, with

169

an eye toward the general election. Lincoln evidently won three-fourths of that "soldier vote." As Lincoln biographer James McPherson notes: "He would have been reelected without the soldier vote. But the most impressive thing about the 1864 election was that the men who would have to do the fighting and dying had voted overwhelmingly for their commander in chief to help him finish the job."[2] Impressive, yes—but we should not follow Lincoln's dictum so closely that we craft his own talents into a requirement for the job. True, we are likely better off when the soldiers support their own commander in chief sufficiently to want him to continue in the job. On the other hand, the tradition of civilian control of the military is at risk if we suppose that nobody not supported by the military should ever occupy the White House.* The fact that service members evidently preferred John McCain over Barack Obama in the 2008 presidential race[3] is interesting but not deeply revelatory: McCain, after all, was a genuine war hero, and Obama an unknown quantity. Whether the level of support for Obama changes in the next election, now that he is President and briskly pursuing the Afghan War and the War on Terror, will perhaps yield more intriguing information.

And not only about the soldier vote. Obama might have run in 2008 as the peace candidate, but next time around he will be running as a war President. This simple truth cannot be avoided. The nation is at war. America has been at war, some

---

*This is one of several reasons that the media did both the military and the country a disservice by playing up, during the second half of the Bush Administration, any disagreement between military leaders and the President. It is indeed the task of the military to tell the President when they think he is wrong. But he is invested by the Constitution with the power to decide. If we take the view that the President's decision to overrule his military commanders is evidence of perfidy or incompetence, we should stop pretending that we believe in civilian control, and stop admiring Lincoln, too, who overruled his generals constantly.

say, since the first attack on the World Trade Center, the car bomb set off in the underground garage in February of 1993. Certainly America has been at war since the second attack in September of 2001. Even a President who inherits a war started under somebody else's watch is known to history as a leader in that war. Consequently, although the next presidential election will doubtless feature bitter disputes over domestic policy, it will also be in part a referendum on Obama as commander in chief of the mightiest armed forces on the face of the globe.

In the conduct of war, the President's judgment matters enormously. Not his intellect, or his charm, or his positions on what we are bold to call the issues—his judgment. His wisdom. His ability to weigh pros and cons and uncover, through a mystic fashion difficult to explain, the proper course of war. I have tried in these pages to offer an account of President Obama's judgment, of what he believes to be worth fighting for. To be sure, the President, like any leader, must weigh politics against his moral sense in reaching his most important decisions, and never more so when he is deciding on war.

Those Presidents who have made war most successfully have not been satisfied to be right. They have determined to make their wars bipartisan. This sense pervaded, for example, Abraham Lincoln's famous Cooper Union address, which biographer Harold Holzer describes, in the subtitle of a book, as the speech that made Lincoln president.[4] The intention of the speech, says one historian, was "to show that the Republican position on slavery was not, as [Stephen] Douglas and the Democrats had been insisting, a departure from that of the nation's founders."[5]

How did Lincoln build the bridge? He began by insisting that he was simply restating the views of "the thirty-nine," as he called them—meaning those who signed the original Constitution, and that these founders never intended to limit the power of the Congress to restrict slavery.[6] That was to reassure the

Whig traditionalists. Next, lest the radicals worry that the potential candidate wanted simply to follow the original understanding of the Constitution, Lincoln insisted that he meant
nothing of the kind: "To do so, would be to discard all the lights
of current experience—to reject all progress—all improve-
ment."[7] Having satisfied the disparate wings of his own party,
he addressed the South. He complimented Southerners on
their reason and justice, then refuted, one by one, the charges
laid against his party: the charge that Republicans represented
only Northern interests, the charge that Republicans were whipping up the antislavery sentiment to get votes, the charge that
Republicans were not conservatives, the charge that Republicans sought war. It was the South, said Lincoln, that was threatening to break up the Union should a Republican win election
to the Presidency.[8] The North was ready to continue matters as
they were, leaving slavery alone in the South while fighting, on
moral grounds, its extension. So far, says Holzer, Lincoln had
"preached political moderation and sectional harmony." Now,
lest the antislavery side feel slighted, he "bristled with barely
contained indignation over the moral outrage of human slavery."[9]

Actually, Lincoln did more than that. He concluded, in
words the newspapers printed in all capitals: "LET US HAVE
FAITH THAT RIGHT MAKES MIGHT, AND IN THAT FAITH, LET US,
TO THE END, DARE TO DO OUR DUTY AS WE UNDERSTAND IT."[10]
This sounds very much like—even though, in terms, it is not—
a willingness to go to war. War for the Union? War against slavery? The speech never says. But Lincoln, by dancing around the
possibility of a conflict, successfully built the bridge—the
bridge, in this case, not between slaveholder and abolitionist,
not between North and South, but between the radicals who
wanted a war to free the slaves, and the moderates who wanted
the Union's peace preserved at all costs.

Surely a degree of Barack Obama's electoral victory was due to his successful effort to persuade voters that he, too, was a builder of bridges. It even looks as if he has; not in domestic policy, which remains as polarized as ever, but in his approach to war. True, there were people on the left and right alike who thought that America had elected an antiwar President, but that simply turned out not be true. Rather, the nation elected a President in the tradition of American wartime leaders: a man ultimately willing, whether or not it was his original intention, to sacrifice idealism for pragmatism in pursuit of his primary duty of keeping the nation safe.

The office of the Presidency, once assumed, transforms the outlook of its holder. What had seemed frivolous becomes frightening. What had seemed nonsense becomes necessary. The world turns out to be a dangerous place after all. The United States turns out to have actual enemies, people who wish the nation harm, and very few of them are moved by personal loathing for any particular resident of the White House. It is invariably saddening, wrote F. Scott Fitzgerald, to look with new eyes at things upon which you have expended your own powers of adjustment. We tend to imagine that the rest of the world views us through the lens of our domestic politics. This is absurd. When you step aside from partisanship, and examine the world afresh, you discover the simple truth that there are people who hate us. Not Bush. Not the Iraq War. Us. America.

If the first job of the executive is the protection of the nation's security, the choices presented when the commander in chief must actually sit in the Oval Office and make a decision turn out to be few. Often none is attractive. But the need to pick from among several unappealing ways to defend the nation's borders is what separates Presidents from pundits. To the outside critic, everything is easy. For the President who takes the job seriously, everything is hard.

I believe that much of the virulent hatred directed at President Obama's predecessor, and at Obama himself, arises from a rejection of this proposition. Hatred in politics often stems from a rejection of rational argument and a refusal to acknowledge reasonable differences of opinion.[11] To the hater, the world is simple not complex. The answers are obvious. "If the President were only as clear-eyed and wise as I am," the protester thinks, "he would see the world as it truly is, and make better decisions." It turns out, however, that in time of war, very different Presidents may see the world in roughly the same way. Again, review what we have seen. President Obama, succeeding President George W. Bush, largely adopted Bush's approach to Iraq; decided to use a version of that approach in prosecuting the war in Afghanistan; and widened the Terror War beyond the targets pursued by the Bush Administration. In the end, the Administration even adopted parts of the Bush Doctrine. True, Obama cast aside the more idealistic aspect of the Doctrine: the effort to use American power to build democracy. On the other hand, President Obama has adopted wholeheartedly what we might call the Bush Doctrine's political science: the determination to fight our enemies overseas, eliminating them where possible, rather than wait to be attacked.

There is a trope about President Obama, a meme he must set himself to battle: the notion that he cares about domestic policy but has no passion even for a war he insists is a necessity. Fouad Ajami put it this way: "He fights the war with Republican support, but his constituency remains isolationist at heart."[12] The claim about Obama's constituency may be true—who knows?—but I see no reason to be skeptical of the President's determination to pursue both the Afghan War and the Terror War. True, for reasons that are not clear, Obama rarely speaks of victory. This is unfortunate. Wars do have victors, and they do have losers, and if you believe in what you are doing then it is better to win than to lose: morally better. If these are unjust wars, then President Obama should stop prosecuting them, immediately, not at some promised future date. If on the other hand they are just wars, then he should articulate a moral obligation to prevail.

Certainly Obama seems to believe that the obligation exists. Indeed, as we have seen, the President's words and actions suggest very few limits on what he is willing to do to win the wars he seems determined to fight. In this, as many critics have pointed out, Obama seems not too different from Bush. Perhaps what were seen in Bush as character flaws—and what are seen in Obama as surprises—should be counted as neither. Perhaps they are simply the measures a reflective leader might reluctantly take to protect a nation under threat from a new kind of enemy. And if some of these measures—the use of prisoner renditions, for example, or the rejection of battlefield equivalence—seem to violate the very theory of just war that the President espouses, the quickest way to end the abuses may be to win.

The Media

Most wars wane in popularity as they drag on. National support for the Civil War all but collapsed in 1863, and revived only after a series of Union victories the following summer. The same was true eighty years later, in the midst of World War II. Indeed, the American public overwhelmingly opposed America's entry into the Second World War, right up until the day Japan attacked Pearl Harbor. It is a dangerous thing to try to fight a war without the public firmly behind you. Thus, President Eisenhower, on the occasion of Britain's disastrous and unpopular Suez campaign in 1956, wrote to a friend: "If one has to fight, then that is that. But I don't see the point in getting into a fight to which there can be no satisfactory end, and in which the whole world believes you are playing the part of the bully and you do not even have the firm backing of your entire people."[13]

This is a sensible statement of political reality. It may even contain a kernel of just war thinking: after all, the tradition holds a war not to be just when there exists no reasonable possibility of success, and a successful war is less likely when your own people and the world are united against you. I mention this proposition because of President Obama's steady insistence that Afghanistan is a war of necessity, and Iraq is not. I explained back in Part I why the distinction may be less compelling than the President implies. But that is beside the point. What matters is what the President believes, because the belief of a President in the justice of a war surely helps to shape public opinion. I say "helps" because public opinion is notoriously fickle. A recent Rand study suggests that the American people tend to support wars as long as America is perceived to be winning.[14] Even high casualty counts seem not to sway support as strongly when the United States seems likely to prevail. The dicier the war, however, the weaker the support. People like to win, and swiftly.

Which leads us to a significant obstacle to modern warfare: how is the public to figure out who's winning? I mean this question quite seriously. How many battles of the Iraq War can the reader name? How many from Afghanistan? Probably few or none. Out of either ignorance or condescension, the modern news media rarely tell us. One night a year or so after the fall of Baghdad, my wife and I were watching the evening news. The anchor recounted a fierce battle in a city in southern Iraq, and told us how many American soldiers died. Here is what he did not tell us: what piece of ground the battle was contesting, what difference it made who prevailed, and who won. That is correct: a major American television network managed to report on a fierce battle in a large war without ever mentioning which side prevailed. This is not, as the right would have it, some mystical antiwar bias. This is simple ineptitude.

Even during the Vietnam War, which many in the media came to oppose, reporters troubled to inform the public on major battles. And we paid attention. After all these years, people in my generation can still name them: Khe Sanh, Dien Bien Phu, the Tet Offensive. How many Americans today can identify Takur Ghar, one of the bloodiest engagements of the Afghan War? Takur Ghar was a small part of Operation Anaconda, an all-out assault on al-Qaeda forces in March of 2002. Takur Ghar was a battle over possession of a mountaintop, a 10,000-foot peak perfect for observation as well as offensive and defensive military operations. Anaconda, usually described as the first major battle of the twenty-first century involving American forces, established an unusual record: never before had American troops engaged in serious warfare at so high an altitude. *Time* magazine described Anaconda as "designed to squeeze the life out of a Taliban and al-Qaeda stronghold dug deep into the Shah-i-Kot mountains of eastern Afghanistan."[15] The battle did not go as planned. The enemy did not play its proper part. The military had grown accustomed to battling Taliban troops, who usually fled when outgunned. But the al-Qaeda forces stood their ground. Much of the engagement was heroically fought by small SEAL teams dropped behind the al-Qaeda lines.

In the end, Anaconda was a mixed success. Military analysts learned a good deal from what went wrong. In the Vietnam era, the public often participated in such debates, because we received blow-by-blow accounts from the battlefield. Many opponents of the war, back then, took pride in following its progress, the better to dissect it. Today is different. Some in the press tried to cover Anaconda, but America seemed to pay little attention. Somehow Anaconda, like the other important engagements of Iraq and Afghanistan, has dropped off the radar. We manage to pronounce upon the war without troubling to understand it.

Let me be clear. I believe, deeply, in dissent. If dialogue is the life's blood of democracy, then dissent is its beating heart.[16] Yes, during the previous Administration, some silly people on the right suggested that protesters were being un-American, and, during the current Administration, some silly people on the left are suggesting much the same. There are authoritarians everywhere, across the spectrum, partisans who wish dissenters would shut up and let them get on with the important work they have to do. Our Constitution, our history, and our core values tend to get in the way of efforts to stifle dissent. As they should.

In time of war, dissent can be of particular importance. I refer here not to the adolescent protest of slogan and hatred and demonization, but to a mature reflective dissent that raises serious questions about principle and policy. The theory of just and unjust wars praised by President Obama rests on the proposition that there are moments when you have no choice but to fight. For exactly this reason, it is a very useful thing for some citizens to suggest, at the dawn of every use of force, that there may be alternatives. True, antiwar dissent can be of the pie-in-the-sky variety. It can be of the I-hate-America variety. But it can also be deep and thoughtful and, for those who believe in dialogue, a vital contribution to debate. Nowhere should our debates be more thorough than when we are deciding to kill.

I mention all this because serious dialogue requires serious information. All too often, alas, the media have been unhelpful in providing information about the nation's wars. When America was on the verge of war in Afghanistan, and then in Iraq, there was little reporting aimed at explaining how terrible a thing is war. One might see in this tendency toward cheerleading in the early stages a kind of pro-military bias. In an odd way, it might have the opposite effect. By refusing to take war seriously enough to warn of its consequences, the media actually enhance the likelihood of public disillusion and outrage when some of the terrible things that happen in every war duly happen.[17]

But put that problem aside. Consider the reporting during times of war. Many reporters are conscientious and try hard, often at risk to their own lives. For this they should be celebrated. Too often, however, especially nowadays, the reporting is unhelpful to those trying to follow the war at home. A couple of years ago, a leading American newspaper ran a front-page story about how the Iraqi army, bogged down in a battle against insurgents, had to call on the American army for support. The implication was that the Iraqis were incompetent. What the reader would not discover, until the jump page (online, the second or third screen, to which hardly anyone reads) were two important facts: first, the call for assistance was in accordance with the operating procedures worked out by the two armies for such circumstances, and, second, the combined Iraqi-American forces won the battle. Yet without a full and accurate picture of what is at stake, not in the war alone but battle by battle, the public can hardly take an informed view.

I remember the news coverage, early in the Iraq War, of the battle for Nasiriyah, where resistance was greater than expected. Some commentators spun this as a sign that the war was going badly,[18] as if, somehow, the only war worth fighting is one where the other side surrenders without a shot. Here is another example of the difficulties resulting from a world in which America fights wars, but too many Americans know next to nothing about war. And here, again, the media could help. Alas, the press seems oddly unwilling to spend much time explaining what war is like—a tale we need to hear before a war begins. For example, millions of Americans know that professional football player Pat Tillman was killed in Afghanistan by friendly fire. The events were tragic but not uncommon. There is no way to

defend the apparent effort of some officials to hide the true circumstances of Tillman's death: such an outrage is perfectly fair
media game. But few stories went on to explain the astonish-
ingly high proportion of casualties in every war that result from
the same cause, in some battles, as high as 50 percent. The Second World War alone featured innumerable friendly-fire incidents, including several that are especially well known among
military buffs, such as the attack on General Omar Bradley's
army by American fighters in Sicily, and the sinking of HMS *Ox-
ley* by a fellow British submarine, which mistook it for a U-boat.[19]
But one need not be much of a buff to be familiar with the sinking of the American submarine *Seawolf,* which was attacked, mis-
takenly, by a British destroyer. Indeed, during the Second World
War, somewhere close to 20 percent of Allied casualties were
likely from friendly fire. (Most military historians reject the official figure of 2 percent as implausibly low.) Korea, Vietnam,
Grenada, and the Gulf War all saw friendly-fire casualty rates
above 10 percent. In the wars in Iraq and Afghanistan, however,
the percentage of friendly-fire deaths among American person-
nel seems to be around 1 percent—by far the lowest in history—a fact that might at least have provided some balance to
the reporting about the Tillman tragedy. (In fairness, the Associated Press did run a dispatch, which was widely ignored.)
Friendly-fire deaths are always great tragedies, and finding ways
to protect against them is a continuing project in the American
military; but friendly fire is also one of the things that happens
in war, and when reporters treat it as sensational they are doing
their jobs poorly.[20]

I worry about whether our claim to support the troops, whatever we think of their mission, has any content beyond its simplicity as a slogan. During the Second World War and the
Korean War, winners of the Medal of Honor were household
names.[21] No longer. Evidently stories of real heroism on the bat-

tlefield are uninteresting to a media obsessed instead with celebrity divorces and how much money political candidates spend on clothes. Even opponents of the Afghan and Iraq Wars have insisted from the start that they support the troops. Fair enough. One way of supporting America's armed forces is to honor their achievements. So, because they receive so little recognition, here are the names of the Americans who have won the Medal of Honor in Iraq, as of this writing:

Jason L. Dunham, Corporal, United States Marine Corps, who was mortally wounded while shielding his fellow Marines from an exploding hand grenade in Karibalah in 2004.

Ross McGinnis, Private First Class, United States Army, who died protecting the crew of his vehicle from an exploding hand grenade in Adhamiyah in 2006.

Michael A. Monsoor, Master-at-Arms, Second Class, United States Navy, a member of a SEAL team, who gave his life to protect his fellow SEALs and the Iraqis accompanying them, in fierce fighting in Ar Ramadi in 2006.

Paul R. Smith, Sergeant First Class, United States Army, who by himself assaulted a vastly superior enemy force that had ambushed his construction crew near Baghdad International Airport in 2003, giving his life to allow the withdrawal of his fellow soldiers, many of them wounded.

And here are the names of those who have won the Medal of Honor in Afghanistan:

Salvatore Giunta, Specialist, United States Army, who in a single engagement risked his life to save a comrade, then risked it a second time to save another. (Giunta is the first living Medal of Honor recipient since Vietnam.)

Robert James Miller, Staff Sergeant, United States Army, who was fatally wounded when, after an ambush, he drew Taliban fire to allow his fellow soldiers to escape.

Jared C. Monti, Sergeant First Class, United States Army, who led his badly outnumbered patrol in resisting an enemy attack, and was mortally wounded trying to bring a wounded comrade to safety.

Michael P. Murphy, Lieutenant, United States Navy, who led a four-member SEAL team that was ambushed by an enemy force at least ten times larger, and, in order to call for assistance, exposed himself to enemy fire and was killed.

These men all died as genuine heroes. Cable networks that have airtime to tell us, quite properly, of heroic rescues in time of disaster, but also of every child saved from a well, could surely take a little while to tell us stories of the heroes of a military we all claim to honor; unless of course the claim to support the troops is a lie.

Still, in these fractious times, even the Medal of Honor awards have seen their share of controversy. The Murphy case in particular has become something of a cause célèbre, because of the way the attack began. The SEAL team, tracking one of the most notorious leaders of the Taliban, encountered a group of goat herders. The members of the team believed that the goat herders, if released, would inform the Taliban of the team's whereabouts. The choice was to kill the goat herders or release them and risk the attack. Lieutenant Murphy decided to let them go, and the ambush followed. Now we come to the controversy: some have insisted that Murphy decided to release the goat herders because of a fear of liability back home, due to the increasing application of the machinery of criminal justice to the operation of the machinery of warfare.[22] This is of course possible, but nothing in the public record supports it. At least equally possible is another scenario: that Lieutenant Murphy decided not to harm the goat herders because to kill them would have been a great moral wrong. If indeed he took the decision for this reason, at risk to his life and the lives of his men, he acted honorably, and in accordance with the highest traditions of the American military. Perhaps the day will come again when the media will contemplate the possibility of reminding us, with our troops in harm's way, what those traditions are.

Here, I think, President Obama could help. We have all seen the passion with which he battles for his vision of what the nation's health care system should look like, or how the financial sector should be regulated. What we need is for him to bring the same passion to his defense of the military and its mission. I refer here not to the routine speeches delivered on the days set aside to honor those who have sacrificed, or even to his addresses, often quite thoughtful, to military audiences. I have in mind, rather, his frequent appearances on the White House lawn and the campaign trail when, with vigor and even anger, he seeks to rally his political base. If he would bring the same impromptu determination and fury to trying to rally the public in support of his wars—yes, his wars now, nobody else's—he would do more than anyone else can to truly support the troops. He might even build the bridge of which Lincoln dreamed, and unite us behind our commander in chief, and the mission on which he has sent our armed forces.

OBAMA'S CHOICES, AND OURS

So here we are, a nation thrice at war. President Obama has told us, as he should, what he believes is worth fighting for, and how. His words tell a part of the story; his actions supply the rest. Our job as citizens is to distill from actions and words alike what we might call Obama's philosophy of war. Back in the introduction, we met the veteran of Iraq who was skeptical of the idea that his friends should die for someone's theory. Yet a war leader must possess one, and should articulate it clearly. This book has been a reflection on Barack Obama's theory.

Abraham Lincoln summarized the rules of war this way: "Civilized belligerents do all in their power to help themselves, or hurt the enemy, except a few things regarded as barbarous or cruel. Among the exceptions are the massacre of vanquished foes, and non-combatants, male and female."[23] Lincoln penned these lines to a political ally who believed that the Emancipation Proclamation was beyond the President's authority. Lincoln answered, on the contrary, that he had freed the slaves as a military necessity—that is, as part of the war effort—and that the act lay within the powers of the President: "I think the constitution invests its Commander-in-chief, with the law of war, in time of war." Why did this matter? Because the slaves were property, wrote Lincoln, and property of the enemy could be confiscated. Then came the lines quoted above: that to win a war, you could do everything that was not "barbarous or cruel." Confiscating property that supported the enemy's war effort, Lincoln concluded, did not fit this exception.

President Obama evidently believes something similar. Within certain limits, Obama believes that his side, at least, can do all in its power to help itself or to hurt its enemy. In his Nobel Address, the President suggested that the theory of just and unjust wars tells us what those limits are. As we have seen from his actions, Obama, like other Presidents before him, actually prefers to adapt the theory to a form best serving the military and political ends of the United States. Perhaps this is inevitable. Perhaps the realists are right, and no great nation ever acts except in its own interest. And yet, if we are to be a moral people, we must develop a serious public ethics and bring it to bear on the great issues of the day. President Obama is right that the most ethically attractive template for the analysis of issues of war and peace is the theory of just and unjust wars. That theory, however, is more coherent in its traditional Christian version than in the watered-down secular form that we bring to our debates. And, in whatever form it is offered, the theory is useful only if its ringing phrases serve as actual guides to action, rather than just words.

Although President Obama, as we have seen, has spoken of the possibility of using military force for humanitarian purposes, he considers defense of the nation his highest duty, and there are few Americans who would disagree. The manner in which he interprets this mandate turns out to be little different from the interpretation offered by President Bush. Both seem willing to do whatever they deem necessary. President Obama has even contended for means that Bush did not—the right to assassinate American citizens, for instance—and seems to have greatly increased the use of everything from remote missile strikes to secret military operations. And, despite his talk of just war, Obama plainly does not believe there is a moral equivalence on the battlefield between our forces and the enemy's; in the present war, at least, he does not think the enemy has the right to do to us what we have the right to do to them.

This is not to say that a different President would behave differently. The rising security state, run by a nearly unfettered executive branch, is a bipartisan creation. The sharp debate over the ways in which Obama has supposedly unraveled Bush policies is, as one observer correctly noted, "mostly window dressing for just what was going on before."[24] And, in the words of the constitutional scholar Jack Balkin, Obama is offering "a liberal, centrist, Democratic version of the construction of these same governing practices."[25]

If the moderately conservative Bush and the moderately liberal Obama wind up reaching the same conclusions about how to defend America, we might begin to call what they are doing a consensus. It turns out that leaders of differing ideologies see certain matters the same way. On matters of the nation's security, at least, the Oval Office evidently changes the outlook of its occupant far more than the occupant changes the outlook of the Oval Office. The existence of a consensus does not mean that the consensus is right: both Presidents could be wrong. (As should by now be clear, on some issues I think they are.) It is the responsibility of every American to be prepared to offer a moral critique of the use (or non-use) of military force. Not a legal critique. A moral critique. We should be engaged in open and public debate over what it is right and wrong for American armed forces to do.

We are a nation founded on the notion of dissent, and trying to control what people can say is wrong. On the other hand, at minimum, the existence of a consensus does suggest that some of the more wildly hyperbolic critics of President Bush may owe him an apology. Otherwise, by muting themselves now, they might seem to be playing partisan games with the lives of American service members—and the lives of those we ask them to kill.

All of which leads us to our final set of questions—questions all of us should be asking, and often, as citizens of the world's only superpower and, at the moment, its indispensable superpower. The first question is whether we should remain a superpower, a status that requires some considerable investment. At the moment, however, I am not sure what the alternative is. Probably—tragically—our leaders have little choice other than to maintain the military at its high level of equipment and training, for all the expense this entails. According to the President, the world is a dangerous place. The history of great powers that have chosen to reduce their readiness for war is inauspicious. As we have seen, Athens lost the Second Peloponnesian War after deciding not to rebuild its military to face new threats. When England, seeking to save money, began reducing the armaments of its forces in Normandy in the fifteenth century, the French saw their opportunity and launched a war.[26] Other powers have had the same experience: the Spanish in the War of Succession, for example, and the French in the Second World War; even the United States itself, which nearly lost the War of 1812 after its disastrous decision to disarm following the successful Revolution. As long as there is a threat, anyone elected to the Presidency is likely to accept the reality that the United States is at war.

Still, all of this argument revolves around the defense of the nation. The theory of just and unjust wars began in the effort not to restrain war but to restrain injustice—including injustice toward others. On that subject, President Obama's words are sharp and hopeful, proposing the necessity of military force to prevent great slaughters. Other Presidents, too, have spoken boldly; but, in the end, each great slaughter of strangers has been allowed to run its course. Perhaps Obama's predecessors simply bowed to political reality. Yet one would wish, sooner or later, for a President who might at least try to rally us to a cause greater than the defense of our own nation.

I do not mean to deny that defending America is the highest duty of our government; of course it is. But just as our wealth creates in us a certain responsibility toward the rest of the world, so does our status as the world's only superpower. Americans will certainly disagree with each other on precisely what that responsibility entails, but we should not pretend that we have none.

At this writing, the Iraq War is winding down. Our military role in Afghanistan may not last much longer. But we will be asked to fight again, perhaps by this President, perhaps by a successor. When that moment arrives—when we are asked, in whatever cause, to risk blood and treasure—we will need a common language in which to debate the wisdom of whatever war is looming. President Obama has proposed that in that moment of decision, we invoke the language of just and unjust wars. We should ask, then, the same questions the just war tradition has been asking for centuries:

> *Is the war for a just cause?* Has the other side done wrong? Are we fighting out of libido or out of charity? (As we have seen, this must include the possibility of fighting not for ourselves but for others.)
>
> *Is the war a last resort?* If the goal is just, is there another way to reach the same result with less suffering? (As we have seen, sanctions are in most cases a way of making ourselves feel good, not a way of solving the problem.)
>
> *Is there a reasonable prospect of success?* (As we have seen, protracted wars sap public support, and without public support, success is difficult.)
>
> *Can we fight the war in a just manner?* (As we have seen, the media and our political leaders tend to do a poor job of informing us what war is really like, so we will likely have to educate ourselves.)

The traditional just war inquiries are only part of where our reflections should take us. As citizens of the most powerful nation on earth, we must ensure that we are fully informed about both the purposes of a war and its likely costs. In the bumper-sticker politics of the present age, this might require a considerable effort, but that hard work is the very least that we should demand of each other. We should demand of any President who seeks to lead us to war a clear vision of the structure of the peace that is to follow. And we should resist absolutely the temptation to partisanship. When the horror of war is upon us, what is right is equally right, whichever party happens to be in charge; and what is wrong is equally wrong.

Through it all, we must be wary, asking ourselves other questions, reflecting on the darker side of our history. Are we fighting, really, for empire? For vengeance? To show the world that we are strong? Then of course we must also look at matters the other way around, asking ourselves why the enemy is fighting, and how the people ranked against us see the world. We might decide to do battle anyway, and the just war tradition teaches that there are times when we must. President Obama has joined the long list of American leaders who insist not only that there is true evil in the world, but that some evils must be combated by force of arms. The future holds as many challenges as the past. More than a few of them will lead to calls for war. When the moment for decision arrives, let us do what we can to ensure that we get there thoughtfully. Shakespeare urged caution in waking the sleeping sword of war. True caution is not timidity, but the art of thinking things through.

Back in the Preface, we met the Iraq War veteran who was upset at the idea that his friends had died for somebody's theory. As I have suggested, however, war without theory is simple slaughter. In these pages, I have accepted the invitation President Obama extended in his Nobel Address to reflect critically upon the lessons just war theory holds for the present age. I have tried to suggest where we as a nation fall short of the requirements of the tradition, and where the tradition falls short of our requirements as a nation. All through American history, when one conflict has ended, the next tidal wave of violence has turned out to be just beyond the horizon. The time to figure out what is worth fighting for is before the flood washes over us.

APPENDIX

The text of President Obama's Nobel Peace Prize acceptance speech, as released by the White House:

For Immediate Release
December 10, 2009
Remarks by the President at the Acceptance of the Nobel Peace Prize

Oslo City Hall
Oslo, Norway

1:44 P.M. CET

THE PRESIDENT: Your Majesties, Your Royal Highnesses, distinguished members of the Norwegian Nobel Committee, citizens of America, and citizens of the world:

I receive this honor with deep gratitude and great humility. It is an award that speaks to our highest aspirations—that for all the cruelty and hardship of our world, we are not mere prisoners of fate. Our actions matter, and can bend history in the direction of justice.

And yet I would be remiss if I did not acknowledge the considerable controversy that your generous decision has generated. (Laughter.) In part, this is because I am at the beginning, and not the end, of my labors on the world stage. Compared to some of the giants of history who've received this prize—Schweitzer and King; Marshall and Mandela—my accomplishments are slight. And then there are the men and women around the world who have been jailed and beaten in the pursuit of justice; those who toil in humanitarian organizations to relieve suffering; the unrecognized millions whose quiet acts of courage and compassion inspire even the most hardened cynics. I cannot argue with those who find these men and women— some known, some obscure to all but those they help—to be far more deserving of this honor than I.

But perhaps the most profound issue surrounding my receipt of this prize is the fact that I am the Commander-in-Chief of the military of a nation in the midst of two wars. One of these wars is winding down. The other is a conflict that America did not seek; one in which we are joined by 42 other countries—including Norway—in an effort to defend ourselves and all nations from further attacks.

Still, we are at war, and I'm responsible for the deployment of thousands of young Americans to battle in a distant land. Some will kill, and some will be killed. And so I come here with an acute sense of the costs of armed conflict—filled with difficult questions about the relationship between war and peace, and our effort to replace one with the other.

Now these questions are not new. War, in one form or another, appeared with the first man. At the dawn of history, its morality was not questioned; it was simply a fact, like drought or disease—the manner in which tribes and then civilizations sought power and settled their differences.

And over time, as codes of law sought to control violence within groups, so did philosophers and clerics and statesmen seek to regulate the destructive power of war. The concept of a "just war" emerged, suggesting that war is justified only when certain conditions were met: if it is waged as a last resort or in self-defense; if the force used is proportional; and if, whenever possible, civilians are spared from violence.

Of course, we know that for most of history, this concept of "just war" was rarely observed. The capacity of human beings to think up new ways to kill one another proved inexhaustible, as did our capacity to exempt from mercy those who look different or pray to a different God. Wars between armies gave way to wars between nations—total wars in which the distinction between combatant and civilian became blurred. In the span of 30 years, such carnage would twice engulf this continent. And while it's hard to conceive of a cause more just than the defeat of the Third Reich and the Axis powers, World War II was a conflict in which the total number of civilians who died exceeded the number of soldiers who perished.

In the wake of such destruction, and with the advent of the nuclear age, it became clear to victor and vanquished alike that the world needed institutions to prevent another world war. And so, a quarter century after the United States Senate rejected the League of Nations—an idea for which Woodrow Wilson received this prize—America led the world in constructing an architecture to keep the peace: a Marshall Plan and a United Nations, mechanisms to govern the waging of war, treaties to protect human rights, prevent genocide, restrict the most dangerous weapons.

In many ways, these efforts succeeded. Yes, terrible wars have been fought, and atrocities committed. But there has been no Third World War. The Cold War ended with jubilant crowds dismantling a wall. Commerce has stitched much of the world together. Billions have been lifted from poverty. The ideals of liberty and self-determination, equality and the rule of law have haltingly advanced. We are the heirs of the fortitude and foresight of generations past, and it is a legacy for which my own country is rightfully proud.

And yet, a decade into a new century, this old architecture is buckling under the weight of new threats. The world may no longer shudder at the prospect of war between two nuclear superpowers, but proliferation may increase the risk of catastrophe. Terrorism has long been a tactic, but modern technology allows a few small men with outsized rage to murder innocents on a horrific scale.

Moreover, wars between nations have increasingly given way to wars within nations. The resurgence of ethnic or sectarian conflicts; the growth of secessionist movements, insurgencies, and failed states—all these things have increasingly trapped civilians in unending chaos. In today's wars, many more civilians are killed than soldiers; the seeds of future conflict are sown, economies are wrecked, civil societies torn asunder, refugees amassed, children scarred.

I do not bring with me today a definitive solution to the problems of war. What I do know is that meeting these challenges will require the same vision, hard work, and persistence of those men and women who acted so boldly decades ago. And it will require us to think in new ways about the notions of just war and the imperatives of a just peace.

We must begin by acknowledging the hard truth: We will not eradicate violent conflict in our lifetimes. There will be times when nations—acting individually or in concert—will find the use of force not only necessary but morally justified.

I make this statement mindful of what Martin Luther King Jr. said in this same ceremony years ago: "Violence never brings permanent peace. It solves no social problem: it merely creates new and more complicated ones." As someone who stands here as a direct consequence of Dr. King's life work, I am living testimony to the moral force of non-violence. I know there's nothing weak—nothing passive—nothing naive—in the creed and lives of Gandhi and King.

But as a head of state sworn to protect and defend my nation, I cannot be guided by their examples alone. I face the world as it is, and cannot stand idle in the face of threats to the American people. For make no mistake: Evil does exist in the world. A non-violent movement could not have halted Hitler's armies. Negotiations cannot convince al Qaeda's leaders to lay down their arms. To say that force may sometimes be necessary is not a call to cynicism—it is a recognition of history; the imperfections of man and the limits of reason.

I raise this point, I begin with this point because in many countries there is a deep ambivalence about military action today, no matter what the cause. And at times, this is joined by a reflexive suspicion of America, the world's sole military superpower.

But the world must remember that it was not simply international institutions—not just treaties and declarations—that brought stability to a post–World War II world. Whatever mistakes we have made, the plain fact is this: The United States of America has helped underwrite global security for more than six decades with the blood of our citizens and the strength of our arms. The service and sacrifice of our men and women in uniform has promoted peace and prosperity from

Germany to Korea, and enabled democracy to take hold in places like the Balkans. We have borne this burden not because we seek to impose our will. We have done so out of enlightened self-interest—because we seek a better future for our children and grandchildren, and we believe that their lives will be better if others' children and grandchildren can live in freedom and prosperity.

So yes, the instruments of war do have a role to play in preserving the peace. And yet this truth must coexist with another—that no matter how justified, war promises human tragedy. The soldier's courage and sacrifice is full of glory, expressing devotion to country, to cause, to comrades in arms. But war itself is never glorious, and we must never trumpet it as such.

So part of our challenge is reconciling these two seemingly irreconcilable truths—that war is sometimes necessary, and war at some level is an expression of human folly. Concretely, we must direct our effort to the task that President Kennedy called for long ago. "Let us focus," he said, "on a more practical, more attainable peace, based not on a sudden revolution in human nature but on a gradual evolution in human institutions." A gradual evolution of human institutions.

What might this evolution look like? What might these practical steps be?

To begin with, I believe that all nations—strong and weak alike—must adhere to standards that govern the use of force. I—like any head of state—reserve the right to act unilaterally if necessary to defend my nation. Nevertheless, I am convinced that adhering to standards, international standards, strengthens those who do, and isolates and weakens those who don't.

The world rallied around America after the 9/11 attacks, and continues to support our efforts in Afghanistan, because of the horror of those senseless attacks and the recognized principle of self-defense. Likewise, the world recognized the need to confront Saddam Hussein when he invaded Kuwait—a consensus that sent a clear message to all about the cost of aggression.

Furthermore, America—in fact, no nation—can insist that others follow the rules of the road if we refuse to follow them ourselves. For when we don't, our actions appear arbitrary and undercut the legitimacy of future interventions, no matter how justified.

And this becomes particularly important when the purpose of military action extends beyond self-defense or the defense of one nation against an aggressor. More and more, we all confront difficult questions about how to prevent the slaughter of civilians by their own government, or to stop a civil war whose violence and suffering can engulf an entire region.

I believe that force can be justified on humanitarian grounds, as it was in the Balkans, or in other places that have been scarred by war. Inaction tears at our conscience and can lead to more costly intervention later. That's why all responsible nations must embrace the role that militaries with a clear mandate can play to keep the peace.

America's commitment to global security will never waver. But in a world in which threats are more diffuse, and missions more complex, America cannot act alone. America alone cannot secure the peace. This is true in Afghanistan. This is true in failed states like Somalia, where terrorism and piracy is joined by famine and human suffering. And sadly, it will continue to be true in unstable regions for years to come.

The leaders and soldiers of NATO countries, and other friends and allies, demonstrate this truth through the capacity and courage they've shown in Afghanistan. But in many countries, there is a disconnect between the efforts of those who serve and the ambivalence of the broader public. I understand why war is not popular, but I also know this: The belief that peace is desirable is rarely enough to achieve it. Peace requires responsibility. Peace entails sacrifice. That's why NATO continues to be indispensable. That's why we must strengthen U.N. and regional peacekeeping, and not leave the task to a few countries. That's why we honor those who return home from peacekeeping and training abroad to Oslo and Rome; to Ottawa and Sydney; to Dhaka and Kigali—we honor them not as makers of war, but of wagers—but as wagers of peace.

Let me make one final point about the use of force. Even as we make difficult decisions about going to war, we must also think clearly about how we fight it. The Nobel Committee recognized this truth in awarding its first prize for peace to Henry Dunant—the founder of the Red Cross, and a driving force behind the Geneva Conventions.

Where force is necessary, we have a moral and strategic interest in binding ourselves to certain rules of conduct. And even as we confront a vicious adversary that abides by no rules, I believe the United States of America must remain a standard bearer in the conduct of war. That is what makes us different from those whom we fight. That is a source of our strength. That is why I prohibited torture. That is why I ordered the prison at Guantanamo Bay closed. And that is why I have reaffirmed America's commitment to abide by the Geneva Conventions. We lose ourselves when we compromise the very ideals that we fight to defend. (Applause.) And we honor—we honor those ideals by upholding them not when it's easy, but when it is hard.

I have spoken at some length to the question that must weigh on our minds and our hearts as we choose to wage war. But let me now turn to our effort to avoid such tragic choices, and speak of three ways that we can build a just and lasting peace.

First, in dealing with those nations that break rules and laws, I believe that we must develop alternatives to violence that are tough enough to actually change behavior—for if we want a lasting peace, then the words of the international community must mean something. Those regimes that break the rules must be held accountable. Sanctions must exact a real price. Intransigence must be met with increased pressure—and such pressure exists only when the world stands together as one.

One urgent example is the effort to prevent the spread of nuclear weapons, and to seek a world without them. In the middle of the last century, nations agreed to be bound by a treaty whose bargain is clear: All will have access to peaceful nuclear power; those without nuclear weapons will forsake them; and those with nuclear weapons will work towards disarmament. I am committed to upholding this treaty. It is a centerpiece of my foreign policy. And I'm working with President Medvedev to reduce America and Russia's nuclear stockpiles.

But it is also incumbent upon all of us to insist that nations like Iran and North Korea do not game the system. Those who claim to respect international law cannot avert their eyes when those laws are flouted. Those who care for their own security cannot ignore the danger of an arms race in the Middle East or East Asia. Those who seek peace cannot stand idly by as nations arm themselves for nuclear war.

The same principle applies to those who violate international laws by brutalizing their own people. When there is genocide in Darfur, systematic rape in Congo, repression in Burma—there must be consequences. Yes, there will be engagement; yes, there will be diplomacy—but there must be consequences when those things fail. And the closer we stand together, the less likely we will be faced with the choice between armed intervention and complicity in oppression.

This brings me to a second point—the nature of the peace that we seek. For peace is not merely the absence of visible conflict. Only a just peace based on the inherent rights and dignity of every individual can truly be lasting.

It was this insight that drove drafters of the Universal Declaration of Human Rights after the Second World War. In the wake of devastation, they recognized that if human rights are not protected, peace is a hollow promise.

And yet too often, these words are ignored. For some countries, the failure to uphold human rights is excused by the false suggestion that these are somehow Western principles, foreign to local cultures or stages of a nation's development. And within America, there has long been a tension between those who describe themselves as realists or idealists—a tension that suggests a stark choice between the narrow pursuit of interests or an endless campaign to impose our values around the world.

I reject these choices. I believe that peace is unstable where citizens are denied the right to speak freely or worship as they please; choose their own leaders or assemble without fear. Pent-up grievances fester, and the suppression of tribal and religious identity can lead to violence. We also know that the opposite is true. Only when Europe became free did it finally find peace. America has never fought a war against a democracy, and our closest friends are governments that protect the rights of their citizens. No matter how callously defined, neither America's interests—nor the world's—are served by the denial of human aspirations.

So even as we respect the unique culture and traditions of different countries, America will always be a voice for those aspirations that are universal. We will bear witness to the quiet dignity of reformers like Aung Sang Suu Kyi; to the bravery of Zimbabweans who cast their ballots in the face of beatings; to the hundreds of thousands who have marched silently through the streets of Iran. It is telling that the leaders of these governments fear the aspirations of their own people more than the power of any other nation. And it is the responsibility of all free people and free nations to make clear that these movements— these movements of hope and history—they have us on their side.

Let me also say this: The promotion of human rights cannot be about exhortation alone. At times, it must be coupled with painstaking diplomacy. I know that engagement with repressive regimes lacks the satisfying purity of indignation. But I also know that sanctions without outreach—condemnation without discussion—can carry forward only a crippling status quo. No repressive regime can move down a new path unless it has the choice of an open door.

In light of the Cultural Revolution's horrors, Nixon's meeting with Mao appeared inexcusable—and yet it surely helped set China on a path where millions of its citizens have been lifted from poverty and connected to open societies. Pope John Paul's engagement with Poland created space not just for the Catholic Church, but for labor leaders like Lech Walesa. Ronald Reagan's efforts on arms control and embrace of perestroika not only improved relations with the Soviet Union, but empowered dissidents throughout Eastern Europe. There's no simple formula here. But we must try as best we can to balance isolation and engagement, pressure and incentives, so that human rights and dignity are advanced over time.

Third, a just peace includes not only civil and political rights—it must encompass economic security and opportunity. For true peace is not just freedom from fear, but freedom from want.

It is undoubtedly true that development rarely takes root without security; it is also true that security does not exist where human beings do not have access to enough food, or clean water, or the medicine and shelter they need to survive. It does not exist where children can't aspire to a decent education or a job that supports a family. The absence of hope can rot a society from within.

And that's why helping farmers feed their own people—or nations educate their children and care for the sick—is not mere charity. It's also why the world must come together to confront climate change. There is little scientific dispute that if we do nothing, we will face more drought, more famine, more mass displacement—all of which will fuel more conflict for decades. For this reason, it is not merely scientists and environmental activists who call for swift and forceful action—it's military leaders in my own country and others who understand our common security hangs in the balance.

Agreements among nations. Strong institutions. Support for human rights. Investments in development. All these are vital ingredients in bringing about the evolution that President Kennedy spoke about. And yet, I do not believe that we will have the will, the determination, the staying power, to complete this work without something more—and that's the continued expansion of our moral imagination; an insistence that there's something irreducible that we all share.

As the world grows smaller, you might think it would be easier for human beings to recognize how similar we are; to understand that we're all basically seeking the same things; that we all hope for the chance to live out our lives with some measure of happiness and fulfillment for ourselves and our families.

And yet somehow, given the dizzying pace of globalization, the cultural leveling of modernity, it perhaps comes as no surprise that people fear the loss of what they cherish in their particular identities—their race, their tribe, and perhaps most powerfully their religion. In some places, this fear has led to conflict. At times, it even feels like we're moving backwards. We see it in the Middle East, as the conflict between Arabs and Jews seems to harden. We see it in nations that are torn asunder by tribal lines.

And most dangerously, we see it in the way that religion is used to justify the murder of innocents by those who have distorted and defiled the great religion of Islam, and who attacked my country from Afghanistan. These extremists are not the first to kill in the name of God; the cruelties of the Crusades are amply recorded. But they remind us that no Holy War can ever be a just war. For if you truly believe that you are carrying out divine will, then there is no need for restraint—no need to spare the pregnant mother, or the medic, or the Red Cross worker, or even a person of one's own faith. Such a warped view of religion is not just incompatible with the concept of peace, but I believe it's incompatible with the very purpose of faith—for the one rule that lies at the heart of every major religion is that we do unto others as we would have them do unto us.

Adhering to this law of love has always been the core struggle of human nature. For we are fallible. We make mistakes, and fall victim to the temptations of pride, and power, and sometimes evil. Even those of us with the best of intentions will at times fail to right the wrongs before us.

But we do not have to think that human nature is perfect for us to still believe that the human condition can be perfected. We do not have to live in an idealized world to still reach for those ideals that will make it a better place. The non-violence practiced by men like Gandhi and King may not have been practical or possible in every circumstance, but the love that they preached—their fundamental faith in human progress—that must always be the North Star that guides us on our journey.

For if we lose that faith—if we dismiss it as silly or naive; if we divorce it from the decisions that we make on issues of war and peace—then we lose what's best about humanity. We lose our sense of possibility. We lose our moral compass.

Like generations have before us, we must reject that future. As Dr. King said at this occasion so many years ago, "I refuse to accept despair as the final response to the ambiguities of history. I refuse to accept the idea that the 'isness' of man's present condition makes him morally incapable of reaching up for the eternal 'oughtness' that forever confronts him."

Let us reach for the world that ought to be—that spark of the divine that still stirs within each of our souls. (Applause.)

Somewhere today, in the here and now, in the world as it is, a soldier sees he's outgunned, but stands firm to keep the peace. Somewhere today, in this world, a young protestor awaits the brutality of her government, but has the courage to march on. Somewhere today, a mother facing punishing poverty still takes the time to teach her child, scrapes together what few coins she has to send that child to school—because she believes that a cruel world still has a place for that child's dreams.

Let us live by their example. We can acknowledge that oppression will always be with us, and still strive for justice. We can admit the intractability of depravation, and still strive for dignity. Clear-eyed, we can understand that there will be war, and still strive for peace. We can do that—for that is the story of human progress; that's the hope of all the world; and at this moment of challenge, that must be our work here on Earth.

Thank you very much. (Applause.)

END

2:20 P.M. CET

AUTHOR'S NOTE

This book is part of a larger project on the application of just war theory to America's use of military force around the world. My interest in the topic began during the Clinton Administration, and I have been teaching the subject since the early years of the Bush Administration. This volume, as I mentioned in the preface, had its genesis during the Bush years, when the nation's response to the 9/11 attacks piqued my interest in the morality of different forms of self-defense. Although I opposed the war in Iraq and questioned the war in Afghanistan, I was nevertheless struck by the similarities between them, as I explain in Part I.

My ultimate goal is to write a treatise on the ethics of war, and to publish several smaller treatments—such as this one—along the way. I recognize that many scholars are skeptics of the effort to develop a concrete ethics of war, preferring to rely on international law rather than moral theory to restrain the instinct of nations to use military force. I suppose that I must be counted as being in the opposite camp—as a skeptic of international law—for reasons unnecessary to adduce here.

I have presented various parts of this book at academic and other institutions around the country, including Columbia Law School, Hartford Seminary, the University of Minnesota School of Law, Yale Law School, the Yale Club of New York, and the Northwestern University School of Law, where earlier versions of Parts II and III formed the heart of my Julius Rosenthal Lectures.

Over the years that I have spent working on this manuscript, I have had the benefit of particular comments, either on the manuscript or on the ideas underlying it, from more of my colleagues than I can remember and thank. I would single out in particular spirited exchanges (from which I learned much) with Bruce Ackerman, Akhil Amar, Heather Gerken, Oona Hathaway, Harold Koh, Daniel Markovits, Tracey Meares, Robert Post, and Kate Stith. I have also had the benefit of comments from editors at *Nomos,* where an earlier version of Part III was scheduled to be published several years ago; alas, after the editing was complete, I found myself unable to make up my mind about certain key questions. And I received any number of incisive comments from my brother, Eric Carter.

Over the past few years, I have had the benefit of exemplary research assistance from many students, including (and I hope I have left no one out) Jessica Chen, Caroline Gross, Margot Kaminski, Mark Totten, and Stephanie Turner. I am grateful, too, for the suggestions of my editor, Harold Evans, and my literary agent, Lynn Nesbit.

And, as always, my most graceful editor, strongest supporter, and most thoughtful critic has been my wife, Enola Aird, who along with our children, Leah and Andrew, represents a blessing of which I can never be worthy.

Cheshire, Connecticut
October 2010

NOTES

I. ELIMINATING ENEMIES

1. Robert Baer, "The Khost CIA Bombing: Assessing the Damage in Afghanistan," *Time,* January 8, 2010.

2. See generally the discussion in Paul W. Kahn, *Sacred Violence: Torture, Terror, and Sovereignty* (Ann Arbor: University of Michigan Press, 2008).

3. I should make clear that my interest as an ethicist is in the product, not the process, of decision making. Thus, although Bob Woodward's book *Obama's Wars* (New York: Simon & Schuster, 2010) illuminates in a quite readable way the battles over policy, it is the policies themselves, and not the players behind them, that are my subject.

4. See Christopher Drew, "Drones Are Playing a Growing Role in Afghanistan," *New York Times,* February 19, 2010.

5. According to Woodward's account, Obama was somewhat surprised by the request by his commanders for more troops in the Afghan theater. He might even have been annoyed by the clumsiness with which it was presented. See Woodward, *Obama's Wars,* pp. 185 ff. But he nevertheless gave them most of what they wanted, a decision consistent with his stated goal of winning the war.

6. See, for example, Mark Mazetti, "U.S. Is Said to Expand Secret Actions in Mideast," *New York Times,* May 24, 2010.

7. Quoted in Ephraim Douglass Adams, *Great Britain and the American Civil War,* (BiblioBazaar, 2006) (first published 1924), p. 486.

8. See Carl Sandburg, *Abraham Lincoln: The Prairie Years and the War Years,* (New York: Harcourt, 1954), p. 614.

9. Barack Obama, *The Audacity of Hope* (New York: Crown, 2006), p. 29.

10. Ibid., p. 45.

11. Thomas Nagel, "War and Massacre," *Philosophy and Public Affairs* 1, no. 2 (1972), p. 123.

12. George W. Bush, remarks made on March 29, 2002.

13. I discuss this disequivalence in my essay "Does Congress Matter?" (unpublished).

14. William Lloyd Garrison, *No Compromise with Slavery: An Address Delivered in the Broadway Tabernacle,* New York, February 14, 1854 (New York: American Anti-Slavery Society, 1854), p. 6.

15. Ibid., p. 10.

16. Ibid., p. 21.

17. Ibid., p. 22. Ironically, Garrison accused the pro-slavery side of being intolerant of other views. Ibid., pp. 23–25.

18. Ibid., pp. 28–29.

19. Ibid., p. 29.

20. Although Catholic just war thinking has dominated Western thought, there are certainly theories of just war in other traditions, even though they are not always as fully worked out. On Islam, see, for example, John Kelsay, *Arguing the Just War in Islam* (Cambridge: Harvard University Press, 2007), a treatment more scrupulously fair-minded than some of what is written on the subject. On Judaism, see, for example, Michael Walzer, "War and Peace in the Jewish Tradition," in Terry Nardin, ed., *The Ethics of War and Peace: Religious and Secular Perspectives* (Princeton: Princeton University Press, 1996), p. 95; and Aviezer Ravitsky, "Prohibited Wars in the Jewish Tradition," in Nardin, *The Ethics of War and Peace,* p. 115. See also George Wilkes, "Judaism and Justice in War," in Paul Robinson, ed., *Just War in Comparative Perspective* (Alershot, England: Ashgate Publishing, 2003), p. 9. Both Walzer and Wilkes contend that Judaism has not traditionally struggled, as Christianity has, with when it is just to go to war. Nevertheless, there are analogues to (and differences from) certain parts of the just war tradition in the rabbinic teachings. A useful compilation of just war arguments from various cultures and religions is Richard Sorabji and David Rodin, eds., *The Ethics of War: Shared Problems in Different Traditions* (Aldershot, England: Ashgate, 2007).

21. An intriguing analogue is the evolution in our understanding of pain imposed by the state. The administration of pain, once viewed as an important function of the state, is now viewed as an aberration to be avoided. For a useful discussion of this evolution, see Karl Shoemaker, "The Problem of Pain in Punishment: Historical Perspectives," in Austin Sarat, ed., *Pain, Death, and the Law* (Ann Arbor: University of Michigan Press, 2001), p. 15.

22. See, for example, Maeve Reston, "Obama Tells Veterans Afghanistan Is a 'War of Necessity,'" *Los Angeles Times,* August 18, 2009.

23. See Richard Norman, *Ethics, Killing, and War* (Cambridge: Cambridge University Press, 1995).

24. See, for example, Stanley Hauerwas, "Should War Be Eliminated? A Thought Experiment," in John Berkman and Michael Cartwright, eds., *The Hauerwas Reader* (Durham, NC: Duke University Press, 2001). In this essay,

originally published in 1984, Hauerwas asserts the duty of the pacifist to make, and refute, the strongest possible case for war, rather than to deny that the case exists.

25. See, for example, Jeff McMahan, "Self-defense and the Problem of the Innocent Attacker," *Philosophy and Public Affairs* 20 (Fall 1991): 301.

26. Ironically, Hitler's claim, although a lie, was not ridiculous. Stalin himself was terrified of war with Germany, but some of his generals were evidently itching for war, so much so that when the first reports of the German advance came in, Stalin's aides suspected that his senior commanders were making them up, to goad him into attacking first. See Anthony Beevor, *Stalingrad* (New York: Penguin, 1998), pp. 8–9.

27. See John Ferling, *Almost a Miracle: The American Victory in the War of Independence* (New York: Oxford University Press, 2007), pp. 21–33.

28. Of course there are endless sources on this point. Among the best is the historian William H. Freehling's gracefully written study, *The Road to Disunion, Volume II: Secessionists Triumphant* (New York: Oxford University Press, 2007). As Freehling points out, many secessionists, long before the attack on Fort Sumter, wanted to seize Washington and the government by force. See especially chapter 17.

29. M. Tullius Cicero, *De Officiis*, bk. 2, sec. 27, in Walter Miller, ed., *De Officiis. With an English Translation* (Cambridge: Harvard University Press, 1913).

30. For a recent, and cautious, defense of at least some preventive attacks as necessary in the contemporary world, see Thomas M. Nichols, *Eve of Destruction: The Coming Age of Preventive War* (Philadelphia: University of Pennsylvania Press, 2008). The preemptive-preventive distinction is drawn in a slightly different way in Alan M. Dershowitz, *Preemption: A Knife That Cuts Both Ways* (New York: Norton, 2006).

31. James Russell Lowell, "Abraham Lincoln 1864–1865," reprinted in *The Harvard Classics* (New York: P. F. Collier & Son, 1909).

32. See *Final Report of the National Commission on Terrorist Attacks Upon the United States,* Executive Summary, available at http://www.9-11commission.gov/report/911Report_Exec.htm.

33. This difficulty has led to some ingenious suggestions, such as the proposal by philosopher Allen Buchanan and political scientist Robert O. Keohane for an "impartial tribunal" to determine, after the fact, the persuasiveness of the evidence on which a preventive war is based. See Buchanan and Keohane, "The Preventive Use of Force: A Cosmopolitan Institutional Proposal," *Ethics and International Affairs* 18, no. 1 (March 2004), p. 1. I am not sanguine about such ideas, perhaps because I am not sanguine about

the potential for impartiality in international institutions generally. In any event, the United States would never submit itself to such a mechanism.

34. Jean Bethke Elshtain, *Just War Against Terror: The Burden of American Power in a Violent World* (New York: Basic Books, 2003), p. 188.

35. See Matthew Barakat, "Obama Called a 'War Criminal' at D.C. Rally," *Salt Lake City Tribune*, March 20, 2010.

36. This is the subject of chapter 1 of Michael Walzer, *Arguing About War* (New Haven: Yale University Press, 2004).

37. Martin Luther, "Whether Soldiers, Too, Can Be Saved," in Theodore G. Tappert, ed., *Selected Writings of Martin Luther, 1529–1546* (Minneapolis: Fortress Press, 1967), p. 436.

38. Thomas Aquinas, *Summa Theologica*, pt. 2–2, Q. 40, trans. Fathers of the English Dominican Province (New York: Benziger Bros., 1948).

39. See, for example, the discussion in Geoffrey Parker, "Early Modern Europe," in Michael Howard, George Andreopoulos, and Mark Shulman, *The Laws of War: Constraints on Warfare in the Western World* (New Haven: Yale University Press, 1997), p. 40.

40. The requirement that any war, even in self-defense, may be undertaken only when there is a reasonable hope of success, leads to some counterintuitive results. When we read the famous account in Thucydides of the negotiations between the Athenians and the Melians, we cheer for the little island of Melos for standing up against the greater might of Athens, which plans to conquer and enslave the Melians for no greater reason than that the prestige of Athens will otherwise suffer. Thucydides, *History of the Peloponnesian War*, trans. Richard Crawley (New York: E.P. Dutton, 1920), pp. 392–401. But the just war theorist should be less certain that the Melians deserve our applause. The Melians possessed no reasonable hope of success. They were destined to lose the battle, especially once the Spartans chose not to come to their aid. Thus the slaughter that ensued, on both sides, could have been avoided, with the same essential result, by surrender.

When I made this point to students in my Just War seminar, they responded by pointing to other possible consequences of the Melians' decision to struggle: faced with an unexpectedly difficult victory, the Athenians might think twice, they suggested, before attacking the next helpless island. Well, yes. They might. Then again, they might not. Just war theory requires a more delicate as well as detailed formulation; the harm to be prevented by engaging in the violence of warfare should never be speculative. The theologian Richard Regan has proposed that war be banned unless the state undertaking the war is 90 percent certain of the truth of the factual assumptions underlying the decision to fight, including facts about the future. Regan would apply his 90-percent standard to humanitarian wars as well. See Richard J. Regan, *Just War: Principles and Cases* (Washington, DC: Catholic University of America Press, 1996), p. 52.

41. St. Thomas Aquinas, *Summa Theologica*, vol. 3, pt. 2–2, Q. 40.

42. For a particularly sharp criticism of the notion that we should treat the just war factors like a legal code, see George Weigel, "Moral Clarity in a Time of War," *First Things*, January 2003.

43. See Jean Bethke Elshtain, *Augustine and the Limits of Politics* (South Bend: Notre Dame University Press, 1998).

44. Wayne A. Meeks, *The Origins of Christian Morality: The First Two Centuries* (New Haven: Yale University Press, 1993), p. 116.

45. Augustine, *Confessions*, trans. Edward Bouverie Posey, bk. 7, xxi (27), *The Harvard Classics* (New York, Collier & Sons, 1909, cq.) p. 202.

46. Meeks, *Origins of Christian Morality*, pp. 118, 119.

47. A useful intellectual history of just war theory after its secularization is Richard Tuck, *The Rights of War and Peace: Political Thought and the International Order from Grotius to Kant* (Oxford: Oxford University Press, 1999). Professor Tuck offers, among other insights, the suggestion that the early modern philosophers wrote so much about international law because they saw in the relationships among independent sovereign states a sort of testing ground for their theories about the interactions among independent sovereign individuals.

48. Aquinas, *Summa Theologica*, vol. 3, pt. 2–2, Q. 40.

49. I owe this point to the work of John Finnis. See Finnis, "The Ethics of War and Peace in the Catholic Natural Law Tradition," in Nardin, ed., *The Ethics of War and Peace*, pp. 15, 17.

50. Augustine, *The City of God*, trans. Marcus Dods, bk. 19, ch. 7, (New York: Modern Library, 1950), p. 683.

51. The general view among scholars is that Grotius dispensed entirely with the criterion that war be waged only when the sovereign possesses the right intention. See, for example, Mohammad Taghi Karoubi, *Just or Unjust War: International Law and Unilateral Use of Armed Force by States at the Turn of 20th Century*, pp. 75–76; Mark Totten, "Using Force First: Moral Tradition and the Case for Revision," *Stanford Journal of International Law* 43, no. 1 (2007). But there are dissenters. See, for example, Christopher A. Stumpf, *The Grotian Theology of International Law: Hugo Grotius and the Moral Fundament of International Relations* (Berlin: Walter de Gruyter GmbH & Co., 2006), pp. 215–216: "The elements of the right authority, the just reason, and the appropriateness of the measures taken can be detected quite easily in Grotius' elaboration of the requisites of a just war. The requirement of the right intention, however, is less easy to identify." Indeed, the general view among

scholars is that Grotius dispensed altogether with the requirement of right intention.

52. Benjamin Franklin, "The Autobiography," in Alan Houston, ed., *Franklin: The Autobiography and Other Writings on Politics, Economics, and Virtue* (Cambridge: Cambridge University Press, 2004), p. 78.

53. One way of thinking about this is in economic terms. The question is whether there is some other good the terrorist would accept as a substitute for the act of terror that you want to prevent. When a hostage is held and threatened with death unless you do X, the substitute is obvious (assuming an honest terrorist). Give him X—money, a colleague held prisoner, whatever—and the hostage survives. Nowadays, however, much of the terror directed against Western interests is built around a complex spectrum of demands. Often it is difficult to see precisely which concessions will lead to the desired result. Moreover, if you give the terrorist what he wants, you make terror a more efficient way to gain one's ends, and others, seeing the likelihood of high returns, become more likely to engage in terrorist activity against you.

On the other hand, there is considerable evidence that raising the price of terrorism to the terrorist, so to speak, by taking precautions or by hunting down terrorists does reduce the incidence. A useful discussion of this approach is in Charles H. Anderton and John R. Carter, *Principles of Conflict Economics* (New York: Cambridge University Press, 2009), especially pp. 132–139. One might reasonably object that this approach assumes that the terrorist acts rationally. Game theory teaches that there are occasions when acting irrationally is a better strategy than acting rationally, a proposition that helps explain why there are bullies: unreasoning anger and threats can get you what you want. But if we assume that the terrorist does not act rationally, there is no obvious reason to try to give him what he wants, as we have no way of knowing whether it will make him stop.

54. See Ron Suskind, *The One Percent Doctrine: Deep Inside America's Pursuit of Its Enemies Since 9/11* (New York: Simon & Schuster, 2006), pp. 61–62 (al-Qaeda), 213 (Iraq). For a nicely nuanced effort to apply international law to the argument, see Matthew C. Waxman, "The Use of Force Against States that *Might* Have Weapons of Mass Destruction," *Michigan Journal of International Law* 31, No. 1 (Fall 2009), p. 1.

55. Roberta Wohlstetter, in her classic study *Pearl Harbor: Warning and Decision* (Stanford: Stanford University Press, 1962), points out that difference between information being present in the system and information making its way to military and political decision makers. Anyone with a serious interest in the problems with intelligence on Iraq should read her book,

with care, and should also be aware that Wohstetter's work, widely viewed as the authoritative analysis, was published two decades after the Pearl Harbor attack. Sometimes, working out exactly what went wrong takes time.

56. There remain some who insist that Saddam Hussein did indeed possess weapons of mass destruction, but that they were moved to Syria before the war began. A former Iraqi Air Force general and a former Syrian intelligence officer are among them. See Georges Sada, *Saddam's Secrets: How an Iraqi General Defied and Survived Saddam Hussein* (Brentwood, TN: Integrity Publishers, 2006). President Bush's top political adviser, Karl Rove, still believes this, and has recently lamented that the Bush Administration did not draw the public's attention to the evidence in support of these claims. See Karl Rove, *Courage and Consequence: My Life as a Conservative in the Fight* (New York: Threshold Editions, 2010).

Certainly one cannot say that this did not occur. But one would expect some further evidence to have turned up by now, either in documentary form or from the interrogations of top Iraqi officials. So far, no such evidence has been publicly released. The Iraq Study Commission did not entirely rule out the possibility that the weapons, if they existed, had been moved, but the report's language on this point was, to say the least, dubitante. See *Comprehensive Report of the Special Advisor to the Director of Central Intelligence on Iraq's Weapons of Mass Destruction*, released September 30, 2004, available at https://www.cia.gov/library/reports/general-reports-1/iraq_wmd_2004/index.html.

Ironically, as this book was going to press, the cache of secret Iraqi documents released by WikiLeaks suggested that there may actually have been large stores of weapons of mass destruction, principally chemical, that had been preserved by Saddam Hussein's regime, even though reported destroyed. See Noah Shachtman, "WikiLeaks Show WMD Hunt Continued in Iraq—With Surprising Results," *Wired* (online), http://www.wired.com/dangerroom/2010/10/wikileaks-show-wmd-hunt-continued-in-iraq-with-surprising-results/.

57. In his initial blog response, Sunstein conceded that Cheney "made a good deal of sense" in arguing that the United States should act on even a 1 percent possibility that al-Qaeda would obtain a nuclear weapon and deploy it against this country. He added, "The problem, of course, is that a firm response might impose costs and create risks of its own." See http://uchicagolaw.typepad.com/faculty/2006/06/the_one_percent.html.

Sunstein then turned his argument into a fascinating book, where he pointed out the same problem that decision theorists always tend to have with overly simple models like the 1-percent rule and the precautionary principle: namely, a failure to consider the cost of the action that will be taken to avoid the potential harm; and, for that matter, a failure to apply to the proposed action the same principle of caution. See Cass Sunstein, *Worst-Case Scenarios* (Cambridge: Harvard University Press, 2009). The warning he sets forth is throughout the book. The particular discussion of Cheney, which in the book is only background for the larger argument, is at pp. 24–27.

58. Another version of this comment comes from a longtime director of Central Intelligence: "Intelligence, unlike many other professions, is not a business in which a few major or even small mistakes in the actual practice of the craft can be chalked up with a smile and wisecracks, such as 'Back to the old drawing board.' It has this in common with the military profession." Allen W. Dulles, *The Craft of Intelligence* (Guilford, CT: Lyons Press, 2006) (first published 1963), p. 174.

59. Sunstein, *Worst-Case Scenarios,* especially chapter 3.

60. See Schelling, *Arms and Influence* (Boulder, CO: ABC-Clio, 1977) (first published 1966), p. 94.

61. Consequences are not everything. I have written earlier, and still believe, that although the invasion of Grenada was arguably just under a traditional understanding of the ethics of war, the invasion of Panama, with its massive destruction aimed at the arrest of one man, clearly was not. See Stephen L. Carter, *God's Name in Vain: The Wrongs and Rights of Religion in Politics* (New York: Basic Books, 2000), p. 134.

62. The definitive account (so far) of why the war went so well for America and its allies is John Keegan, *The Iraq War* (New York: Random House, 2004). As Keegan notes, the war was no walkover. The Iraqis fought back hard. Nevertheless, Keegan points out that no seriously contested war had ended so swiftly since the second half of the nineteenth century. He emphasizes training, flexibility, and technology as the keys to the victory.

63. Former intelligence officers have told journalists that Porter Goss, who headed the Central Intelligence Agency for part of President George W. Bush's administration, purged senior staff who disagreed with him. Many believed that he considered it the Agency's duty to provide intelligence confirming what the White House wanted confirmed. See, for example, the account in Tim Weiner, *Legacy of Ashes: The History of the CIA* (New York: Random House, 2007), especially pp. 580–583. As Weiner's own research makes clear, alas, these stories, if true, would hardly distinguish the Bush Administration from any other, because, says Weiner, for much of its history, the Agency has seen its principal mission as pleasing the White House, especially under Presidents Kennedy, Johnson, and Reagan.

64. John Keegan, *Intelligence in War: The Value—and Limitations—of What the Military Can Learn About the Enemy* (New York: Alfred A. Knopf, 2003)

65. Alissa J. Rubin and Mark Mazzetti, "Afghan Base Hit by Attack Has Pivotal Role in Conflict," *New York Times,* December 31, 2009.

66. Greg Miller, "Confusion Grows over How Bomber Infiltrated CIA Base in Afghanistan," *Los Angeles Times,* January 6, 2010.

67. Weiner, *Legacy of Ashes,* p. 450.

68. See Robert Baer, *See No Evil: The True Story of a Ground Soldier in the CIA's War on Terrorism* (New York: Crown Books, 2002), pp. 66–68.

69. Weiner, *Legacy of Ashes,* pp. 452–453.

70. David Vessel, "Conducting Successful Interrogations," *FBI Law Enforcement Bulletin,* October 1998.

71. Warren D. Holmes, *Criminal Interrogation: A Modern Format for Interrogating Criminal Suspects Based on the Intellectual Approach* (Springfield, Illinois: Charles C. Thomas, 2002), p. xi.

72. See Arthur S. Aubry Jr. and Rudolph R. Caputo, *Criminal Interrogation* 3d. ed. (Springfield, IL: Charles C. Thomas, 1980), p. 210.

73. Vessel, "Conducting Successful Interrogations."

74. Aubry and Caputo, *Criminal Interrogation,* pp. 114–118.

75. Vessel, "Conducting Successful Interrogations."

76. See the discussions in Walzer, "Emergency Ethics," in his *Arguing About War,* p. 33, and Walzer, *Just and Unjust War* (New York: Basic Books, 2006) pp. 251–68. I discuss the problem of emergency in detail in Part II.

77. Kahn, *Sacred Violence,* p. 80.

78. Elaine Scarry, *The Body in Pain: The Making and Unmaking of the World* (New York: Oxford University Press, 1985), p. 61.

79. A useful summary of the details of recent allegations of torture against the United States government, although its prose is occasionally overheated, is Laurel E. Fletcher and Eric Stover, *The Guantanamo Effect: Exposing the Consequences of U.S. Detention and Interrogation Practices* (Berkeley: University of California, 2009). The research should be chilling to any reader, no matter his or her predisposition on the various controversies arising from the War on Terror. The reader should be cautioned, however, that the book documents allegations. This may matter because al-Qaeda training manuals advise operatives that, if captured, they should always allege torture. On the other hand, not everything can be an invention, and the authors produce a useful set of documents that lay out what American interrogators were permitted to do.

For a thoughtful and stirring, if ultimately unsatisfying, argument on behalf of the use of personal narrative to understand violence generally, and torture in particular, see Irene Matthews, "Translating/Transgressing/Torture . . ." in Marguerite Waller and Jennifer Rycenga, eds., *Frontline Feminisms: Women, War, and Resistance* (New York: Routledge, 2001), p. 83.

80. See Scarry, *The Body in Pain,* pp. 45–51.

81. John Langbein, "The Legal History of Torture," in Sanford Levinson, ed., *Torture: A Collection* (New York: Oxford University Press, 2004), p. 101.

82. Treatises on interrogation urge the opposite, and one wishes their advice were more closely heeded by police departments. See, for example, Aubry and Caputo, *Criminal Interrogation,* p. xii: "Every detail of a man's confession must be checked and rechecked by investigation and reinvestigation."

83. Weiner, *Legacy of Ashes,* pp. 394–396.

84. Scarry, *The Body in Pain,* p. 28.

85. Elaine Scarry, "Five Errors in the Reasoning of Alan Dershowitz," in Levinson, ed., *Torture: A Collection,* p. 281.

86. Richard Posner, "Torture, Terrorism, and Interrogation," in Levinson, ed., *Torture: A Collection,* p. 292.

87. From what I can tell, Professor Dershowitz's argument has been more talked about than read. For his own detailed presentation, see Alan M. Dershowitz, *Why Terrorism Works: Understanding the Threat, Responding to the Challenge* (New Haven: Yale University Press, 2002), passim, but especially chapter 4. For his response to his critics, see Dershowitz, "Tortured Reasoning," in Levinson, ed., *Torture: A Collection,* p. 257. The controversy became one of public moment following Professor Dershowitz's publication of what was actually quite a thoughtful op-ed essay during the run-up to the 2008 presidential campaign. See Alan Dershowitz, "Democrats and Waterboarding," *Wall Street Journal,* November 7, 2007.

88. Elaine Scarry, "Five Errors in the Reasoning of Alan Dershowitz," in Levinson, ed., *Torture: A Collection,* p. 281.

89. Jean Bethke Elshtain, "Reflection on the Problem of 'Dirty Hands,'" in Levinson, ed., *Torture: A Collection,* pp. 77, 83. We might look similarly askance at the otherwise plausible suggestion that we develop a set of legitimating rules to create a sort of due process prior to attempting to assassinate terrorist leaders. See, for example, Richard Murphy and Afsheen John Radsan, "Due Process and Targeted Killing of Terrorists," *Cardozo Law Review* 31 (2009), p. 405.

90. See Guido Calabresi, *Ideals, Beliefs, Attitudes, and the Law: Private Law Perspectives on a Public Law Problem* (Syracuse, NY: Syracuse University Press, 1985), p. 167, n. 240 (discussing Charles Black, "Mr. Justice Black, the Supreme Court, and the Bill of Rights," *Harper's Magazine,* February 1961, p. 63).

91. Posner, "Torture, Terrorism, and Interrogation" in Levinson, ed., *Torture: A Collection,* p. 294.

92. U.S. Department of Justice, press release, August 24, 2009.

93. See, for example, Greg Miller "Obama Preserves Renditions as Counter-terrorism tool," *Los Angeles Times,* February 1, 2009.

94. I do not mean to suggest that nobody noticed. The American Civil Liberties Union issued several scathing press releases, for instance. The *New York Times* ran a front-page story on Obama's decision to allow rendition to continue. See David Johnston, "U.S. Says Rendition to Continue, but with More Oversight," *New York Times,* August 24, 2009. *Mother Jones* accused the Obama Administration of a cover-up of continuing torture. See Nick Baumann, "Obama Still Fighting to Cover Up Rendition-to-Torture," *Mother Jones,* October 28, 2009. Even Al-Jazeera did a major feature. See "Obama to Continue 'Renditions,'" August 25, 2009, available in English at http://english.aljazeera.net/news/americas/2009/08/200982515611934234.html. The campuses of America, however, remained uncharacteristically silent.

95. Article 17 states: "No physical or mental torture, nor any other form of coercion, may be inflicted on prisoners of war to secure from them information of any kind whatever. Prisoners of war who refuse to answer may not be threatened, insulted, or exposed to unpleasant or disadvantageous treatment of any kind." If prisoners who answer questions get better accommodations than prisoners who refuse, then the ones who refuse are suffering "disadvantageous treatment." Although this proposition seems to some of us quite obvious, it has by no means gained widespread acceptance.

96. See David S. Cloud and Julian E. Barnes, "U.S. May Expand Use of Its Prison in Afghanistan," *Los Angeles Times,* March 21, 2010.

97. See Eric Schmitt, "U.S. to Expand Detainee Review in Afghan Prison," *New York Times,* September 12, 2009. The proposition that the Bagram prison population may be increased as other facilities shut down is somewhat buried, down in the third paragraph from the end of the article: "Officials say the importance of Bagram as a holding site for terrorism suspects captured outside Afghanistan and Iraq has risen under the Obama administration, which barred the Central Intelligence Agency from using its secret prisons for long-term detention and ordered the military prison at Guantánamo closed within a year."

98. See David S. Cloud and Julian E. Barnes, "U.S. May Expand Use of Its Prison in Afghanistan," *Los Angeles Times,* March 21, 2010. (See note 96.)

99. See, for example, the discussion in Alan B. Krueger, *What Makes a Terrorist: Economics and the Roots of Terrorism* (Princeton: Princeton University Press, 2007), especially chapter 1.

100. Anderton and Carter, *Principles of Conflict Economics,* chapter 8.

101. Schelling, *Arms and Influence,* p. 2.

102. See David Day, *Conquest: How Societies Overwhelm Others* (New York: Oxford University Press, 2008), especially the later chapters.

103. Barbara Ward, *Nationalism and Ideology* (New York: Norton, 1966), chapter 8, and passim. Ward's lectures were an effort to understand what would bind people into nations once nationalism died as a force. She gave enormous credence to the power of ideas, especially when melded with a sense of history. Her vision was a bit Hegelian for my taste: she saw great conflicts leading to fresh syntheses, which in turn found a place in the narratives people used to define themselves. Ward also worried that too much faith in technology, or in economics or in other means of using learning to bind us together, would distract from the actual effort of building the structures of peace. In this she was undoubtedly correct.

104. This distinction, introduced in Walzer's book *Just and Unjust Wars*, pp. 251–268, and refined in his more recent essay "Emergency Ethics," republished in his monograph *Arguing About War*, p. 33, proposes a greater range of moral possibilities when the community faces extinction.

II. NO EQUIVALENCE

1. Although at present the United States has disclosed no plans to do so, the Reaper could in theory be armed with a single small nuclear warhead. The nuclear warhead once carried by the Tomahawk missile weighed under 300 pounds, but it is not clear how easily it could be adapted for a drone. Although the United States has tested nuclear weapons weighing in the vicinity of 100 pounds, the lightest nuclear weapon the nation has ever placed in widespread deployment was evidently the MK-57, which weighed about 500 pounds, and had an explosive force of under 20 kilotons. The mainstay of the current American nuclear arsenal is the B-61, Mod 11, which weighs about 1,200 pounds. The maximum yield of the B-61 is classified, but is thought to be about 340 kilotons. Megaton weapons—the stuff of the titanic city-destroying explosions seen in movies—weigh many thousands of pounds, and could not be carried by any remote-controlled aircraft currently in operation, whether in the American or any other arsenal. Consistent rumors have claimed that Israel is developing drones capable of delivering nuclear warheads, but so far no public evidence has been adduced. Israel recently introduced its largest drone, the Eitan, capable of delivering a payload weighing a ton. In theory, this would be sufficient to deliver a small (kiloton-range) nuclear warhead.

Although there are no known plans for the United States to develop a

UAV capable of carrying a large nuclear warhead, the Obama Administration is permitting the Air Force to press ahead with plans to create a drone that is nuclear-powered, and can therefore stay aloft indefinitely.

2. John Finnis, "The Ethics of War and Peace in the Catholic Natural Law Tradition," in Terry Nardin, ed., *The Ethics of War and Peace: Religious and Secular Perspectives* (Princeton: Princeton University Press, 1996), pp. 15, 26 (emphasis in original).

3. Walzer, *Just and Unjust Wars*, pp. 138–145.

4. George Orwell, "Looking Back on the Spanish War," in *George Orwell, A Collection of Essays* (San Diego: Harvest, 1981) (reprint; first published 1946), pp. 188, 194. Walzer, in the pages just cited, also discusses the Orwell essay.

5. At the beginning of any American combat operation, rules of engagement are distributed to all service members participating. The rules of engagement for Operation Desert Storm (the ground stage of the 1991 Gulf War) provided as follows: "Do not engage anyone who has surrendered, is out of battle due to sickness or wounds, is shipwrecked, or is an aircrew member descending by parachute from a disabled aircraft." These restrictions track the Geneva Conventions. Note that they do not prohibit engaging— nor does the Law of Armed Combat generally prohibit—enemy soldiers who are retreating. Under both international law and the ethics of war, retreat and surrender are entirely different things.

6. An excellent account of the debate, and of many of the attacks, is Jane Mayer, "The Predator War," *New Yorker*, October 26, 2009.

7. I say "de facto" because the Administration, at this writing, has been reluctant to support its use of drone attacks on pure self-defense grounds, preferring to rely on United Nations authorizations. See Kenneth Anderson, "Targeted Killing in U.S. Counterterrorism Strategy and Law," working paper, May 11, 2009. This is surely, at best, justification rather than explanation. Were the Security Council suddenly to revoke the resolutions on which the Administration relies, it is difficult to imagine that the drone attacks would stop.

8. See, for example, the account in "The Rise of the Pilotless Planes," *The Week*, April 9, 2009.

9. Augustine, "To Count Boniface," in Arthur F. Holmes, ed., *War and Christian Ethics: Classic and Contemporary Readings on the Morality of War* (Great Rapids: Baker Books, 1975), p. 63.

10. Walzer, *Just and Unjust Wars*, p. 36.

11. See John Keegan, *The Face of Battle* (New York: Penguin, 1976), pp. 320–325, and passim.

12. In international law, the usual way out of this mess is for one side to declare that the other side's forces are themselves unjust combatants; that is, they do not qualify for the status of belligerents under the practices of war. This was the attitude of General Ulysses S. Grant at Fort Donelson, the battle that was the turning point in the western theater of the Civil War and, possibly, of the war itself. When the defenders of Fort Donelson sought to negotiate surrender terms, Grant refused. They were rebels, he said, and therefore not belligerents with rights of negotiation under the laws of war. The astonished Confederate general then surrendered unconditionally, although chastising Grant for his "ungenerous and unchivalrous" attitude. See John Keegan, *The Civil War* (New York: Knopf, 2009), pp. 126–128. Similarly, many international lawyers (including, particularly, those who happen to be employed by the United States government) argue that terrorists, as well as the irregulars fighting on behalf of the Taliban, are unlawful combatants, meaning that they have no legal right to bear arms at all. They lack what are known as belligerent rights. Belligerent rights are necessary to conduct lawful war.

The international lawyer might argue, and the ethicist would agree, that terrorists are not, for instance, fighting on behalf of a sovereign. (Remember, the import of the traditional requirement that war be legally declared is that one has gone to war for the prince and not a pirate or brigand.) They are not fighting in uniform or trying to spare civilians. (More on this problem below.) In short, they do not meet the tests we have already seen for fighting a just war and, under international law, meet none of the tests for lawful belligerence. Consequently, whatever they do in battle, whether in Afghanistan or here, is equally unlawful.

Well, maybe. Bear in mind, however, that it is precisely this view that those on the other side are fighting lawlessly that leads to the conclusion that if they happen to be captured they are not protected by the Geneva Conventions. Besides, even if this view of international law is correct, I doubt it makes much political difference. Politicians who rush to condemn the attacks on our forces are not worrying themselves about the niceties of international law. And to the ethicist, concerned not about legal and illegal but about right and wrong, the question of equivalence is still worth pursuing. Indeed, just war theory may offer a more intellectually satisfying answer than international law to the problem.

13. Kahn, *Sacred Violence*, p. 14. For a thoughtful effort to find a balance between, on the one hand, the harm that terrorists might do and, on the other, the amount of violence we should expend in defending ourselves, see Michael Ignatieff, *The Lesser Evil: Political Ethics in an Age of Terror* (Princeton, NJ: Princeton University Press, 2004).

14. See, for example, Andrew Sola, "The Enlightened Grunt? Invincible Ignorance in the Just War Tradition," *Journal of Military Ethics* 8 (2009), p. 48.

15. Although the *ad bellum–in bello* distinction possesses a clear logic, there is a certain peculiarity, as Richard Norman has pointed out, in holding that Germany was wrong to fight but its soldiers had the right to kill. See Norman, *Ethics, Killing, and War,* pp. 166–167.

16. Jeff McMahan, *Killing in War* (New York: Oxford University Press, 2009).

17. See, for example, Richard Overy, *Why the Allies Won* (New York: Norton, 1996), particularly chapter 9. Says Overy (p. 286): "The belief that their cause was on the side of progress on world history gave a genuine moral certainty to the Allies, which the Axis populations largely lacked. Popular commitment to the war in the aggressor states was half-hearted and morally ambiguous. In the Allied communities, on the other hand, there was a powerful crusading rejection of the forces of fascist darkness."

18. See Joseph T. Glatthaar, *Forged in Battle: The Civil War Alliance of Black Soldiers and White Officers* (Baton Rouge: Louisiana State University Press, 2000), pp. 155–156.

19. See Keegan, *The Iraq War,* pp. 1–8.

20. Walzer, *Just and Unjust Wars,* p. 31.

21. See, for example, Andrew Sola, "The Enlightened Grunt? Invincible Ignorance in the Just War Tradition." See also Helene Ingierd and Henrik Syse, "Responsibility and Culpability in War," *Journal of Military Ethics* 4, no. 2 (2005), p. 85. For an argument that the access of American forces to greater sources of information adds to the moral culpability of at least most officers in the particular case of the Iraq War, see J. Joseph Miller, "*Jus ad bellum* and an Officer's Moral Obligations: Invincible Ignorance, the Constitution, and Iraq," *Social Theory and Practice* 40, no. 4 (October 2004), p. 457. For a strong argument the other way—that is, in favor of the tradition of moral equivalence—see Dan Zupan, "The Logic of Community, Ignorance, and the Presumption of Moral Equality: A Soldier's Story," *Journal of Military Ethics* 6, no. 1 (2007), p. 41.

22. See David Rodin, *War and Self-Defense* (Oxford: Oxford University Press, 2002), especially pp. 166–172.

23. Ibid., p. 170. This model is not as effective as it may appear. It ignores the Bayesian notion of the interplay between statistical inference and the state of background knowledge of the observer. For the model to work, "rightness" and "wrongness" must be randomly distributed across possible sides in a war. But suppose they are not. Suppose the soldier is asked to fight for a country that he believes, based on experience, is almost always correct

in its assessment of the justice of any given war. Now he has a reason to do battle even if he himself is not certain of the rightness of the war. And, at the other extreme, a soldier may be asked to fight for a country he believes is almost always incorrect. He should obviously not fight. The soldier to whom Rodin's model applies, then, is the soldier who satisfied two criteria: (1) he himself is not certain of the justice of the war, and (2) his own knowledge and experience provide no basis on which to judge whether his government as a general matter is able to make accurate assessments of the justice of wars. I suspect that in the current era, few American soldiers believe that criterion (2) is satisfied.

24. McMahan, *Killing in War,* p. 154.

25. Letter, Oliver Wendell Holmes Jr. to Frederick Pollock, February 1, 1920, reprinted in Richard A. Posner, ed., *The Essential Holmes: Selections from the Letters, Speeches, Judicial Opinions, and Other Writings of Oliver Wendell Holmes, Jr.* (Chicago: University of Chicago Press, 1992), p. 102. The topic of the letter was the nature of war, and Holmes, who claimed to abhor war, also offered the ultimate realist analysis of it: "[B]etween two groups that want to make inconsistent kinds of world I see no remedy except force." He added: "[E]very society rests on the death of men." Ibid., p. 103.

26. *Ex parte Quirin,* 317 U.S. 1, 31 (1942): "Lawful combatants are subject to capture and detention as prisoners of war by opposing military forces. Unlawful combatants are likewise subject to capture and detention, but in addition they are subject to trial and punishment by military tribunals for acts which render their belligerency unlawful."

The historian Louis Fisher has argued persuasively that the decision to use military tribunals to try saboteurs was taken principally for political reasons. See Louis Fisher, *Nazi Saboteurs on Trial: A Military Tribunal and American Law,* 2d. ed. (Lawrence: University of Kansas Press, 2005).

27. I should add that McMahan's fine book *Killing in War* offers the argument in far more nuanced form. And he does not suggest this theory as a defense of American military activities in the Terror War.

28. Deborah Madsen, *American Exceptionalism* (Edinburgh: Edinburgh University Press, 1998).

29. See, for example, the discussion in Steven R. David, "Israel's Policy of Targeted Killing," *Ethics and International Affairs* 17 (2003), p. 111.

30. An account of the decline of assassination (along with sabotage) is in John Keegan, *War and Our World* (New York: Knopf, 2001).

31. See the discussion in John Keegan, *The Mask of Command* (New York: Penguin, 1987), particularly his comparison of Alexander and Wellington in part 2.

32. Among the many sources for this proposition, one of the most eloquent, almost poetic, accounts may be found in Norbert Elias, *The Civilizing Process: Sociogenetic and Psychogenetic Investigations,* trans. Edmund Jephcott, (Oxford: Blackwell, rev. ed., 2000), pp. 162–172. Of course, as the philosopher Charles Taylor has pointed out, one consequence of the celebration of the warrior ethic, all through history, has been to give a "subordinate and largely ancillary role to women." Charles Taylor, *The Sources of the Self: The Making of the Modern Identity* (Cambridge: Harvard University Press, 1989), p. 100.

33. There is an unsophisticated argument available to the effect that assassination is murder, and is therefore banned. I have even seen it in print, although I will not embarrass anyone by saying where. Note that the argument is fallacious, in that it assumes the conclusion: the goal is to figure out *whether* assassination is murder.

34. Whitley R. P. Kaufman, "Rethinking the Ban on Assassination: Just War Principles in the Age of Terror," in Michael W. Brough, John W. Lango, and Harry Van der Linden, eds., *Rethinking the Just War Tradition* (Albany: State University of New York Press, 2007), pp. 171, 180.

35. See the discussion in Jeff McMahan, "Realism, Morality, and War," in Nardin, ed., *The Ethics of War and Peace,* p. 78. See in particular p. 90: "The case in which it is most obviously permissible intentionally to attack or kill a morally noninnocent noncombatant in war is that in which the assassination of a political leader who bears moral responsibility for his country's unjust aggression would be sufficient to stop that aggression, thereby eliminating the need to kill a large number of that country's soldiers."

36. See, for example, Kaufman, "Rethinking the Ban on Assassination"; Gross, "Self-defense against Terrorism—What Does It Mean? The Israeli Perspective," *Journal of Military Ethics* 1, no. 2 (July 2002), p. 91; and Casper Weinberger, "When Can We Target the Leaders?" *Strategic Review* (Spring 2001), p. 21.

37. Available at http://www.state.gov/s/l/releases/remarks/139119.htm.

38. Unless there is a classified addition, the relevant executive orders—numbers 11905 (Ford), 12036 (Carter), and 12333 (Reagan)—all have effectively similar (and similarly vague) language. Thus, Reagan's executive order reads: "No person employed by or acting on behalf of the United States Government shall engage in, or conspire to engage in, assassination." Carter's was identical; Ford's lacked the reference to persons acting on behalf of the United States. None of the orders define their terms.

39. This point was made immediately after the speech by, among others, Anthony Dworkin of the European Council on Foreign Relations. See his commentary at http://www.crimesofwar.org/news-obama2.html.

40. See Scott Shane, "U.S. Approves Targeted Killing of American Cleric," *New York Times,* April 6, 2010.

41. For Lincoln's assertion of his "broader powers," see, for example, William Lee Miller, *President Lincoln: The Duty of a Statesman* (New York: Random House, 2008), p. 101. Lincoln used the phrase to justify the extraordinary measures he took to defend Washington from invasion in the early days of the Civil War. I choose Miller's book almost at random; most Lincoln biographers quote the same language.

42. See Sandburg, *Abraham Lincoln: The Prairie Years and the War Years,* p. 239.

43. M. Tullius Cicero, *De Officiis,* bk. 3, sec. 107, in Walter Miller, ed., *De Officiis. With an English Translation* (Cambridge: Harvard University Press, 1913). One should note that although Cicero argued that pirates lacked all moral and legal standing, he did not believe they lacked all morality. On the contrary, Cicero offered a version of an argument that would come to be associated with Augustine, that, among themselves, "robbers even have a code of laws to observe and obey." Ibid., bk. 2, sec. 40.

44. The Bush Administration's resurrection of the term *hostis humani generis* has caused some confusion. There is a distinction, occasionally still mentioned in international law but dating back to Roman law, between an enemy who is *hostis* and an enemy who is *inimicus. Hostis* denotes a "public" enemy, usually one who is an enemy because of his status, as a soldier or even a subject of an enemy state. *Inimicus* denotes a private enemy, who wants to do someone harm because of personal enmity. The point is that the enemy who is *hostis* is not presumed to have any enmity, but is merely doing his duty, unlike the enemy who is *inimicus.* Of the many sources on this point, a classic text that the reader will find particularly clear and accessible is *Halleck's International Law,* vol. 2 (4th ed., London: Kegan, Paul, Trench, Trubner & Co., 1908), chapter 19.

45. True, the pirate and the brigand fought for booty and plunder, too, but this was not the principal distinction, given that the poorly paid foot soldiers of the sovereign often fought for the same thing.

46. To be sure, the border between a major and a minor terror incident is not an easy one to sketch. As terrorism expert Heather Hurlburt has pointed out, we should not assume that "lethality" and "societal disruption" will run in tandem. She adds: "I don't think there is a threshold. There's no number [of casualties] you can pick out. It's much more about how the government responds and how non-government entities respond, and how different societal actors respond." "Roundtable: America 2021: The Military and the World," *Democracy: A Journal of Ideas* (Summer 2010), pp. 15, 21.

47. For an argument that this blurring of the roles of combatant and

noncombatant may be an inevitable consequence of the rise of various re-
sistance movements in the decades after the Second World War, see George
J. Andreopoulos, "The Age of National Liberation Movements," in Howard,
Andreopoulos, and Shulman, p. 191.

48. Judith Jarvis Thomson, "Self-Defense," *Philosophy and Public Affairs*
20 (Fall 1991), p. 297.

49. Augustine, "To Count Boniface," in Holmes, ed., *War and Christian
Ethics*, p. 63.

50. See Sanford H. Kadish, "Respect for Life and Regard for Rights in
the Criminal Law," *California Law Review* 64 (July 1976), pp. 871, 878–881.

51. See the discussion in George P. Fletcher and Jens David Ohlin, *Defending Humanity: When Force Is Justified and Why* (New York: Oxford University Press, 2008).

52. Thomson, "Self-Defense," p. 293.

53. For an argument that it is nevertheless impermissible to kill a by-
stander, see Larry Alexander, "Self-Defense, Justification, and Excuse," *Philosophy and Public Affairs* 22 (1993) Professor Alexander's argument depends
on the distinction, unknown to everyday conversation but crucially important in philosophy and law, between "justification" and "excuse." Loosely
speaking, an act that is justified leaves the actor morally blameless. An act
that is excused means that the actor has indeed committed a morally blame-
ful act, but that, under the circumstances (to borrow from theology rather
than philosophy), the act is forgiven. One way of conceptualizing the difference is to think of acts that are justified as acts we might encourage, even
when they are violent; whereas acts that are excused we might allow but dis-
courage. See, for example, the discussion in Claire O. Finkelstein, "Self-
Defense as a Rational Excuse," *University of Pittsburgh Law Review* 57 (1996),
p. 621.

54. A similar but more sophisticated argument, aimed at Allied tactics
during World War II, and taking the traditional view of Catholic natural law
thinking, is John C. Ford, S. J., "The Morality of Obliteration Bombing," in
Richard B. Miller, ed., *War in the Twentieth Century: Sources in Theological Ethics*
(Louisville: Westminster/John Knox Press, 1992), p. 138. The essay was originally published in 1944.

55. One might of course decide that the time has come to update Augustine to take into account the complexities of our world. The foremost
thinker on this point is Jean Bethke Elshtain. See especially her books *Just
War Against Terror* and *Augustine and the Limits of Politics*.

56. Anthony T. Kronman, *Education's End: Why Our Colleges and Universities
Have Given Up on the Meaning of Life* (New Haven: Yale University Press,
2007), p. 77.

57. See Talal Asad, *On Suicide Bombing* (New York: Columbia University Press, 2007).

58. As Paul Kahn has pointed out, sacrifice is central the idea of citizenship—not only in war but in the living of a common life. See Kahn, *Sacred Violence*, especially chapter 4. On the sacrifice of war, see also pp. 150–153, and passim.

59. Asad, *On Suicide Bombing*, p. 63.

60. Augustine, "Contra Faustum," trans. Richard Stothert, book XXII, para. 74, in Philip Schaff, ed., *Nicene and Post-Nicene Fathers,* Vol. 4. (Buffalo, NY: Christian Literature Publishing Co., 1887), p. 301.

61. The philosopher Nicholas Fotion, commenting on the tendency of the guerilla to blur the traditional definition of who is a legitimate target and who is innocent, has this to say: "It is as if the narrowing of meaning takes place in order to make palatable the maiming and killing of those whom the rebels have chosen to maim and kill." Nicholas Fotion, *War and Ethics: A New Just War Theory* (London: Continuum, 2007), p. 123.

62. Some studies suggest that levels of religious belief in the armed forces are higher than in the public at large. See, for example, the data reported in Peter D. Feaver and Richard H. Kohn, "The Gap: Soldiers, Civilians, and their Mutual Misunderstanding," *National Interest,* Fall 2000, p. 29. (The Feaver and Kohn data are only for military officers, not enlisted.) There are polling data to the contrary (see, for example, the survey summarized at http://militarytimes.com/projects/polls/2007activepoll_religion.php), but the wording of the questions might have influenced the results.

63. The proposed Protocol I of the Geneva Convention, adopted in 1977 but never ratified by the United States, would in certain circumstances extend the protections of the Conventions to those who do not fight in uniform. For reasons stated below, I think the United States is correct not to endorse it.

64. Asad, *On Suicide Bombing*, p. 67.

65. Fotion, *War and Ethics,* p. 128. Fotion, a philosopher, offers the view that just war theory is underused. I think this is half correct. I agree with the theologian Stanley Hauerwas that just war theory is actually overused, so much talked about that it has become simply another set of legalist hoops for a self-interested state to jump through on its way to doing what it intends to do anyway. Michael Walzer has expressed the view that there is progress in the fact that everyone at least talks about just and unjust wars, whatever errors they may make. I share this view, which is why I think Fotion half correct.

66. *Army Field Manual,* para. 25.

67. Ibid., paras. 39, 40.

68. Ibid., para. 43.

69. Terry Nardin has put the point nicely: "Implicit in the idea of atrocity is the principle that innocent people should not be deliberately killed or abused." Terry Nardin, "International Political Theory," in Scott Burchill et al., eds., *Theories of International Relations*, 4th ed. (New York: Palgrave Mac-Millan, 2009), pp. 284, 290.

70. To qualify for combatant status under Protocol I, the guerilla fighter would have to carry weapons openly immediately before, and also during, an engagement. One immediately spots the bizarre asymmetry. A soldier in uniform may be targeted in war without regard to whether he is, at that moment, carrying a weapon. Under Protocol I, however, the guerilas would be indistinguishable from civilians until they chose to display their arms, and could melt invisibly into a crowd of noncombatants immediately after.

71. McMahan, *Killing in War*, p. 30.

72. A useful history of the efforts to assess guerrilla activity (including the question of wearing uniforms) through the lens of the laws of war is George J. Andreopoulos, "The Age of National Liberation Movements," in *The Laws of War*, p. 191.

73. As Alfred-Maurice de Zayas has pointed out, a guerilla movement often benefits from provoking the other side to attack civilians, and might therefore be more likely to hide among them: "[T]heir goal of revolutionizing the civilian population becomes easier to achieve if numerous civilian victims result from a State's anti-guerilla measures." Alfred M. de Zayas, "Combatants" in *Encyclopedia of International Law*, vol. 1 (Amsterdam: Elsevier, 1992), p. 670.

74. See Zayas, "Combatants," p. 668.

75. The argument to the contrary, which admittedly has much currency among international lawyers, is that even those who have not fought in uniform are protected by Article 3 of the Fourth Geneva Convention, which protects "Persons taking no active part in the hostilities, including members of armed forces who have laid down their arms" once they have fallen into the hands of a warring power. The key argument is over whether those who do not fight in uniform are "members of armed forces" in the first place. If they are, then they are in any case lawful combatants. The other exception is this, from Article 4: "Nationals of a State which is not bound by the Convention are not protected by it." Note that the protection depends on nationality, meaning that one cannot decide that the provision does not apply merely by pointing out that the captive is a member of a group that itself is fighting outside the Geneva Conventions, as long as he is a national of a state that is within them.

76. Claude Pilloud et al., International Committee of the Red Cross, *Commentary for International Committee of the Red Cross on the Additional Protocols of 8 June 1997 to the Geneva Conventions of 12 August 1949* (1987).

77. Bacque's central error seems to be his assumption that the category of DEF, for "disarmed enemy forces" (which he says, incorrectly, was created by Eisenhower), was designed in order to classify the captured soldiers as something other than enemy combatants protected by the Geneva Conventions, so that they might freely be mistreated. According to the historian Earl Zimke, however, the DEF category was actually created in order to assure "an early and rapid disbandment of the German forces." Earl F. Zimke, book review, *Journal of American History* 80, no. 4 (March, 1994), p. 1526. See generally the essays in Gunter Bischof and Stephen E. Ambrose, eds., *Eisenhower and the German POWs: Facts Against Falsehood* (Baton Rouge: Louisiana State University Press, 1992).

78. See, for example, Albert E. Cowdrey, "A Question of Numbers," in Bischof and Ambrose, *Eisenhower and the German POWs*, p. 78; and Rüdiger Overmans, "German Historiography, the War Losses, and the Prisoners of War," in Bischof and Ambrose, p. 127.

79. Cowdrey, "A Question of Numbers," p. 92. Overmans, after careful research into primary German sources, concludes that "the maximum possible number of casualties in Western Allied hands is in the ten thousands—but not 800,000 or a million." Overmans, "German Historiography, the War Losses, and the Prisoners of War," p. 167.

80. Cowdrey, "A Question of Numbers," p. 92.

81. Another tactic used on German prisoners of war, arguably a less objectionable one, was to force thousands to enroll in a reeducation program that aimed at turning them into Western-style liberal democrats. See Ron Robin, *The Barbed-Wire College: Reeducating German POWs in the United States During World War II* (Princeton: Princeton University Press, 1995). A principal purpose of this process, says Robin, was "the transformation of the German enemy into a made-to-order ally," p. 29. The intention of the program was in most ways admirable, but it was likely illegal under the Geneva Conventions, which prohibit exposing prisoners to propaganda. (Ironically, the prisoners were taught that the American political spectrum was relatively narrow, and that we tended to emphasize our similarities rather than our differences. See pp. 83–86 and passim. Would that it were so.)

82. See, for example, the discussion in Gavin Daws, *Prisoners of the Japanese: POWs of World War II in the Pacific* (New York: William Morrow, 1994). It is worth nothing that Daws is no Japan-basher. On the contrary, he condemns at some length the racism he believes motivated much of America's war policy in the Pacific Theater.

83. Orwell, "Looking Back on the Spanish War," p. 191. He adds, perhaps a bit mordantly: "But unfortunately the truth about atrocities is far worse than that they are lied about and made into propaganda. The truth is that they happen." Ibid., p. 292.

84. See Walzer, *Just and Unjust Wars,* pp. 46–47.

85. Quoted in Harry S. Stout, *Upon the Altar of the Nation: A Moral History of the Civil War* (New York: Penguin, 2006), p. 325.

86. Walzer, *Just and Unjust Wars,* p. 32.

87. Keegan, *The Face of Battle,* p. 322.

88. Walzer, *Just and Unjust Wars,* p. 307. In war there is often a mirror-image insanity back home, as commanders imagine the situation on the ground to be better than it is. An officer sent from the front to brief Hitler during the battle of Stalingrad, the turning point of World War II, described in detail the desperate situation of the German forces. Hitler listened for a bit, then turned to his map, where he pointed to flags marking the positions of nonexistent divisions ready to come to the aid of his beleaguered army. The officer remembered later: "I saw that he had lost touch with reality. He lived in a fantasy world of maps and flags." Quoted in Anthony Beevor, *Stalingrad* (New York: Viking Penguin, 1998), p. 345.

89. If better training of soldiers can indeed help avoid atrocities, one way to achieve the goal might be to spread the blame for atrocities upward. See, for example, the discussion in Neta C. Crawford, "Individual and Collective Moral Responsibility for Systemic Military Atrocity," *Journal of Political Philosophy* 15, no. 2 (2007), p. 187.

90. See Keegan, *The Iraq War,* pp. 187–188.

91. See Glatthaar, *Forged in Battle,* p. 200.

92. Scarry, *The Body in Pain,* p. 59.

93. Donald W. Shriver Jr., *An Ethic for Enemies: Forgiveness in Politics* (New York: Oxford University Press, 1995), p. 77.

94. Glatthaar, *Forged in Battle,* p. 200.

95. Abraham Lincoln, "Message to Congress," July 4, 1861, in Roy P. Basler, ed., *The Collected Works of Abraham Lincoln,* vol. 4 (New Brunswick: Rutgers University Press, 1953) p. 430 (emphasis in original).

96. An excellent introduction to this and other concepts of game theory as applied to war is Anderton and Carter, *Principles of Conflict Economics.* Of particular interest is the discussion in chapter 8 on why reciprocity is relatively unsuccessful in dealing with terrorism. True, tit-for-tat is not the only winning strategy. As Thomas Schelling points out, the threat of irrationality can sometimes be even better. See Schelling, *Arms and Influence,* pp. 99–125. For example, in a game of chicken, where two cars head straight toward each other, each driver tries to persuade the other that he will not turn away; and

the first to turn loses. If one driver believes that the other is not rational, the rational driver will turn away and the irrational driver will win.

Schelling famously applies this logic to the Cuban Missile Crisis, to explain why Kruschev blinked. Schelling also believes that a degree of irrationality is inevitable in the conduct of international affairs, including war: "While it is hard for a government, particularly a responsible government, to appear irrational whenever such an appearance is expedient, it is equally hard for a government, even a responsible one, to guarantee its own moderation in every circumstance." Ibid., p. 41.

97. I am of course aware of the claim, common among legal scholars, that the Conventions and their Additional Protocols have become part of customary international law, and are therefore binding even on nonsignatories. And not just by scholars. Consider this, for example, from the government of Switzerland: "Today, the Geneva Conventions of 1949 and the two Additional Protocols of 1977 are by and large regarded as customary international law binding on all states and all parties to conflicts" (http://www.eda.admin.ch/eda/en/home/topics/intla/humlaw/gecons.html). Note the use of the passive tense, leaving unclear who exactly is doing the regarding. Switzerland has for years worked closely with the International Committee of the Red Cross (ICRC), seeking to persuade the rest of the world that the Additional Protocols should be treated as binding provisions of customary international law. For the views of the ICRC, see, for example, Jean-Marie Henckaerts, Louise Doswald-Beck, Carolin Alvermann, *Customary International Humanitarian Law, Volume I: Rules* (New York: Cambridge University Press, 2005), especially the introduction, but also the many references to the Additional Protocols as "adopted by consensus." With respect, I must dissent. I tend to be Kantian on these questions, meaning that I remain unpersuaded of the legal force of treaties on countries that have never ratified them.

Many scholars offer a more nuanced view of the binding character of the Additional Protocols. See, for example, Steven R. Ratner and Jason S. Abrams, *Accountability for Human Rights Atrocities in International Law: Beyond the Nuremberg Legacy* (New York: Oxford University Press, 2001), pp. 86–89 and elsewhere, taking the position that the Additional Protocols are binding on all states insofar as they reflect customary international law as it existed at the time of their ratification, but, beyond that, are binding only on the signatories. Another approach may be found in C. P. M. Cleiren and M. E. M. Tijssen, "Rape and Other Forms of Sexual Assault in the Armed Conflict in the Former Yugoslavia: Legal, Procedural, and Evidentiary Issues," in Roger S. Clark and Madeline Sann, eds., *The Prosecution of International Crimes: A Critical Study of the International Tribunal for the Former Yugoslavia* (New Brunswick, NJ: Transaction Publishers, 1996), p. 257. Cleiren and Tijssen approach Protocol I by asking which parts of it represent interpretative readings of the original Geneva Accords. They point out, too, that many of those who drafted and ratified the Additional Protocols seemed to think the provisions would not apply to most noninternational conflicts. (Cleiren and Tijssen are not the first to make either of these claims; but they make them quite interestingly.)

98. There is some reason to believe that Lincoln considered the enlistment of colored troops as a matter not of equality but of necessity. He evidently later told the governor of Pennsylvania: "[W]e must avail ourselves of this element, or in all probability go under." Quoted in Douglas L. Wilson, *Lincoln's Sword: The Presidency and the Power of Words* (New York: Knopf, 2006), p. 139.

99. See the discussion in James M. McPherson, *Tried by War: Abraham Lincoln as Commander in Chief* (New York: Penguin, 2008), pp. 203–205.

100. See the many accounts of this phenomenon in Noah Andre Trudeau, *Like Men of War: Black Troops in the Civil War, 1862–1865* (Boston: Little Brown, 1998).

101. McPherson, *Tried by War,* p. 248.

102. Champ Ferguson, a raider for the Southern side but not a member of the regular armed forces, was hanged in 1865 for the Saltville Massacre. Although soldiers participated in the massacre, none were brought to justice. Evidently, Robert E. Lee, commanding the Confederate forces, did at one point direct that a General Felix H. Robertson, accused of massacring black prisoners in a separate incident, be placed on trial, but Robertson escaped to a different military jurisdiction and resumed the war. He became insubordinate, however, and the Confederate Congress declined to agree formally to his promotion to brigadier general, apparently because of the massacre. Robertson was wounded, and retired, but was never further punished, by either side. See Thomas D. Mays, "The Battle of Saltville," in John David Smith, *Black Soldiers in Blue: African American Troops in the Civil War Era* (Chapel Hill: University of North Carolina Press, 2003), pp. 200, 217–222.

103. McPherson, *Tried by War,* pp. 214–216.

104. See, for example, the discussion of Douglass in John David Smith, "Let Us Be Grateful That We Have Colored Troops That Will Fight," in Smith, *Black Soldiers in Blue,* pp. 1, 50.

105. Frank A. Haskell, "Frank A. Haskell's View," in Richard Harwell, ed., *Two Views of Gettysburg* (Chicago: Lakeside Press, 1964), pp. 95, 217. The 1964 volume is evidently a reprint of an earlier book, but contains no evidence by which it might be dated.

106. I discuss this concept further in my monograph *The Dissent of the Governed: A Meditation on Law, Religion, and Loyalty* (Cambridge: Harvard University Press, 2000).

107. But see Elaine Scarry, *Thinking in an Emergency* (forthcoming, W.W. Norton in February 2011); lectures delivered in 1997.

108. See Walzer, *Just and Unjust Wars*, pp. 251–268. See also Walzer, "Emergency Ethics," in *Arguing About War,* p. 33.

109. Walzer, "Emergency Ethics," p. 34.

110. A particularly astute critique is Christopher Toner, "Just War and the Supreme Emergency Exception," *Philosophical Quarterly* 55 (October 2005), p. 545. Toner's particular concern is the War on Terror. I do not agree with all of Toner's conclusions (and, as my text suggests, neither does President Obama), but the essay will greatly repay a serious reading. Another fine response is in Brian Orend, *The Morality of War* (Peterborough, Ontario: Broadview, 2006), pp. 127–133.

111. Martin L. Cook, "Michael Walzer's Concept of 'Supreme Emergency,'" *Journal of Military Ethics* 6 (2007), p. 138.

112. Alex J. Bellamy, "The Ethics of Terror Bombing: Beyond the Supreme Emergency," *Journal of Military Ethics* 7 (2008), p. 41.

113. See Walzer, "Emergency Ethics," pp. 41–44.

114. Augustine, *The City of God,* book 19, ch. 12.

115. Aquinas, *Summa Theologica,* vol. 3, pt. 2–2, Q. 40.

116. See, for example, Brian Orend, "Justice After War," *Ethics and International Affairs 16* (Spring, 2002), p. 45.

117. One might argue of course that the timetable on which Obama is withdrawing is not entirely Bush's. After all, the Status of Forces Agreement was not finalized until the interregnum between the 2008 presidential election and the end of Bush's term. No doubt the coming change in Administrations was a factor. But whether it was a large one or a small one nobody who was not there can say.

118. See Walzer, *Just and Unjust Wars,* pp. 117–123.

119. See ibid., passim, and especially p. 120: "It was the crime of the aggressor to challenge individual and communal rights, and states responding to aggression must not repeat the challenge once basic values have been upheld."

120. Ibid., p. 122.

121. Ralph B. Potter Jr., "The Moral Logic of War," reprinted in Miller, *War in the Twentieth Century,* pp. 198, 212. The essay was originally published in 1970.

122. See Eric Patterson, "*Jus Post Bellum* and International Conflict: Or-

der, Justice, and Reconciliation," in Michael W. Brough, John W. Lango, and Harry Van der Linden, eds., *Rethinking the Just War Tradition* (Albany: State University of New York Press, 2007), p. 35. As Patterson notes, the peace may require some sort of punishment of the aggressors.

123. In addition, the end of the war places any number of moral and legal obligations upon the victor, from the maintenance of order to the support of the defeated population. These propositions are well known to international law, but they are also important to the ethics of war. See, for example, Rebecca Johnson, "*Jus Post Bellum* and Counterinsurgency," *Journal of Military Ethics* 7 (2008), p. 215.

124. Obama, *The Audacity of Hope*, p. 495.

125. Helene Cooper and Mark Landler, "U.S. Eyes New Sanctions over Iran Nuclear Program," *New York Times*, February 9, 2010.

126. See the discussion in Tuck, *The Rights of War and Peace.*

127. Roland H. Bainton, *Christian Attitudes Toward War and Peace: A Historical Survey and Critical Re-Evaluation* (Eugene, OR: Wipf and Stock Publishers, 2008), p. 220.

III. THE RIGHTS AND DIGNITY OF STRANGERS

1. For details, visit http://www.ushmm.org/conscience/sudan/darfur. At this writing, the genocide is taking about 10,000 lives each month. The author is a former member of the committee, but this essay represents my own views only.

2. Samantha Power, *A Problem from Hell: America in the Age of Genocide* (New York: Harper Collins, 2002), p. 511. I am aware that some defenders of the Iraq War described it as a humanitarian intervention, aimed at overthrowing a leader whose regime ruthlessly suppressed its own people and had arguably engaged in genocide against the Kurds. Unlike some critics, I do not think this argument ridiculous. But I also do not find it persuasive.

3. For a spirited challenge to our tendency to take the moral right to self-defense as axiomatic, for individuals and states alike, see Richard Norman, *Ethics, Killing and War,* especially chapter 4.

4. In the typology of the philosopher Jeff McMahon, the invader is the "Just Attacker" and the putative sovereign who is oppressing his people is the "Culpable Attacker," who possesses, in just war terms, no right of self-defense. See Jeff McMahan, "Innocence, Self-Defense and Killing in War," *Journal of Political Philosophy* 2 (1994): p. 193; and McMahan, "Self-Defense and the Problem of the Innocent Attacker," p. 301.

5. See Human Rights Watch, *Leave None to Tell the Story: Genocide in Rwanda* (1999).

6. Quoted in Jean Hatzfeld, *Machete Season: The Killers in Rwanda Speak,* trans. Linda Coverdale (New York: Farrar, Straus and Giroux, 2005), p. 25.

7. Obama, *The Audacity of Hope,* p. 45.

8. Sean D. Murphy, *Humanitarian Intervention: The United Nations in an Evolving World Order* (Philadelphia: University of Pennsylvania Press, 1996), p. 12. Many pro-interventionist scholars would agree that efforts to redress a sovereign's violations of human rights are "the only legitimate reasons" for humanitarian warfare. See Julie Mertus, "Reconsidering the Legality of Humanitarian Intervention: Lessons from Kosovo," *William and Mary Law Review* 41 (May 2000): 1743, 1751.

9. W. Michael Reisman, "Why Regime Change Is (Almost Always) a Bad Idea," *American Journal of International Law* 98 (July 2004), p. 520.

10. Walzer, *Just and Unjust Wars,* p. 101. Earlier I mentioned the problem of sovereignty, the virtual wall that international law builds around each state. Walzer is among those who believe that when a government commits acts sufficiently horrific, it ceases to be sovereign. Ibid.

11. Ibid., p. 106.

12. Ibid., p. 107.

13. See, for example, Michael Walzer, *Arguing About War,* chapter 5.

14. Michael Walzer, "Arguing for Humanitarian Intervention," in Nicolaus Mills and Kira Brunner, eds., *The New Killing Fields: Massacre and the Politics of Intervention* (New York: Basic Books, 2002), pp. 19, 22.

15. This is why some scholars continue to insist that humanitarian interventions violate international law. See, for example, Oscar Schachter, *International Law in Theory and Practice* (Boston: Martinus Nijhoff Publishers, 1991), pp. 123–126.

16. See V. S. Naipaul, "Columbus and Crusoe," in *The Writer and the World: Essays* (New York: Knopf, 2002), p. 301.

17. John Howard Yoder, *When War Is Unjust: Being Honest in Just-War Thinking* (Eugene, OR: Wipf and Stock, 1996), pp. 100–101. On the subject of refugees, we often give insufficient attention to the use of force against them—not by those who are fleeing them, but by those are protecting them. The internal rules governing the operation of a refugee camp have the practical effect of law, and the fact that the organization running the camp might have an entirely humanitarian motivation should not free the rules from moral and political criticism. See Michel Agier, "Humanity as an Identity and Its Political Effects (A Note on Camps and Humanitarian Government)," *Humanity: An International Journal of Human Rights* 1, no. 1 (Fall 2010), p. 29.

18. For a useful recent discussion of their complexity and duration, see the recent Rand report, James Dobbins et al., *America's Role in Nation-Building: From Germany to Iraq* (Santa Monica: Rand, 2003).

19. Reisman, "Why Regime Change Is (Almost Always) a Bad Idea," p. 517.

20. See, for example, Fernando R. Tesón, *A Philosophy of International Law* (Boulder: Westview, 1998).

21. For a dated but still useful and quite influential discussion, see Thomas M. Franck, "The Emerging Right to Democratic Governance," *American Journal of International Law* 86 (1992), p. 46. See also Thomas M. Franck, "The Democratic Entitlement," *University of Richmond Law Review* 29 (1994), p. 1.

22. See, for example, Anthony D'Amato, "The Invasion of Panama Was a Lawful Response to Tyranny," *American Journal of International Law* 84 (April 1990): pp. 516, 519.

23. Human Rights Watch, among other groups, has asserted that France has violated international human rights through its policies. See http://hrw.org/english/docs/2004/02/26/france7666.htm.

24. I personally am "shocked," but I am an outlier, for I am shocked by the relentless secularism of American schools, too, a factor that I do believe deprives both parents and children of a fundamental human right. For some of my reasons (which are, I think, unlikely to persuade one who does not begin in agreement, or at least dubitante), see Stephen L. Carter, *God's Name in Vain: The Wrongs and Rights of Religion in Politics* (New York: Basic Books, 2000), especially chapters 11 and 12.

Given this claim, one might reasonably ask how many people need be shocked in order to justify intervention. But, as will be seen, I am more interested in explaining it than justifying it; or, put otherwise, because just war thinking appeals to conscience and not to law, it may be enough that a single individual, the sovereign, is shocked, and so decides to act rather than withhold. This puts to the rest of the world the decision whether to aid him, oppose him, or, most often, to sit quietly on the sidelines, waiting to see which way the momentum runs.

25. See, for example, Jean Bethke Elshtain, *Just War on Terror: The Burden of American Power in a Violent World* (New York: Basic Books, 2003), p. 57 and passim.

26. Luther, in a sixteenth-century essay, rejects the right to rebel against constituted authority, even when that power is used to oppress. "[T]o be right and to do right do not always go together," he writes, adding: "[I]t is right that subjects patiently suffer everything and do not revolt." God, he

says, has taken the power of the sword from those who are subjects. Should they wield the power God has removed, "then before God they are worthy of condemnation and death." Martin Luther, "Whether Soldiers, Too, Can Be Saved," in Theodore G. Tappert, ed., *Selected Writings of Martin Luther, 1529–1546* (Minneapolis: Fortress, 1967), pp. 433, 466.

This judgment might seem harsh, but Luther opens an intriguing door. True, the people of the oppressive leader are not to revolt. But a neighboring ruler might intercede:

> There are some who abuse this office, and strike and kill people needlessly simply because they want to. But that is the fault of the persons, not of the office. ... They are like mad physicians who would needlessly amputate a healthy hand just because they wanted to. Indeed, they themselves are a part of that universal lack of peace which must be prevented by just wars and the sword and be forced into peace. ... In the end God's justice finds them and strikes, as happened to the peasants in the revolt.

Ibid., p. 437. Consider the logic of this argument. There is no right, says Luther, to rebel against constituted authority, for authority is given by God Himself. That is why the oppressed subjects must suffer patiently. But the ruler who oppresses them is answerable to another authority—to God, says Luther—and the just war is a tool that God might use against the unjust ruler, in the same way that even a just ruler might use force to control the peasants. If the just war is God's tool, then God approves of it, and even directs it, through the prince of some other land, who sees what is happening, and refused to countenance it. For Luther, this foreign prince, interceding to overthrow the first, is acting according to God's law of peace. Thus, for Luther, the just war, fought by an outside power, is the only way to overcome an oppressive ruler—a very far cry from the current understanding, in which the outside power is seen as presumptively unjust in its interference across borders.

27. Jean Bethke Elshtain, "Just War and Humanitarian Intervention" *American Society of International Law Proceedings* 95 (2001), pp. 1, 4.

28. A good recent example is George R. Fletcher and Jens David Ohlin, *Defending Humanity: When Force Is Justified and Why* (New York: Oxford University Press, 2008), especially chapter 6.

29. See, for example, Fernando R. Tesón, *A Philosophy of International Law* (Boulder: Westview, 1998).

30. Some scholars have argued that we should consider even under less

onerous conditions the possibility that the sovereign has lost its right to govern. For example, Michael Walzer contends that the sovereign has a responsibility to create conditions in which it is possible to struggle politically for change. See Walzer, *Just and Unjust Wars,* especially chapter 6. Fernando Tesón, in *A Philosophy of International Law,* places an interesting gloss on Walzer's argument. As I read Tesón, he would limit any intervention according to the principle that an outsider must not disturb "rights and local institutions that represent [the people's] freely chosen life in common." Tesón, p. 62, and ff. Taking the example of Iraq (and writing five years before the Anglo-American invasion), he argues that it would be permissible for an outsider to aid a popular insurrection, or perhaps to engage in a surgical military strike to destroy a site for building weapons of mass destruction. An invasion would be a different matter, unless the state itself (as against the government) proved illegitimate. Surgical strikes (and weapons of mass destruction) to one side, a popular uprising offers no guarantee about the "freely chosen life in common" of the people. Like the early Walzer, Tesón may be a bit of a romantic on the matter of "the people," for they are rarely as united, or as mutually concerned for one another's welfare, as in their models; at the moment of revolution, very often, their level of mutual concern is less, not more. Nevertheless, in the end, Tesón would recognize only sovereigns who respect rights in the Western sense. Lea Brilmayer, among others, has warned that this approach tends to demean the genuine feelings of attachment to nation that make a people a people, replacing loyalty to a group with a "watery liberal facsimile." See Lea Brilmayer, *American Hegemony: Political Morality in a One-Superpower World* (New Haven: Yale University Press, 1994), p. 184. Brilmayer makes an intriguing point. But, again, we do not know precisely where Obama stands on the problem, and we will not know until he acts.

31 Fletcher and Ohlin, *Defending Humanity,* pp. 131–132. On the practical level, as the authors concede, if the Genocide Convention does not mandate the prevention of genocide, it becomes much cheaper for Western powers to charge others with genocide: after all, the words cost a good deal less than they would if existence of genocide gave rise to a responsibility to act.

32. A fear of intervention is not of course the only reason that a state might choose, against its inclinations, to respect the human rights of its people. Reputational capital might also be at stake, although not every nation responds in the same way to this particular incentive. See, for example, the discussion in Oona A. Hathaway, "Two Cheers for International Law," *Wilson Quarterly,* Autumn 2003.

33. I explain below why intervention by local peacekeepers represents an unserious effort to deal with the catastrophe.

34. Indeed, we are more likely to err when we rush. Were I so bold as to propose an amendment to the traditional *jus ad bellum* criteria, I would add that the justice of a war is at least enhanced if it has been launched following a process of reasonable deliberation.

35. I am not suggesting a moral equivalence between the Soviet attack on Afghanistan and the Anglo-American attack on Iraq. The procedural similarities, however, are striking: each invasion was launched by a superpower in the teeth of opposition by most of the world. And the world could do nothing about either one.

36. I do not share the view, proposed by George Fletcher and Jens David Ohlin, that the humanitarian intervention rationale for the Iraq War fails because Saddam Hussein's massacre of his own people, specifically the Kurds, occurred fifteen years prior to the Anglo-American invasion. Fletcher and Ohlin, *Defending Humanity*, pp. 153–154. This conclusion is in keeping with the theory that prevention of genocide is the only cause for which an outside intervention might be justified. But that is not their theory. Fletcher and Ohlin contend, and I agree, that the outsider may intervene when the people would themselves have a right of self-defense against the state. The fundamental difference between my view and theirs is that I believe this right of self-defense applies to far more than a threat of annihilation, or of the other possibilities listed in the Genocide Convention.

37. Power, *A Problem from Hell*, pp. 504–506.

38. Obama, *The Audacity of Hope*, p. 495.

39. For a particularly sobering look at the epidemic, see Jeffrey Gettleman, "Africa's Forever Wars: Why the Continent's Conflicts Never End," *Foreign Policy*, March/April 2010. I should add, lest there by any confusion, that Gettleman was not the journalist on the panel.

40. "Spreading Genocide to Chad," editorial, *New York Times*, March 20, 2006.

41. Paul Johnson, "Obama Has to Be World Sheriff," *Forbes*, April 23, 2009.

42. Quoted at http://www.blackfive.net/main/2005/03/after_action_re.html.

43. For a firsthand account of such an attack into the ambush in Iraq, see http://www.michaelyon-online.com/men-of-valor-part-iii.htm.

44. Although the matter is not without controversy, many security specialists swear by this scheme for everyone from police to bodyguards.

45. A good discussion of the advantages enjoyed by the American military is Eliot Cohen, "The Military," in Peter H. Schuck and James Q. Wilson,

eds., *Understanding America: The Anatomy of an Exceptional Nation* (New York: Public Affairs, 2008), p. 247.

46. To take an example that might seem trivial but is actually crucial, the Department of Defense spends an estimated $20 billion a year fighting rust on its equipment. Many countries spend little or nothing, and so their stock of materiel, no matter how fancy when purchased, quickly deteriorates.

47. See, for example, the discussion in Wyatt Kash, "Military's Technological Might Is Slipping, Navy Under Secretary Says," *Defense Systems* (online magazine), April 15, 2010, available at http://defensesystems.com/articles/2010/04/15/militarys-technology-might-is-slipping-says-navy-undesecretary.aspx.

48. See International Institute for Strategic Studies, *The Military Balance 2010* (Routledge, 2010); available for download at http://www.iiss.org/publications/military-balance/.

49. See Richard A. Clarke, *Cyber War: The Next Threat to National Security and What to Do About It* (New York: Ecco, 2010), pp. 186–187, and elsewhere.

50. This is a point Obama made long before he was President. In his autobiography he wrote: "I might have had arguments with the size of Reagan's military buildup, but given the Soviet invasion of Afghanistan, staying ahead of the Soviets militarily seemed a sensible thing to do." Obama, *The Audacity of Hope*, p. 452.

51. Quoted in Richard Rhodes, *Dark Sun: The Making of the Hydrogen Bomb* (New York: Simon & Schuster, 1995), p. 434.

52. Not all supporters of such a force believe that the United Nations should control it. Jeff McMahan, for example, refers only to "a special force under international control." McMahan, "Killing in War," Nardin, ed., *The Ethics of War and Peace*, pp. 100–101. I should note that McMahan is no believer in pie in the sky, for he adds: "There is of course no such force, nor is there likely to be anytime soon." Ibid., p. 101.

53. The literature lists several. Principal among them is that an army tends to thrive because of those who choose to make it a career. A career spent in the military nevertheless gives you plenty of opportunities to be stationed in your home country. An international force could not offer this. Enlistments would likely be short, and the soldiers would be fighting for money rather than for their countries. It is a matter of history that mercenary armies with short enlistments have had considerable problems of discipline, and worse.

54. Thomas M. Nichols, *Eve of Destruction: The Coming Age of Preventive War* (Philadelphia: University of Pennsylvania Press, 2008), p. 139.

55. For a guardedly optimistic (I emphasize "guardedly") account of what the Security Council might be able to do with a unified force under its com-

mand, see Adam Roberts, "Proposals for UN Standing Forces: A Critical History," in Vaughan Lowe, Adam Roberts, Jennifer Welsh, and Dominik Zaum, eds., *The United Nations Security Council and War: The Evolution of Thought and Practice Since 1945* (New York: Oxford University Press, 2008), p. 99. The volume contains several assessments of the failures of the United Nations when it has used military force, including in the former Yugoslavia. One author suggests that the real problem was not the United Nations but the unwillingness of the United States to commit ground troops. See Susan L. Woodward, "The Security Council and the Wars in the Former Yugoslavia," ibid., p. 406. If so, this strengthens the notion that nobody else in the world is actually equipped to stop genocide.

56. After all, we contract out so much of warfare already. See the discussion in P. W. Singer, *Corporate Warriors: The Rise of the Privatized Military Industry* (Ithaca: Cornell University Press, 2003). If you need a reason to despair, take a close look at chapter 14.

57. See Samuel P. Huntington, *The Soldier and the State: The Theory and Politics of Civil-Military Relations* (Cambridge: Harvard University Press, 1957), pp. 143–162.

58. Elshtain, "Just War and Humanitarian Intervention."

59. Michael Walzer, *Arguing About War,* p. 101.

60. See, for example, the discussion in Bainton, *Christian Attitudes Toward War and Peace,* chapter 14.

61. Donald Kagan, *On the Origins of War and the Preservation of Peace* (New York: Doubleday, 1995), p. 572.

62. Norman, *Ethics, Killing, and War,* p. 214.

63. Available at http://www.eia.doe.gov/emeu/25opec/anniversary.html.

64. Lisette Alvarez, "Britain Says U.S. Planned to Seize Oil in '73 Crisis," *New York Times,* January 2, 2004.

65. Political scientist Dankwart Rustow, quoted in Franklin Tugwell, *The Energy Crisis and the American Political Economy: Politics and Markets in the Management of Natural Resources* (Stanford: Stanford University Press, 1988), p. 97.

66. Uzi B. Arad, "The Short-Term Effectiveness of an Arab Oil Embargo," in Haim Shaked and Itamar Rabinovich, eds., *The Middle East and the United States: Perceptions and Policies* (New Brunswick, NJ: Transaction Books, 1980), pp. 241, 244.

67. On the incentive point, see, for example, McMahan, "Killing in War," in *The Ethics of War and Peace,* pp. 218–219.

68. See Richard H. Speier et al., "Nonproliferation Sanctions," RAND Corporation, 2001, available at http://www.rand.org/pubs/monograph_reports/MR1285/.

69. See, for example, the discussion in William H. Kaempfer and Anton D. Lowenberg, "The Theory of International Economic Sanctions: A Public Choice Approach," *American Economic Review* 78 (September 1988), p. 786.

70. The story of America and Israel should give pause to those who continue to insist on the efficacy of sanctions. Over the last few decades, the United States has frequently been threatened with boycotts, and intermittently boycotted, in retaliation for its support of Israel. And yet the support is unstinting. (I might add that, unlike an awkwardly large number of academics, I am not in the least embarrassed by the relationship between America and Israel. I am old-fashioned enough to be proud that we continue, in the teeth of world opinion, to support the only true democracy in the region.)

71. For a discussion of the role of externalities in war generally, and also in sanctions regimes, see Anderton and Carter, *Principles of Conflict Economics*.

72. This is the well-known calculation of Gary C. Hufbauer, Jeffrey J. Schott, and Kimberly Ann Elliott, *Economic Sanctions Reconsidered: History and Current Policy* (3d ed., Washington, DC: Peterson Institute, 2007). The Hufbauer, Schott, and Elliott data are considered authoritative, and widely relied upon in testing other hypotheses about sanctions.

73. See Robert A. Pape, "Why Economic Sanctions Do Not Work," *International Security* 22 (1997), p. 90. See also Robert A. Pape, "Why Economic Sanctions Still Do Not Work," *International Security* 23 (1998), p. 66.

74. This brief summary is based on the more formal analysis presented in Dean Lacy and Emerson M. S, Niou, "A Theory of Economic Sanctions and Issue Linkage: The Roles of Preferences, Information, and Threats," *Journal of Politics* 66 (February 2004), p. 25. Some theorists would argue that sanctions may be a weak form of action, but that efforts to change another country's behavior through reliance on rewards rather than threats fare even worse. See, for example, Howard Chang, "Carrots, Sticks, and International Externalities," *International Review of Law and Economics* 17 (September 1997), p. 309.

75. See, for example, Shane Bonetti, "A Test of the Public Choice Theory of Economic Sanctions," *Applied Economics Letters* (1997), no. 4, p. 729; and David Lektzian and Mark Souva, "The Economic Peace Between Democracies: Economic Sanctions and Domestic Institutions," *Journal of Peace Research* 40 (November 2003), p. 641. Lektzian and Souva's paper tries to explain why democracies are more likely than countries with other forms of government to impose sanctions. Their thesis is, in part, that democracies must worry more than other regimes about balancing the competing claims of different interest groups, typically "one force pushing them toward the use of sanctions to satisfy domestic interest group pressure and the other pulling

them toward the welfare benefits of free trade," and therefore will prefer "smart sanctions" that impose smaller costs on their own publics. Ibid., pp. 645–646, and passim. Bonetti's paper (which, like Lektzian and Souva's, relies on the Hufbauer, Schott, and Elliott data) suggests that, at least for export sanctions, strong trade relations between the countries in question make the sanctions less likely.

76. See Jo Becker and Ron Nixon, "U.S. Enriches Companies Defying Its Policy on Iran," *New York Times*, March 6, 2010.

77. Another reason the oil companies would not have supported the Iraq War might be bad memories of the Gulf War. After the American-led coalition pushed the Iraqi forces out of Kuwait, the reconstituted Kuwaiti government "consistently voted to keep international investment in its state-controlled oil industry to a minimum." Arik Hesseldahl, "Iraq's Postwar Oil Opportunities," *Forbes*, March 6, 2003.

78. See Michael Makovsky, "There Will Be Oil," *New Republic*, January 27, 2010.

79. Henry A. Kissinger, "Obama's Foreign Policy Challenge," *Washington Post*, April 22, 2009.

80. Norman, *Ethics, Killing and War*, p. 214.

81. One of the ironies of sanctions is that, once you threaten to impose them, you must. By imposing them, you are really trying to change not the behavior of the target country, but the behavior of other countries that might see what you are doing and worry about the prospect of the same thing happening to them. Thus sanctions are, in reality, a general rather than a specific deterrent; they are not really aimed at the target country, another aspect that suggests a violation of *jus in bello*.

83. Here Walzer offers a partial dissent. In his essay "Emergency Ethics" (discussed above), he defends the firebombing of the German cities during the Second World War in order to break the German will to resist. Such an act, he concedes, would ordinarily constitute an offense against the law and ethics of war. But we should evaluate ethical questions differently, says Walzer, when a nation faces an existential threat.

83. See Paul Ramsey, *The Just War: Force and Political Responsibility* (Lanham, MD: Rowman & Littlefield, 2002) (reprint; originally published 1968), p. 492. To similar effect is George Weigel, *Tranquillitas Ordinis: The Present Failure and Future Promise of American Catholic Thought on War and Peace* (New York: Oxford University Press, 1987), which argues that just war theory implicitly contains a requirement of *jus ad pacem*, or "justice in peace." If peace as well as war can result in injustice, an unjust peace is not necessarily better than an unjust war. See especially pp. 357–359.

84. Here I refer to the sort of pacifism associated with a generalized opposition to violence in general, and to the violence of war in particular. In the Christian tradition, this strand of pacifism stems from the determination to live as Christ lived. For an argument that in an age of modern weaponry, Christian pacifism might require that the Christian allow his own country to be conquered, see Robert Drinan, "Is Pacifism the Only Option Left for Christians?" in Arthur F. Holmes, ed., *War and Christian Ethics: Classic and Contemporary Readings on the Morality of War,* 2d ed. (Grand Rapids, MI: Baker Academic), p. 318. Drinan presents the possibility that it is licit to resist a conqueror only through nonviolent means.

It is important to note that there are also other forms of pacifism, including notably "the claim that other structures can and should be put into place that would provide alternative means for resolving conflicts in more orderly and less destructive ways than war offers." Theodore J. Koontz, "Christian Nonviolence: An Interpretation," in Nardin, ed., *The Ethics of War and Peace,* pp. 169, 183.

85. Aquinas, *Summa Theologica,* vol. 3, art. 2, part 2–2, Q. 40.

86. See the discussion in John Mark Mattox, *Saint Augustine and the Theory of Just War* (London: Continuum, 2006), especially pp. 104–110.

87. Reinhold Niebuhr, "Why the Christian Church Is Not Pacifist," in Robert McAfee Brown, ed., *The Essential Reinhold Niebuhr: Selected Essays and Addresses* (New Haven: Yale University Press, 1986), pp. 102, 117. The essay was originally published in 1948.

88. Walzer, *Just and Unjust Wars,* p. 334.

89. For a controversial but well-documented argument that much of the German population was also delighted with the slaughter, see Daniel Goldhagen, *Hitler's Willing Executioners: Ordinary Germans and the Holocaust* (New York: Knopf, 1996).

90. Quoted in Arthur Herman, *Gandhi & Churchill: The Epic Rivalry That Destroyed an Empire and Forged Our Age* (New York: Bantam, 2008), p. 445.

91. George Orwell, "Reflections on Gandhi," in *A Collection of Essays* (New York: Harvest, 1981) (first published 1946), pp. 171, 177–178. For an effort to answer some of these questions, albeit without explicit reference to either Gandhi or Orwell, see Richard B. Miller, *Interpretations of Conflict: Ethics, Pacifism, and the Just-War Tradition* (Chicago: University of Chicago Press, 1991).

92. See Alex Von Tunzelmann, *Indian Summer: The Secret History of the End of an Empire* (New York: Picador, 2007), pp. 110–112.

93. See Herman, *Gandhi & Churchill,* p. 446 and elsewhere. Critics of Gandhi are often accused of taking these and other comments about Hitler and the Jews out of context, the theory being that they should be considered

against the backdrop of his general ideology of nonviolence, and his consistent condemnation of Hitler. Maybe so. Still, the comments do suggest that Gandhi viewed Hitler and Naziism quite differently from the way the rest of the world saw them. Says Herman: "Paradoxically, Gandhi's spiritual strength was also his intellectual blind spot." Ibid., p. 447. Perhaps this explains why, in the aftermath of World War II, Gandhi argued that war is "a crime against God and humanity," and, therefore, "Roosevelt and Churchill are no less war criminals than Hitler and Mussolini." Quoted in Stanley Wolpert, *Gandhi's Passion: The Life and Legacy of Mahatma Gandhi* (New York: Oxford, 2002), p. 213.

94. Herman, *Gandhi & Churchill,* p. 448.

95. See Edith Wyschogrod, *An Ethics of Remembering: History, Heterology, and the Nameless Others* (Chicago: University of Chicago Press, 1998), especially her discussion of what she calls "cataclysm," in chapter 1 and elsewhere. The reader will have to excuse Professor Wyschogrod's frequent lapses into jargon, and her tendency, in an otherwise compelling treatment, to express her skepticism that history in the traditional sense of telling us what happened is even possible. For a stirring defense of the view that the historian must do precisely that, see Gordon S. Wood, *The Purpose of the Past: Reflections on the Uses of History* (New York: Penguin, 2008).

96. Diane Ackerman, *An Alchemy of Mind: The Marvel and Mystery of the Brain* (New York: Scribner, 2004), p. 186.

97. Elaine Scarry, *The Body in Pain,* especially pp. 115–118.

98. Elie Wiesel and Richard D. Heffner, *Conversations with Elie Wiesel* (New York: Schocken Books, 2001), p. 14.

99. Walzer, "The Politics of Rescue," in *Arguing About War,* pp. 67, 81.

100. Wiesel and Heffner, *Conversations with Elie Wiesel,* p. 14.

101. Ackerman, *An Alchemy of Mind,* p. 186.

IV. THE AMERICAN PROVISO

1. Quoted in Carl Sandburg, *Abraham Lincoln: The Prairie Years and the War Years,* p. 579.

2. McPherson, *Tried by War,* p. 250. A slightly contrary opinion is offered by Lincoln biographer Benjamin Thomas in his classic *Abraham Lincoln: A Biography* (Southern Illinois University Press, 2008) (first published 1952). Wrote Thomas of Lincoln's 1864 reelection: "The soldier vote was an important factor in his triumph," p. 453.

3. *Military Times* poll, October 2008. Results available at http://www.

militarytimes.com/static/projects/ pages/081003_ep_2pp.pdf. See Brendan McGarry, "Military Times Poll: Troops Backing McCain," *Military Times,* October 9, 2008. It should be noted that these results are based on voluntary responses from *Military Times* subscribers. The methodology section of the results notes that the average respondent was significantly older than the average military member and that junior enlisted troops, women, and racial and ethnic minorities were underrepresented in the poll.

4. See Harold Holzer, *Lincoln at Cooper Union: The Speech That Made Abraham Lincoln President* (New York: Simon & Schuster, 2004).

5. Douglas L. Wilson, *Lincoln's Sword: The Presidency and the Power of Words* (New York: Alfred A. Knopf, 2006), p. 43.

6. Abraham Lincoln, "Address at Cooper Union, New York City," in Basler, ed., *The Collected Works of Abraham Lincoln,* vol. 3, pp. 522, 523–532.

7. Ibid., p. 535.

8. Ibid., p. 542.

9. Holzer, *Lincoln at Cooper Union,* p. 115.

10. Lincoln, "Address at Cooper Union," p. 550.

11. The secular prophet of this contention was Richard Hofstadter. See Hofstadter, "The Paranoid Style in American Politics," *Harper's Magazine,* Nov. 1964, p. 77, and Hofstadter, *Anti-Intellectualism in American Life* (New York: Vintage, 1966).

12. Fouad Ajami, "Afghanistan and the Decline of American Power," *Wall Street Journal,* April 9, 2010.

13. Quoted in Stephen E. Ambrose, *Eisenhower: Soldier and President* (New York: Simon & Schuster, 1990), p. 429.

14. Eric V. Larson and Bogdan Savych, "American Public Support for U.S. Military Operations from Mogadishu to Baghdad," Rand Corporation, 2005, available at http://www.rand.org/pubs/monographs/2005/RAND_MG231.pdf.

15. "Operation Anaconda," *Time,* available at http://www.time.com/time/covers/1101020318/popup/index.html.

16. How central is dissent to a democracy? In my Massey Lectures at Harvard, I argued that tolerance of and engagement with dissent is the best measure of the health of a democracy. Precisely because of the risk of stifling dissent, I contended, those holding the reins of power "have a moral obligation to be cautious rather than reckless in its exercise." Carter, *Dissent of the Governed,* p. 85.

17. Some commentators suggest that the ubiquity of the news media have reduced the incidence of outrages committed by the United States and its allies. For example, Nicholas Fotion argues in *War and Ethics* (p. 134) that

"since the Vietnam War when television cameras appeared on the battle-field" it has become "almost impossible for western forces to fight 'dirty' wars."

18. The military historian John Keegan points this out in his splendid book *The Iraq War*, pp. 148–149. Keegan includes several examples of media miscoverage in Iraq. Among the most significant was a pause early in the war (late March of 2003), as Allied commanders waited for resupply, a pause that journalists treated as some sort of military setback. See ibid., pp. 183–186.

19. A fascinating account of the tragedy is in Edmund L. Blandford, *Fatal Decisions: Errors and Blunders in World War II* (Annapolis: Naval Institute Press, 1999), pp. 4–7. He discusses other friendly-fire incidents as well.

20. Ironically, some analysts believe that friendly fire deaths are likely to be higher on the side with the greater firepower, for the simple reason that most of the bombs and shells and bullets flying around the battlefield will be from that side.

21. The "Congressional" Medal of Honor so frequently referenced in novels and films does not exist. The misnomer comes about because the ci-tation states that the President awards the medal in the name of Congress.

22. See, for example, John Yoo, "My Gift to the Obama Presidency," *Wall Street Journal*, February 24, 2010.

23. Abraham Lincoln to James C. Conkling, August 26, 1863, in Basler, *The Collected Works of Abraham Lincoln*, vol. 6, p. 406.

24. Quoted in Charlie Savage, "To Critics, New Policy on Terror Looks Old," *New York Times*, July 1, 2009.

25. Quoted in ibid.

26. See the account in Trevor Royle, *Lancaster Against York: The Wars of the Roses and the Foundation of Modern Britain* (Palgrave MacMillan 2008), pp. 120–126.

INDEX